Phonology in Multilingual Grammars

Phonology in Multilingual Grammars

Representational Complexity and Linguistic Interfaces

JOHN ARCHIBALD

OXFORD
UNIVERSITY PRESS

Oxford University Press is a department of the University of Oxford. It furthers the University's objective of excellence in research, scholarship, and education by publishing worldwide. Oxford is a registered trade mark of Oxford University Press in the UK and certain other countries.

Published in the United States of America by Oxford University Press
198 Madison Avenue, New York, NY 10016, United States of America.

© John Archibald 2024

All rights reserved. No part of this publication may be reproduced, stored in a retrieval system, or transmitted, in any form or by any means, without the prior permission in writing of Oxford University Press, or as expressly permitted by law, by license, or under terms agreed with the appropriate reproduction rights organization. Inquiries concerning reproduction outside the scope of the above should be sent to the Rights Department, Oxford University Press, at the address above.

You must not circulate this work in any other form
and you must impose this same condition on any acquirer.

Library of Congress Cataloging-in-Publication Data
Names: Archibald, John, author.
Title: Phonology in multilingual grammars : representational complexity and linguistic interfaces / John Archibald.
Description: New York : Oxford University Press, 2024. |
Includes bibliographical references and index.
Identifiers: LCCN 2023014238 (print) | LCCN 2023014239 (ebook) |
ISBN 9780190923341 (paperback) | ISBN 9780190923334 (hardback) |
ISBN 9780190923365 (epub)
Subjects: LCSH: Grammar, Comparative and general—Phonology. | Multilingualism.
Classification: LCC P217 .A77 2023 (print) | LCC P217 (ebook) |
DDC 414—dc23/eng/20230628
LC record available at https://lccn.loc.gov/2023014238
LC ebook record available at https://lccn.loc.gov/2023014239

DOI: 10.1093/oso/9780190923334.001.0001

Paperback printed by Marquis Book Printing, Canada
Hardback printed by Bridgeport National Bindery, Inc., United States of America

*I syng of a mayden
that is makeles.*

For Martha

'Everything is learnable by somebody'.

—David Birdsong
Universal Learnability Hypothesis

CONTENTS

List of Figures xiii
List of Tables xv
Preface xvii
Acknowledgements xix
List of Abbreviations xxi

1. Overture 1
   1.1 Introduction 1
   1.2 Traditional Context of L2 Speech 2
   1.3 L2 Phonology 3
      1.3.1 Background in Learnability 6
   1.4 Interlanguage Grammars 7
      1.4.1 Sources of Knowledge 8
         1.4.1.1 Universal Grammar 8
         1.4.1.2 Input Effects 9
         1.4.1.3 Components of L1 Knowledge (a.k.a. Transfer) 11
   1.5 Phonological Knowledge 13
      1.5.1 Externalism 13
      1.5.2 Emergentism 13
      1.5.3 Essentialism 14
      1.5.4 Phonology as Cognition 16

2. Phonological Grammars 17
   2.1 Introduction 17
      2.1.1 The Deficit Hypothesis 17
      2.1.2 Phonological Features 18
      2.1.3 Robust Cues 20
   2.2 Methodological Issues 22
      2.2.1 Discrimination 22
      2.2.2 Lexical Selection 23
   2.3 L2 Empirical Studies 23
      2.3.1 Features 23
      2.3.2 Non-robust Cues 24
      2.3.3 Syllables 25
         2.3.3.1 Markedness 25
         2.3.3.2 Typological Universals 26
      2.3.4 Differing Repair Strategies 28

2.4	Ultimate Attainment 34	
	2.4.1	Full Transfer / Full Access in Phonology? 36
2.5	Accessing Grammars 38	
	2.5.1	Deficits Revisited 38
	2.5.2	Stress Deafness 38

2.4 Ultimate Attainment 34
    2.4.1 Full Transfer / Full Access in Phonology? 36
2.5 Accessing Grammars 38
    2.5.1 Deficits Revisited 38
    2.5.2 Stress Deafness 38
        2.5.2.1 Literature Review 38
        2.5.2.2 Acoustic Properties of Stress 39
        2.5.2.3 Tasks 39
        2.5.2.4 What about Representation? 46
        2.5.2.5 Linguistic Assumptions 46
    2.5.3 Acquiring Stress 50
        2.5.3.1 Chinese and Japanese and Stress Deafness 50
2.6 Individual Differences 52
    2.6.1 Working Memory 54
    2.6.2 Phonological Processing 55
2.7 Preserving L1 Features in an L2: A Look at Chain Shift 58
2.8 Intra-constituent Licensing (Redeployment) 60
    2.8.1 Korean Phonology 62
    2.8.2 Finnish Phonology 62
    2.8.3 L2 Data 63
    2.8.4 Finnish Borrowings 64
    2.8.5 Sonorant Voice Structure 64
    2.8.6 A Parsing Comparison 66
2.9 Phonological Parsing 70
2.10 Representational Realism 75
    2.10.1 Results 77
    2.10.2 Summary 78
2.11 Conclusion 79

3. The Phonetics/Phonology Interface 80
3.1 Introduction 80
3.2 Abstract Representations 80
    3.2.1 Background 81
3.3 Perceptibility 82
    3.3.1 Calculating Auditory Distance 86
    3.3.2 Empirical Results 88
    3.3.3 Concerns 89
    3.3.4 Differential Substitution 92
3.4 Mechanisms of Acquisition 92
3.5 Intake Frequency: Acquisition by Phonetics 93
    3.5.1 Inaccuracies on Non-L1 Features 95
    3.5.2 Accurate Perception of Non-L1 Features 96
    3.5.3 Properties of the Input Signal 97
    3.5.4 Intake 97
    3.5.5 Philosophical Grounds 98

Contents

3.5.6 Frequency Redux 99
3.5.7 The Mechanism 102
3.6 Redeployment: Acquisition by Phonology 103
   3.6.1 L2 Acquisition of Length 103
      3.6.1.1 Tasks and Stimuli 104
      3.6.1.2 AXB Auditory Discrimination 104
      3.6.1.3 Lexical Knowledge Task 105
      3.6.1.4 Picture Identification Task 105
      3.6.1.5 Results and Discussion 105
      3.6.1.6 Picture Identification Results 108
      3.6.1.7 Why Do They Get Better? 108
3.7 Illusory Vowels in Production and Perception 110
   3.7.1 Escher's Problem 111
   3.7.2 Perceptual Illusions 111
   3.7.3 Redeployment Redux 113
      3.7.3.1 Persian and Arabic 113
      3.7.3.2 Subjects and Tasks 114
      3.7.3.3 Discrimination 114
      3.7.3.4 Forced Choice 114
      3.7.3.5 Sentence Reading 115
      3.7.3.6 Picture Naming 115
      3.7.3.7 Nonce Word Writing 116
      3.7.3.8 Elicited Imitation 116
      3.7.3.9 Discussion 120
   3.7.4 'Hearing' sC Sequences 121
   3.7.5 What about Production? 121
   3.7.6 Redeployment of Features 123
   3.7.7 Direct Mapping of Acoustics onto Phonology (DMAP) 125
   3.7.8 Universals 126
      3.7.8.1 Differing Repair Strategies as Evidence of Knowledge
         of Markedness 126
3.8 Conclusion 127

4. The Phonology/Morphology Interface 129
4.1 Introduction 129
4.2 The Prosodic Transfer Hypothesis 130
4.3 Right-Edge Clusters 131
4.4 Morphological Theories 133
   4.4.1 Distributed Morphology 133
4.5 Case I: Word Recognition and the Bilingual Lexicon 134
   4.5.1 Phonology Meets the Lexicon 136
   4.5.2 Psycholinguistic Methods 137
   4.5.3 The Bilingual Lexicon 138
   4.5.4 The Role of Phonology 139
   4.5.5 Competition for Root Insertion 140

4.6 Case II: Abrahamsson Revisited: A Distributed Morphology Analysis of Swedish Codas 141
    4.6.1 The Data 143
    4.6.2 A Distributed Morphology Reanalysis 143
4.7 Case III: L2 Allomorphy 145
    4.7.1 L2 Learners 149
        4.7.1.1 Methodology 149
        4.7.1.2 The Task 151
        4.7.1.3 Phonology, Silent Reading, and Lexical Activation 152
        4.7.1.4 Bilingual Lexicon and Non-selective Access 152
        4.7.1.5 Results 152
        4.7.1.6 No Impossible (L2 Turkish) Grammars 154
        4.7.1.7 Secondary Feature Spreading 155
        4.7.1.8 No Crossing Constraint 155
        4.7.1.9 No Impossible (L2 German) Grammars 156
    4.7.2 Poverty of the Stimulus 156
    4.7.3 Summary 157
4.8 Case IV: Intraword Codeswitching 157
    4.8.1 ICS and Phonology 158
    4.8.2 Why No Phonological Switching? 160
    4.8.3 Summary 162
4.9 Conclusion 163

5. The Phonology/Syntax Interface 164
5.1 Introduction 164
5.2 L2 Sentence Processing 164
    5.2.1 The Reading Process 165
    5.2.2 The Sentence Parser 165
    5.2.3 Prosodic Constraints on Reanalysis 166
    5.2.4 Relative Clause Attachment Preferences and Prosody 166
    5.2.5 Phonological Coding 168
    5.2.6 The Implicit Prosody Hypothesis 168
    5.2.7 Phonological Coding and Hearing Loss 171
        5.2.7.1 The Subjects and Methods 172
        5.2.7.2 Prosodic Constraint on Reanalysis in Hard of Hearing 172
        5.2.7.3 Offline Results 173
        5.2.7.4 Eye-Tracking and Reanalysis 173
        5.2.7.5 Implicit Prosody and RC Attachment in Hard of Hearing 174
        5.2.7.6 Results: Offline Tasks 174
        5.2.7.7 Results: Online Tasks 174
        5.2.7.8 ASL Phonology 175
        5.2.7.9 Summary 176

Contents

5.3 L2 WH-Questions 176
    5.3.1 Contiguity Theory 177
    5.3.2 Match Theory 182
    5.3.3 What Is to Be Acquired? 187
    5.3.4 Methodology 190
        5.3.4.1 The Task 190
        5.3.4.2 The Structure of the Argument 191
        5.3.4.3 Interlanguages as Natural Languages 192
    5.3.5 The Role of Input 193
    5.3.6 Shallow Structure 193
    5.3.7 Phonetics and Phonology 194
    5.3.8 Results 194
        5.3.8.1 Pitch Boost 194
        5.3.8.2 Prosodic Structure 196
        5.3.8.3 Architectural Implications 196
        5.3.8.4 Effects of Instruction / UG-Constrained
              Interlanguage 197
    5.3.9 Interfaces 198
        5.3.9.1 Phonetics and Phonology 199
        5.3.9.2 Return to Learnability 200
    5.3.10 Summary 200
5.4 Conclusions 201

6. Underture 202
6.1 Introduction 202
    6.1.1 Bayesian Epistemology 203
6.2 Why Is GenSLA Phonology the Pariah? 205
6.3 GenSLA and Pedagogy 206
6.4 Wrapping Up 207
6.5 Epilogue 210

Appendix A: Reading Sentences 213
Appendix B: Subject Profiles 217
References 219
Index 245

FIGURES

1.1 Components of language acquisition 3
1.2 The SPE Main Stress Rule 6
1.3 Modelling SLA 6
1.4 Dual thresholds in SLA 10
1.5 Less robust vs. more robust transition 11
1.6 Levels in the prosodic hierarchy 16
2.1 Structure of the Japanese/Chinese single liquid 18
2.2 Brown's discrimination results 19
2.3 Brown's lexical selection results 19
2.4 Japanese learners of Russian 21
2.5 Articulator vs. terminal nodes in English 21
2.6 Spanish acquisition of Yucatec Maya ejectives 24
2.7 The Sonority Sequencing Principle 25
2.8 Markedness and consonant clusters 26
2.9 Production accuracy by cluster type 30
2.10 Perception accuracy and input frequency 31
2.11 Transition bursts in consonant clusters 31
2.12 Overall error frequencies (deletion + epenthesis), development over time 32
2.13 Proportion of epenthesis to deletion errors, development over time 33
2.14 Number of errors by task type 33
2.15 Number of epenthesis errors by task type 34
2.16 Nativelike vowel production by Age of Acquisition of the vowels [i] and [ɪ] 35
2.17 Intelligibility by Age of Acquisition for the vowels [i] and [ɪ] 36
2.18 Summary of Birdsong's near-native speaker findings 37
2.19 Discrimination results by acoustic cue 44
2.20 Error rates for stress vs. phoneme contrasts 45
2.21 Scores on different phonological tasks 55
2.22 The 'Puzzle, Puddle, Pickle' problem 58
2.23 Preferential feature preservation 58

2.24	Preferential preservation of [COR]	59
2.25	Korean L2 chain shift	59
2.26	Preferential preservation of [+anterior]	60
2.27	Intra-constituent syllabic licensing	61
3.1	Different release bursts	84
3.2	Consonant to vowel recovery cues	85
3.3	Transition to sonorant vs. obstruent	85
3.4	Auditory distance scale	87
3.5	Feature hierarchies of two three-vowel systems	90
3.6	Auditory discrimination of L2 ejectives	99
3.7	Acoustic signature of ejective vs. plain stop	100
3.8a	Non-strident ejectives in coda position	101
3.8b	Strident ejectives in coda position	101
3.9	The mechanism of intake frequency	102
3.10	Visual illusions by M. C. Escher	111
3.11	Pictures of *slippers* and *stars* used in the informal production task	116
3.12	Right-edge appendices in Persian at the syllable and foot levels	117
3.13	Proposed structure of an initial English sC cluster	118
3.14	Production vs. perception for Persian L1 subjects	119
3.15	Production vs. perception for the Arabic L1 subjects	120
3.16	Persian production and perception at different proficiency levels	122
3.17	Alveolar and palatal stops	123
3.18	[posterior] in English	124
3.19	Phonetics as input to the phonological grammar	127
4.1	The prosodic hierarchy	130
4.2	Priming studies	137
4.3	Picture task	150
5.1	Pitch boost on a WH-question	179
5.2	Lack of pitch boost on a declarative sentence	179
5.3	Pitch track of the WH-question shown in (137)	188
5.4	Pitch track of declarative sentence of (138) with DP object	189
5.5	A native speaker recorded in our study demonstrating pitch compression	189
5.6	Native speaker pitch rise in declarative sentence	190
5.7	Visualization of the pitch patterns in a non-native speaker	191
6.1	The periodic table of elements	208
6.2	A unified architecture for L2 I-language	209
6.3	Domains of inquiry	210

TABLES

2.1	Consonant cluster frequency	29
2.2	The distribution of sC clusters across different corpora	30
2.3	Acoustic and phonological properties of stress systems	41
2.4	Error rates by language group	42
2.5	Cross-linguistic metrical parameters	48
2.6a	Japanese loanword stress applied to the English word *agenda*	51
2.6b	Japanese loanword stress applied to the English word *venison*	51
2.7	Working memory tasks in L1	54
2.8	Working memory and phonology scores	56
2.9	Processing speed and different tasks	56
2.10	Finnish error rates	63
2.11	Kabak and Idsardi research design	77
2.12	Possible responses in a discrimination task	78
2.13	Discrimination accuracy of different consonantal sequences	78
3.1	Feature weight scale	88
3.2	Auditory distance machinery	88
3.3	New segments based on an L1 feature	95
3.4	Features causing inaccurate perception	95
3.5	Cases of successful acquisition of new features	96
3.6	Experimental population for L2 length contrasts	103
3.7	Interpreting ranked data	106
3.8	Auditory discrimination results	106
3.9	Comparison of different subject groups	107
3.10	Picture identification task results	108
3.11	Performance by proficiency level	108
3.12	Native vs. non-native consonantal length contrasts	110
3.13	Non-native vocalic length contrasts	110
3.14	Perception errors correlated with linguistic properties	113
3.15	Persian and Arabic tasks	114
3.16	Perception errors correlated with linguistic properties revised	117
3.17	Syllabic properties of two Saudi Arabic dialects	119

3.18	Accuracy scores of two Saudi dialects 120
3.19	Perception of palatal stops 124
4.1	Interlingual homographs and homophones 135
4.2	Interlingual homophones and interlingual homographs 138
4.3	Polysemes and homophones 139
4.4	Translation equivalents 139
4.5	Final -r words in Swedish 142
4.6	Present and Plural Morphemes in Swedish 142
4.7	Patty's past and plural markings 145
4.8	German plural variants 145
4.9	Multiple exponence in German plural 146
4.10	Phonology in silent reading 152
4.11	Accuracy rates and error patterns 152
4.12	Chi-squared results of Type A vs. Type B errors 153
4.13	Well-formed (Type A) errors which are not in the input 154
5.1	Attachment preferences of three groups 174
5.2	WH vs. DP pitch levels (in semitones) by sentence pair 195
5.3	Pitch levels (in semitones) between WH and [+Q] 196
5.4	Sentential pitch patterns 196
5.5	Native vs. non-native pitch patterns 197

PREFACE

The main goal of this book is to probe questions about the nature of an interlanguage (IL) grammar (i.e. the grammar of a bilingual or multilingual). To do so, I frame my questions within a cognitive science perspective which draws upon abstract representational structures in demonstrating that phonological *knowledge* underlies second language (L2) speech. Specifically, the book will demonstrate that IL grammars are not 'impaired' (Hawkins and Chan 1997), 'fundamentally different' (Bley-Vroman 1990, 2009), or 'shallow' (Clahsen and Felser 2017). The results of these studies will bolster the position that IL grammars are complex mental representations governed by the principles of linguistic theory. This is societally important, especially in North America, where sometimes it is assumed that monolingualism is the norm and that second language learners speak 'deficient' versions of the target language. This project will help us argue against these views. Furthermore, the book seeks to highlight that phonology is critical to properly understanding the production and perception of syllables, words, and phrases in an additional language. Each strand makes falsifiable claims to argue that interlanguage grammars are best explained by abstract phonological categories.

Thus, my goal is to show the utility and indeed necessity of an essentialist representational approach to the generative grammar of second language phonology. Current linguistic cartography is well represented by many neo-empiricist stances, and I believe the time is ripe to present a counter-model. By doing so, I hope to show the centrality of phonology to many L2 phenomena. This is necessary perhaps because of the peculiar history of the discipline. In the heyday of *contrastive analysis*, L2 speech was crucial to many of the arguments made. Throughout the days of *error analysis*, morphological and syntactic phenomena were considered but largely atheoretically (in linguistic terms). With the emergence of GenSLA (generative approaches to second language acquisition), concurrent with Government and Binding Theory and the Principles and Parameters Model L2 syntax climbed up on a pedestal which it really has yet to relinquish. The study of L2 speech continues to flourish though somewhat removed from phonological theory.

A preface to a book on L2 phonology is not the place to survey linguistic history, but let me note a few (relatively) uncontroversial points.

- Language has evolved in humans and not in other species.
- The central mechanism is recursive Merge to generate hierarchical phrases.
- Multilingualism is more common than monolingualism.
- Phonology is invoked to spell out the morphological feature bundles found in the syntactic trees.

Perhaps slightly more controversially, I will argue that phonology is part of the Language Faculty Narrow (Dresher 2018). Phonology is cognition; phonology is grammar. The study of phonology requires abstract hierarchical representations. Furthermore, phonology cannot just be viewed as a computational system to generate single word forms.

The study of grammatical interfaces reveals not just a potential locus of optionality in L2 performance (as foregrounded in the work of Sorace 2011) but, more strikingly, the necessary *design conditions* for an internally consistent architecture of a comprehensive model of second language speech. The resulting empirically motivated model is parsimonious in accounting for all aspects of L2 speech from feature to sentence.

What all levels of representation show is *recursion*, or the creation of hierarchical constituent structure. This is well documented in the literature on Merge (e.g. Watumull et al. 2014) but is just as relevant to the domain of phonology and, indeed, to the domain of L2 phonology. We see it in syllable structure, word structure, and the licensing of syntactic structure.

What this book isn't: a balanced survey or state of the art that could be used to teach an introductory second language acquisition course or even an undergraduate L2 phonology course (though I know these are thin on the ground).

What this book is: an extended argument for (a) the centrality of phonology to the understanding of second language acquisition, (b) the need for abstract representational phonology in interlanguage grammars, and (c) the idea that we can build a unified, internally consistent model of SLA in which phonology, morphology, and syntax are all governed by the same principles of representation and processing.

ACKNOWLEDGEMENTS

There are many people who have played a part over the years in helping me to formulate the ideas presented here. Elan Dresher planted the seed of probing the learnability of phonology in a grad course (long ago) at the University of Toronto. Gary Libben has been a role model in diligence, the pursuit of Big Questions, and humane scholarship. Martha McGinnis has been a great resource in helping me to delve into (or at least scratch the surface of) the intricacies of morphological and syntactic theory. I think her answer to every one of my questions began, 'Well, it's complicated . . .'

I would also like to thank the reviewers of the manuscript for their careful readings and suggestions. They saved me from not a few blunders and helped to make the content and arguments clearer (I hope) to more readers (I hope).

Over the years, I have had the pleasure of interacting with many, ahem, senior scholars in the field who were very generous with their time and support: Susanne Carroll, Jim Flege, Allan James, Roy Major, Wayne O'Neil, and Martha Young-Scholten.

I have had wonderful interactions with many people interested in similar questions to mine at conferences or down the hall in linguistics departments: Nic Abrahamsson, Ocke Bohn, Jen Cabrelli, Walcir Cardoso, Juli Cebrian, Laura Colantoni, Isabelle Darcy, Laurent Dekydtspotter, Fred Eckman, Paola Escudero, Heather Goad, Kevin Gregg, Izabelle Grenon, Bill Idsardi, Tanja Kupisch, John Matthews, Murray Munro, Mary O'Brien, William O'Grady, Öner Özçelik, Norvin Richards, Jason Rothman, Mike Sharwood Smith, Bonnie Schwartz, Christine Shea, Rex Sprouse, Jeff Steele, Sara Stefanich, Steve Weinberger, Lydia White, Magdalena Wrembel, and Mary Zampini.

There were my students at the University of Calgary: Susan Armstrong, Susan Atkey, Leslie Blair, Antonio González Poot, Sue Jackson, Karen Jesney, Jen Mah, Teresa Merrells, Seiko Sagae, Fumiko Summerell, and Silke Weber. And at the University of Victoria: Amjad Alhemaid, Eloisa Cervantes, Martin Desmarais, Jie Deng, Emma Hayter, Dustin Hilderman, Keun Kim, Mitchell Li, Silas Romig, Noah Rummel-Lindig, Adam Steffanick, Lisa Suessenbach, Junyu Wu, Marziyah Yousefi, and Sophia Yuan.

And then there were the good buddies in Calgary who were always there for conversation and friendly interaction: Darin Flynn, Brian Gill, Martha McGinnis, Mary O'Brien, Doug Walker, and Nick Zekulin.

And colleagues here at UVic who helped me bring some of these projects to fruition: Peter Gölz, Hossein Nassaji, Matt Pollard, Patrick Rysiew, Ulf Schütze, and Su Urbanczyk.

Some of this work has been published earlier in my career. I thank the publication venues and the reviewers who provided feedback to improve the pieces. Finally, I would like to thank the team at Oxford University Press, including Meredith Keffer and Vicki Sunter, for seeing the project through, and the production team at Newgen (thanks, Koperundevi). Thanks also to Judy Nylvek for producing such a fine index under very tight time constraints. Finally, I give the highest praise to the diligent and hawk-eyed copyediting of Carrie Watterson.

ABBREVIATIONS

AP	adjective phrase
AoA	Age of Acquisition
BE	Bayesian epistemology
BP	Brazilian Portuguese
C	consonant
CP	complementizer phrase
CS	codeswitching
DEC	Derived Environment Constraint
DH	Deaf and Hard-of-Hearing
DM	Distributed Morphology
DP	determiner phrase
EI	elicited imitation
EP	European Portuguese
ERP	Event-Related Potential
FLA	first language acquisition
GASLA	Generative Approaches to Second Language Acquisition
GenSLA	generative approaches to second language acquisition
GP	Government Phonology
HA	high attachment
HPVT	high phonetic variability training
ICS	intraword code switching
IL	interlanguage
IPH	Implicit Prosody Hypothesis
ISI	Interstimulus Interval
LA	low attachment
LF	logical form
L1	first language
L2	second language
L2ers	second language speakers
L3A	third language acquisition
MaxEnt	maximal entropy

MEG	magnetoencephalography
MSD	minimal sonority distance
NNS	non-native speaker
NP	noun phrase
NS	native speaker
PCR	Prosodic Constraint on Reanalysis
PF	phonetic form
PLD	primary linguistic data
PN	post-nuclear
PTH	Prosodic Transfer Hypothesis
PWd	Prosodic Word
RC	relative clauses
RT	response time
SLA	second language acquisition
SLM	Speech Learning Model
SSH	Shallow Structure Hypothesis
SSP	Sonority Sequencing Principle
SV	Sonorant Voice
UG	Universal Grammar
V	vowel
VP	verb phrase
WSP	Weight-to-Stress Principle

1
Overture

1.1 INTRODUCTION

The primary goal of this book is to articulate a unified architecture for a model of second language phonology. By explicitly addressing the phonological interfaces, I will show how a common set of principles can account for diverse phenomena from phonetics to morphology and syntax. As we shall see, phonology is critical to these interfaces. I also hope to demonstrate that the empirical evidence strongly suggests that the phonological grammars of L2 learners are composed of rich, abstract, complex, hierarchical representations.

Currently, the state of theories of L2 phonology and its interfaces is something like shopping in a department store. We might find Stratal OT phonology (Bermúdez-Otero 2017) in Aisle 1, a derivational lexicon (Aronoff 1994) in Aisle 2, and Phase-Based Syntax (Chomsky 1999) in Aisle 3. The non-selective bilingual lexicon (Van Heuven, Dijkstra, and Grainger, 1998) is showcasing specials at the front of the store, and the phoneticians (Bohn 1995) are lurking in the basement. As cognitive scientists, however, we cannot just pick and choose from the shelves as we build our theories. The architecture is not constructed by tossing a phonological model, a morphological approach, and a syntactic theory into our shopping basket. Crucially, there is more at stake than just the isolation of research camps or researchers into silos. We want to try to understand how all the pieces fit together. Indeed, we want to make sure that they *do* fit together. It is understandable that in attempting to account for the intricacies and complexities of a particular domain (say, phonology), the literatures of other domains (say, syntax) are not probed in depth. Yet the concern is deeper in that the components may well be built upon incompatible models. In this book, I will demonstrate how a unified model of second language phonology can be constructed if we take seriously the interface conditions of phonetics, morphology, and syntax.

There is also a broader reason that I wanted to assemble these studies in book form. The literature in more applied approaches to the study of L2 speech (e.g. Munro 2003) clearly demonstrates that listeners sometimes judge accented speech negatively. Furthermore, around the world we're seeing a rising trend

Phonology in Multilingual Grammars. John Archibald, Oxford University Press. © John Archibald 2024.
DOI: 10.1093/oso/9780190923334.003.0001

of political backlash against migrants (and their children), who are viewed as speaking simplified, or lesser, versions of the majority language. When combined with certain empirical claims that interlanguage grammars are 'impaired' or 'shallow', I believed, there was utility in marshalling the arguments that interlanguage phonological grammars are *not* shallow. In this respect, I am hopeful that the book may have some potential for pedagogic implication and societal change.

1.2 TRADITIONAL CONTEXT OF L2 SPEECH

Much of the work on L2 speech has focussed on the intricacies of speech perception and the psycholinguistics of probing these processes. Although the Speech Learning Model (Flege 1995; Flege and Bohn 2021) and Perceptual Assimilation Model-L2 (Best and Tyler 2007) have revealed much about L2 speech, there is more yet to be accounted for. In this book, I seek to illustrate the centrality of phonology to many components of what we may broadly refer to as *L2 speech*.

What I propose is a cognitive model which builds on the insights from Laboratory Phonology (Pierrehumbert, Beckman, and Ladd 2000) and from Exemplar Theory (Johnson 2005) with respect to the role of phonetic detail in phonological *learning*. Such a mental model, supported by cognitive neuroscience, is rich representationally and looks to the architectural interfaces with phonetics, morphology, and syntax. This book is concerned with the *how* and *what* of second language acquisition (SLA). It is uncontroversial to say that any theory of SLA will have to include a theory of phonological representation (i.e. what is acquired) and a theory of how the linguistic environment influences that knowledge (i.e. a theory of input processing). The launching point for this project is L2 phonology—by which I mean a phonological *grammar* and all that entails (see Gregg 2006, on the notion of L2 grammar). Of course, what becomes more controversial are notions of what exactly is represented and how exactly input influences representation. Although there are many models or theories of SLA (e.g. Competition (MacWhinney 1987), the Modular Cognition Framework (Sharwood Smith and Truscott 2014), Processability (Pienemann 1998), and Autonomous Induction (Carroll 2001, etc.)), the goal of this book is not to develop a comprehensive model of second language learning or even of speech perception. The more modest goal is to take L2 phonology as the starting point and to probe key interfaces, which will allow us to take the first step in developing such an integrated architecture.

Many conceive of L2 phonology, at first blush, to be an esoteric, specialized niche. What I hope to demonstrate here is (a) the centrality of phonology to the understanding of many aspects of linguistic knowledge and ability, and (b) the contributions that the study of L2 phonology can make to the general cognitive science enterprise (see de Almeida and Gleitman 2017).

1.3 L2 PHONOLOGY

To position L2 phonology within a framework of cognitive science, let us begin by covering the tenets of language *learnability* (Wexler and Culicover 1980; Pinker 1989). When we recognize that second language learners have *grammars* (what I will call *interlanguage* grammars (Selinker 1972)) then we can begin to question how such knowledge is acquired, processed, and used. Of course, phonology is part of grammar. My goal here, then, is to model the acquisition of L2 phonology. Consider a model of language acquisition (L1 or L2 or Lx) shown in Figure 1.1.

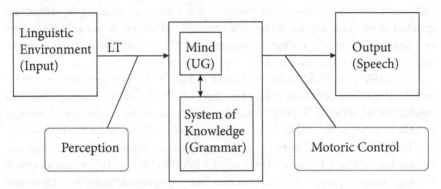

Figure 1.1. Components of language acquisition

Any cognitive domain contains a system of knowledge that is mentally represented. In the case of language, this is called a grammar. Given that humans are the only species to acquire language, it has long been assumed that something in our genetic makeup must lead to the expression of this trait. The species-specific property has been referred to as the language faculty (a cognitive module in the sense of Fodor 1983), a module which other species lack (see Berwick and Chomsky 2016).

The initial state of this faculty (in the absence of experience) is referred to as Universal Grammar (UG). UG characterizes the invariant properties that all human languages share. Now, of course, there are many different languages on the planet, so clearly there is an effect of experience, an effect of the environment. Babies who are exposed to French acquire French. Babies who are exposed to Japanese acquire Japanese. Environments are complex and include more than language. There are faces, music, sounds, smells, and many other influences on cognitive development. We refer to the subset of the environmental input that is language as the *input*. Perception of the spoken input is handled by both general auditory processes and language-specific processes (Jusczyk 1997). Philosophers have tackled the question of how knowledge relates to experience for centuries (and I will not delve too far into the larger issues here). Two broad approaches are *rationalist* and *empiricist* theories of mind. Both have had a strong influence in the field of linguistics. Let me outline them both briefly. On the one hand, an empiricist account of the acquisition of knowledge (Hume, Skinner) emphasizes the environment as the driver for acquisition. Domain-general learning theories (relying heavily on pattern association and associative memory) proceed by induction (specific exemplars in the environment which must be generalized to rules or patterns). The linguistic input imprints upon the hot wax of the empiricist mind to shape our knowledge. Negative feedback and training are crucial to the learning algorithm in such approaches. On the other hand, a rationalist account of the acquisition of knowledge (Chomsky, Descartes) emphasizes the role of innate structure triggered by environmental cues as the main process of the acquisition of linguistic knowledge. Domain-specific learning theories (relying heavily on computational processes and procedural memory) proceeding by deduction (general constraints on the shape of a grammar which guide the representation and analysis of specific strings encountered in the environment) trigger innate structures in the dark museum of the rationalist mind.

Fodor (1983) in *The Modularity of Mind* and in *The Language of Thought* (1975) sets the stage for examining the architecture of what he calls the computational/ representational mind. This approach is also found in the foundational work of Pylyshyn (1984) as well as in their joint work such as Fodor and Pylyshyn (1988). The basic ideas are that there are (a) mental representations which encode our knowledge in what Chomsky would call the mind/brain, and (b) processes which act upon those representations. Processes take representations as their input and create new representations. This symbolic architecture has been central to cognitive science for many years (see Marr 1982). Evidence has accumulated over the years that language processes act upon abstract representations (Ding et al. 2015; Phillips et al. 2000; Poeppel, Idsardi, and van Wassenhove 2008). Two recent studies are particularly intriguing. Farris-Trimble and Tessier (2019) in an eye-tracking study demonstrate that fixation times were different on words which had Canadian Raising (e.g. 'right' [rʌjt] compared to 'ride' [rajd]), indicating that it took longer to calculate a mapping from the surface form to more abstract representations. Within a derivational model, the [ʌj] in 'right' is derived from an underlying /aj/ which makes it more complex than the [aj] in 'ride' which is identical to the underlying /aj/. However, even finding data consistent with abstract representation is not tackling the thornier question which Gallistel (2017) raises, and that is determining what the material realization of symbols in the brain is. As Gallistel (2017: 276) says, 'If there were symbols, then they must reside in memory, because the basic function of a symbol in a computing machine is to carry information forward in time in a computationally accessible form.' He argues that there is very little evidence for the synaptic theory of memory (Gallistel and King 2010), but what alternative is there? Tantalizingly, and I quote at length (Gallistel 2017: 277), he argues:

> We have been looking in the wrong place—for both the symbols and the machinery that operates on them. The symbols are not in the synapses, and the machinery that operates on them is not (primarily) in the neural circuits.

The symbols are in molecules inside the neurons, and the machinery that operates on them is intracellular molecular machinery.

On this view, each neuron is a computational machine. It takes in information through its dendrites, processes that information with complex information processing machinery implemented at the molecular level within the neuron itself, and, at least sometimes, it then generates a signal that carries the encoded results of its processing to other neurons by means of a patterned train of nerve impulses. On other occasions, it may only update its memories and not send out any signal. Because symbolic memory is an indispensable component of any computing machine (Gallistel and King 2010), the molecular-level information processing machinery inside each neuron has, as one of its most basic constituents, molecules whose form may be altered by experience in such a way as to encode acquired information, information that has been conveyed to the cell through its synaptic inputs. These intracellular memory molecules carry the acquired information forward in a form that makes it accessible to the molecular computing machinery.

What this suggests is that we are poised to postulate a representational theory not just of mind but of brain.

Learnability approaches are designed to formulate a *learning theory* which connects a specific linguistic environment to a specific grammar. Lidz and Gagliardi (2015) refer to the learning theory as an *inference* engine by which the learner compares input with expectations informed by both the current grammar and UG. Finally, the grammar is accessed when the speaker engages in some sort of linguistic behaviour such as talking. Chomsky (2018: 26) aptly notes:

> Evidently, the input and output (production) systems are linked. No one understands only Japanese and speaks only Swahili. The natural assumption . . . is that language is a module of a 'central system', which is accessed in the many kinds of use of language, including input analysis and externalization in production.

Although I have been outlining this schema to illustrate child language acquisition, it is also directly relevant to the study of second language acquisition in general, and the study of L2 phonology in particular. I could repeat the previous paragraph and insert the phrase *L2 phonology*, but that would be too repetitive. Suffice it to say that the L2 learner is exposed to L2 linguistic input which is the raw material used to set up an interlanguage phonological grammar which, in turn, is accessed when L2 speech is produced.

Drawing on an insight of Chomsky's (1986), we can categorize two interesting areas of L2 phonology foundational to this book: Plato's Problem and Orwell's Problem. Plato's Problem is that we acquire aspects of linguistic knowledge which are either completely absent from, or impoverished in, the input available to the learner. Orwell's Problem is that we fail to acquire some knowledge that is abundantly present in the input.

1.3.1 Background in Learnability

To delve into these questions, let me provide a bit more background to the study of language learnability (Gold 1967; Pinker 1984; Wexler and Culicover 1980). In the early days of generative linguistics, much effort was spent on crafting a descriptively and explanatorily adequate account of what native speakers of a language knew. In syntax, this included many transformations with such names (the details are unimportant) as Do-insertion, Affix Hopping, and Subject-Aux inversion. In phonology, this included many abstract rules and representations (such as those found in Chomsky and Halle 1968). For example, the Main Stress Rule of Sound Patterns of English was one of the first successful attempts to find patterns in English stress placement. It is reproduced in Figure 1.2.

$$V \rightarrow [1\ stress]\ /\ \left[X \underline{\quad} \left\{ \begin{array}{l} C_0 \left[\begin{array}{c} -\text{tense} \\ V \end{array} \right] C_0^1 \left[\begin{array}{c} \alpha voc \\ \alpha cons \\ -ant \end{array} \right]_0 \\ C_0 \end{array} \right\} \right.$$

$$/ \underline{\quad} \left\{ \begin{array}{l} +C_0 \left[\begin{array}{c} -\text{tense} \\ V \end{array} \right] C_0]_{NA} \\ \left[\begin{array}{c} -\text{tense} \\ V \end{array} \right] C_0]_N \end{array} \right\}$$

Figure 1.2. The SPE Main Stress Rule
SOURCE: Chomsky and Halle (1968)

As Kaye (1990) observes, if this is a possible rule, what isn't? And how could a child learn it? The point is that from this moment on linguists began to realize that grammatical models must be *learnable* based on the input learners are exposed to. And this is where we find ourselves in the field of SLA today, as represented in Figure 1.3.

Figure 1.3. Modelling SLA

The top arrows indicate the notion of developmental path. Learners proceed from an initial state grammar (which under models of Full Transfer (Schwartz and Sprouse 1996) would be identical to the grammar of their L1). The target of their acquisition is the grammar of the L2, which would be as described by linguistic descriptions of native speakers of that target language. The bottom arrows indicate that the intermediate grammars may be representations which are neither L1-like nor L2-like.

Plato's Problem. As Chomsky (1986) points out, we acquire knowledge for which the environmental evidence may be severely impoverished in that it is insufficient to account for the final state of the grammar achieved. Learners may end up representing such abstract elements as metrical feet, or traces of movement, or moraic weight even though there are no direct acoustic cues that signal the need for these elements. In phonology, it has been argued that although both French and English have a phonemic /p/-/b/ contrast, French represents the phonological feature [voice] while English represents the feature [spread glottis] (Iverson and Salmons 1995). Somehow L1 children acquiring those languages are exposed to the relevant input data and acquire the target-like representation. L2 learners face the same task, and the cue to this feature may be subtle. The same would be true of the morphological acquisition problem facing someone who has L1 [aspect] and needs to acquire L2 [tense]. The relevant cues in the input may be subtle.

Orwell's Problem. Chomsky (1986) also indicates that, at times, we are resistant to the acquisition of knowledge which is quite frequent in the environment. There may be lots of [h] sounds in the input learners are exposed to, and yet native speakers of French may be resilient to the acquisition of /h/ (Mah, Goad, and Steinhauer 2016). There may be many tokens of the plural in the input, and yet plural marking is frequently omitted.

This book addresses both of these problems. The treatment of Plato's Problem focusses on representational issues (abstract phonology and Distributed Morphology), while the treatment of Orwell's Problem focusses on the construct of Intake Frequency.

1.4 INTERLANGUAGE GRAMMARS

In a book focussing on second language speech, we must confront early on the question of whether multilingualism is the norm or the exception globally. While difficult to quantify, I side with Grosjean (2012) when he notes that monolingual brains are less common on the planet than multilingual ones. Second language learning is not a specialized skill available to only the academically elite. For me, this means that the default of the lexicon, and the grammatical system, is to assume that more than one grammar will be represented (see also Amaral and Roeper 2014, on multiple grammars). López (2020) talks of this as an integrated grammar, but I will not delve into that deeply here. In Nakayama and Archibald (2005) we first proposed this notion to incorporate language tags (in I-language) as a diacritic feature available via UG. Humans arrive on this planet with the ability to represent more than one language. If the environment triggers this feature, it is activated. This theme is pursued in Archibald and Libben (2019).

1.4.1 Sources of Knowledge

Let us step back epistemologically and ask what sources of knowledge an L2 learner would have to establish new knowledge.

1. Universal Grammar (i.e. *biology*)
2. Input effects (i.e. *environment*)
3. Components of L1 knowledge (i.e. *grammar*)

Let us examine each of these in a bit more detail.

1.4.1.1 UNIVERSAL GRAMMAR

If there is a phrase that is more contentious in the study of language acquisition, or maybe even language itself, I'm not sure what it is. There was a rich and productive debate in SLA in the 1990s concerning the question of whether interlanguage grammars were governed by (or had 'access to') Universal Grammar. Exchanges between opposing sides could be, shall we say, quite heated. Even more recently the debate in both the popular and the academic press as to whether the Amazonian language Pirahã displays the property of recursion was quite inflammatory (Everett 2005; Nevins, Pesetsky, and Rodrigues 2009).

Chomsky at his most neutral would say something like, *well, language is unique to* Homo sapiens, *so we can assume that there is something special and unique in the minds/brains of our species which allows for this trait to emerge in infancy. If we label this unique asset the language faculty then it is an empirical question to ask what the state of this language faculty is at birth, that is to say, prior to exposure to the different languages of the environment. Let us call the properties and principles of this domain-specific faculty Universal Grammar.* The devil is, however, in the details, it seems. Is there a universal set of functional categories or phonological features? Are there operations which apply only to language and not to other cognitive domains?

Let us take a hypothetical example from L2 syntax and then one from phonology to illustrate the point. Imagine that your L1 lacks overt WH-movement but your L2 allows such movement. In languages which allow overt WH-movement, there are constraints on what can move where. In a lovely example from Steven Pinker, consider that in English it is grammatical to say, 'What did you eat eggs with ___?' (a fork) but not 'What did you eat eggs and ___?' (bacon). The UG-related question is whether second language learners will ever generate sentences such as 'What did you eat eggs and?' If they never entertain such hypotheses, then then question is, *where did this knowledge of ungrammaticality come from?* The differences between well- and ill-formed WH-questions cannot be a property transferred from the L1 grammar because the L1 does not allow overt WH-movement. Another possible source of knowledge is UG; L2 learners (like L1 learners) do not consider hypotheses which are not sanctioned in natural languages.

The phonological analogue would be something along these lines. Imagine that your L1 lacks onset consonant clusters; all syllable onsets contain a maximum of one consonant. The L2 that you are acquiring, however, allows complex onsets with more than one consonant (e.g. [fr], [kl] or [str]). In acquiring the grammar of

Interlanguage Grammars

the L2, the learner will move from a grammar where clusters are ill formed (*CC) to a grammar where clusters are well formed (CC). The question is, will they acquire *all* CC clusters at the same time, or will some be acquired before others? If the CC acquisition is, in fact, incremental, then will the order of acquisition match the universal patterns observed in other natural languages? For example, there are languages which allow [str] and [tr] clusters but no language which allows only [str] but not [tr] clusters. Could there be an interlanguage grammar which allows [str] but not [tr]? Not if IL grammars are constrained by UG, but if IL grammars are constructed by domain-general hypothesis testing, then yes.

1.4.1.2 INPUT EFFECTS

Clearly the ambient language also affects the makeup of the IL grammar. Most explicitly, I will return to this in Chapter 3, Section 3.5 (intake frequency), and Chapter 3, Section 3.7.8.1 (markedness in syllable structure), but for now let us start at a high level. Most obviously, as with L1 acquisition, the linguistic environment (a.k.a. primary linguistic data) has a *triggering* effect on the learner. Children will not acquire a /θ/ unless they hear a [θ]. L1 learners will not set up grammars with overt WH-movement or onset consonant clusters unless they are exposed to them in the input. Similarly, L2 learners (whose L1s lack overt WH-movement and onset consonant clusters) will not represent these properties unless they occur in the input.

There are other ways in which the input might affect grammar learning. I will introduce two notions here: input *frequency* and input *saliency*. I use the common term 'saliency' here in a specific sense which refers to a phonetic property of the input that I will refer to as *robustness* (following Wright 2004) for the remainder of the book. I do this to avoid potential ambiguity in the term where a sound might be referred to as salient unto itself (i.e. a property of the signal) or salient to the listener (i.e. an artefact of perception). The notion of frequency is relatively straightforward. Imagine a counter that ticks once every time you hear an [x] or an irregular plural. It is a key construct in usage-based approaches (e.g. Wulff and Ellis 2018). Stated simply, we might assume that, all other things being equal, items which are frequent in the input will be acquired earlier than items which are infrequent.

Frequency has been demonstrated to play a role in irregular morphology. For example, high-frequency irregulars are more resistant to language change than low-frequency irregulars. Compare *went* (high-frequency irregular past-tense of *go*) with *strove* (low-frequency irregular past tense of *strive* which is more likely to be regularized to *strived*). Low-frequency irregulars also tend to have longer response times on a variety of lexical tasks. For example, if asked to produce the plural of a low-frequency noun which has an irregular plural marker such as *larynx*, the response time is usually longer than when asked to produce the plural of a low-frequency noun such as *quodlibet* which takes regular morphology (*larynges* vs. *quodlibets*).

Frequency has also been shown to affect child language acquisition in a number of domains. Legate and Yang (2007) showed that 60% of child-directed utterances in Spanish unambiguously support a grammar with a [tense] feature, compared to only 6% of child-directed utterances in English. Spanish-speaking children begin to regularly mark tense around the age of 2 years of age, while English-speaking children begin to mark it consistently around the age of 3 years, 5 months. In the domain of phonology, it has been reported (Pye, Ingram, and List 1987) that Quechua-speaking children start producing a [tʃ] consistently earlier than English-speaking children do. Pye suggests this is because of the greater input frequency of [tʃ] in Quechua.

The connection to language change, noted above, is not accidental. The fields of historical linguistics, child language acquisition, and second language acquisition share a concern with explaining how grammars change. How did Old English become Middle English? Why does the 5-year-old child sound different than the 3-year-old child? What happens to my L2 Spanish the more I speak or study it? In this respect, then, these fields of developmental linguistics are concerned with formulating a theory not just of a grammar at a particular moment in time—what has been called a *property* theory—but also a theory of the developmental path—what has been called a *transition* theory (Cummins 1983).

In early work (Archibald 1994, 1997b), I proposed one simple model to account for the observed patterns of change over time. The formal model (complemented by a theory of lexical dependency) was proposed at a time when the dominant linguistic theory was Principles and Parameters (Roeper and Williams 1987). Parameters were the cognitive devices designed to account for variation between languages. Allow overt WH-movement? Yes/no. Allow branching onset clusters? Yes/no. Note, however, that in a parameter-setting model, if a switch had been set to, say, branching onsets (yes) then it was a challenge to account for variable performance in which a learner might sometimes produce a branching onset and sometimes modify a branching onset. What I had suggested was that the learning curve of parameter setting was not linear but, rather, S-shaped, as shown in Figure 1.4.

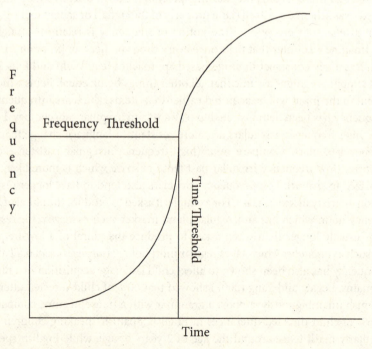

Figure 1.4. Dual thresholds in SLA

Interlanguage Grammars

What this visual metaphor (based on the seminal work by Saleemi 1992) suggests is that at early stages of acquisition (when the slope is flat) the behaviour will be relatively stable (and most likely influenced by the L1 setting). Similarly, at later stages of acquisition (when the slope is again flat) the behaviour will also be relatively stable (and influenced by the L2 setting). However, in the middle stages (when the slope is steep) there is a period of variation, or vacillation, or oscillation between the L1 and L2 settings, which reflects that the learner has not yet decided about the appropriate parameter setting. Thus, there is what I called a *dual* threshold of frequency and time which influences when a decision is made. This sort of model ascribes a major role to input frequency. At early stages, each occurrence of a particular structure (say, branching onsets) will add to a counter but not lead to instantaneous parameter resetting. This is a good thing and avoids what David Lightfoot (1991) called the Evil Neighbour Syndrome, where the evil neighbour leans over the fence and says to someone learning English (either as a first or additional language), 'Your house green lovely is.' If the learner has hair triggers, then this malicious input (which could also be found—more benignly—in speech errors directed to the learners) could cause them to mis-set their parameters. But in Figure 1.4 we see that after a certain number of items which have branching onsets, the transition will be rapid. Yet in that transitional stage we may see variation or optionality. This notion is also articulated in Yang's (2018) Tolerance Principle, which formulates how many exceptions a particular grammar will accept before making a change.

In addition to frequency, *robustness* is a property of the signal which may make it easier to perceive by all human ears. As Wright (2004) defines it, a robust signal resists environmental masking. That is to say, it can stand out in a noisy environment. For example, the transition from a voiceless stop to a vowel (e.g. [ta]) is more robust than the transition from a liquid to a vowel (e.g. [la]), as can be seen in the waveforms in Figure 1.5.

s l a t   s t a p

Figure 1.5. Less robust vs. more robust transition
SOURCE: Adapted from Cardoso, John, and French (2009)

I will return to robustness when it comes to the discussion of intake frequency. However, now let us turn to the third component under consideration as sources of knowledge: the L1.

1.4.1.3 COMPONENTS OF L1 KNOWLEDGE (A.K.A. TRANSFER)
One of the central issues in the field of SLA has been the notion of transfer (see Major 2008 for an overview). It is certainly clear in L2 phonology that the L1 can act

as a strong influence on both the perception and production of the L2. Weinreich (1953), Nemser (1971), Lado (1957), and Scovel (1988) all talk about elements of this sort of transfer. Perhaps most obviously, this phenomenon makes its presence felt in the realm of second language accent: English speakers can readily identify a French as opposed to a German accent in an L2 speaker. For example, the English word *have* [hæv] might be pronounced as [haf] by a German speaker and [av] by a French speaker. Both L1s, lacking the [æ] vowel may substitute [a]; the German speaker might devoice the syllable final [v] to produce [f] (as would happen in German); the French speaker would not produce a [h] given its absence from the French consonantal inventory. The work of Scovel (1988) and others focusses on the underlying etiology of this trait and falls within the general rubric of the Critical Period Hypothesis. Treated under the broad category of *age effects in SLA* (Birdsong 1992; Harley 1986; Herschensohn 2000; Hyltenstam and Abrahamsson 2000; Meisel 2011; Singleton 1989), the key questions would be (a) are these accentual patterns correlated with or caused by the Age of Acquisition, (b) what other components of the grammar are implicated, and (c) what function might this trait serve?

Scovel is of the opinion that a second language accent in production serves an anthropological, or perhaps even evolutionary, function. Across the species, our ability to detect foreign accents is acute, and Scovel suggests that the purpose is to identify in-group and out-group members of a social order. This kind of fascinating speculation reminds us that we can transfer our perceptual properties as well. Transfer does not merely implicate a late production routine. Rochet (1995) provides a nice example when it comes to the perception of the high front rounded vowel [y] by English and Brazilian Portuguese (BP) speakers. English speakers tend to mishear the [y] as [u], while the BP speakers hear it as [i].

Under a model of Full Transfer (Schwartz and Sprouse 1996), is it unsurprising that the initial state of L2 acquisition will be the final state of L1 acquisition. As we will see, this position does have some intricate implications when we consider the Redeployment Hypothesis (in Chapter 3, Section 3.6), but right off the bat, we are faced with the more straightforward question of looking at the developmental path in SLA and the question of how cross-linguistic equivalencies are assigned.

Examples from Phonology
L1 [b]: L2 [p]
L1 [e]: L2 [ɛ]

Examples from Morphology
L1 [+perfect]: L2 [+past]

Thus, learners will initially set up equivalencies or correspondences between L2 features and L1 features. As a result, it is unsurprising that our L1 experience and

Phonological Knowledge 13

grammatical system influence our L2 production and perception at the beginning stages of SLA.

1.5 PHONOLOGICAL KNOWLEDGE

In this book, I am focussing on the role of phonology in language. My broad starting point is that phonology is grammar; phonology is knowledge. Couched in these terms, we need to step back and look at some issues related to the acquisition of knowledge. This is a field that many philosophers have explored.

Scholz, Pelletier, and Pullum (2022) outline three schools of thought which are well represented in the philosophy of linguistics: externalism, emergentism, and essentialism.

1.5.1 Externalism

The locus of inquiry and explanation under this approach is to account for the actual utterances of speakers. The *explanandum* (what is to be explained) could be referred to as the E-language, or the corpus. A critical part of the *explanans* (the explanation) would be the distributional properties found in the corpus and the pattern-association skills of the language learner. Such an approach in linguistics is manifested in usage-based approaches (Bybee 2010). De Almeida (2017: 11) points out the difficulty usage-based models have in accounting for the productivity of the human language capacity:

> If cognitive systems aren't productive, how do we manage to say, understand, and think expressions we never said, understood or thought before? . . . It is not only connectionism that fails to account for the productivity of mental representations: a variety of frameworks (e.g. usage-based language representation, embodied cognition) do too. . . . [T]he finite elementary symbols/ representations ought to yield for an infinite capacity and the only way known to humankind that this can be achieved is by assuming that cognitive capacities are truly productive (and compositional and systematic), which thus far . . . only symbolic architectures do.

1.5.2 Emergentism

The locus of inquiry here is more a domain-general account which seeks to understand how language fits into the broader architecture of cognition (see MacWhinney and O'Grady 2015, for an overview). Researchers probe the properties of communication systems and look to see how interfaces with other cognitive modules such as working memory might explain linguistic behaviour. Exemplar theorists assume that abstractions (prototypes) emerge as a result of the processing of phonetically detailed representations. Such models (e.g. Adriaans and Kager 2010; Albright 2009; Coleman and Pierrehumbert 1998) achieve generalization by methods of (largely domain-general) pattern association.

1.5.3 Essentialism

The locus of inquiry here is on the machinery which accounts for the knowledge of well-formed versus ill-formed linguistic strings at the level of word and phrase. Actual utterances are taken to be epiphenomenal. Furthermore, an essentialist approach to the study of L2 phonology would accommodate abstract phonological representations. Generative phonology (e.g. Dresher 2009; Hale and Reiss 2000) posits abstract representations which are not directly connected to phonetic substance or directly read off the input. Hale and Reiss (2000), however, note that substance affects learning but not representation.

The work of Berent (2018) presents cogent arguments for what she calls *algebraic* phonology: phonology which operates on abstract variables. This architecture assumes categories such as 'sonorant' or 'onset' or 'syllable' or 'foot'. We will see throughout the book much empirical support for the existence of these types of phonological categories in interlanguage grammars. Berent also acknowledges that algebraic phonology, while necessary to account for phonological knowledge and behaviour, is not sufficient. She notes that phonological grammar interfaces with other cognitive and physical systems particularly when engaged in acquisition and production. Consistent with what I am arguing in this book, the gradual and gradient effects that are witnessed in acquisition and production, which are central to exemplar-based models, are accounted for by these interface conditions without the need to abandon categorical, symbolic representation. For example, we know that there is a developmental path to acquisition; not all new structure is acquired simultaneously. Take the example given in González Poot (2011; 2014) where L1 Spanish speakers are acquiring L2 Yucatec Mayan ejectives. He shows, as we will see in more detail in Chapter 3, Section 3.5.1, that subjects do not acquire the plain/ejective contrast for all obstruents at the same time. The learning path is gradual, but the end state of L2 knowledge is categorical phonological representation.

There are both empirical and philosophical reasons to adopt the Essentialist Model. From at least the time of Sapir (2008/1933), we have sought and found evidence that abstract representations such as the phoneme are necessary. More recently, Lago and colleagues (2015), drawing on Phillips and colleagues' (2000) insights, conducted brain scanning studies which rely on the brain's ability to detect unusual stimuli. The studies show that outliers are identified at a *phonemic* level, thus demonstrating that constructs such as the phoneme are real in terms of cognitive neuroscience. Work in the school of Dresher's (2009) Contrastive Hierarchy also establishes the need of abstract phonological features. For example, Dyck (1995) shows that languages which represent a feature such as [+high] on an [i] vowel behave differently than languages which do not (in terms of such processes as feature spreading). It is, therefore, *not* the acoustic signal properties of the [i] vowel which predict its behaviour but rather the mental representation. This mental representation is abstract. Hestvik and Durvasula (2016) conducted an Event-Related Potential (ERP) study which demonstrated that the learners were behaving in a manner consistent with phonological underspecification of the feature ([spread glottis]) phonologists argue is responsible for representing the English voicing contrast in pairs like /b/-/p/. Broś and colleagues (2021) demonstrate via an ERP study that regular Spanish stress is computed based on abstract phonological representations and not stored lexically.

Cutler (2012: 419) can be seen to sum up, while acknowledging the existence and function of veridical traces in memory, that 'evidence from L2 learning makes it clear that lexical phonological representations are abstract'.

Evidence for abstract representations in L2 learners can be found in Archibald (1993a, 2005). In these works, I show that such constructs as extrametricality (where syllables are invisible to the algorithm which determines stress placement), metrical foot structure (as a trochaic foot which is prominent on the left, or an iambic foot which is prominent on the right), and derived sonority (which shows that the phonetic property of sonority is governed by abstract phonological features) explain the properties of L2 grammars. None of these properties can be read directly off the input signal; these constituents are not labelled by an invariant acoustic cue to guide the learner. Weber (2014) shows that foot structure (not segmental properties) is critical to understanding the differential effects on intelligibility of different kinds of stress errors (e.g. 'diRIgent' vs. 'diriGENT' when compared to the actual form 'DIrigent'—*conductor*). Evidence for knowledge of abstract phonological structures can also be found in Özçelik and Sprouse (2016), Özçelik (2017b), Monahan, Lau and Idsardi (2013), Steinberg, Truckenbrodt, and Jacobsen (2010), Cabrelli Amaro (2017), and Lahiri and Reetz (2002, 2010). This is consistent with work in disparate frameworks (Archibald 2023; Pulleyblank 2006) which argue that the mapping of features to segments is a *learning* problem. This mapping is neither provided by UG nor something that needs to be 'noticed' in the input (see Carroll 2001; Rast 2008). This is also developed in the work of Dresher (2018), who argues that actual features are neither innate nor emergent. What is innate is something like the Successive Division Algorithm, which is a learning procedure to arrive at a Contrastive Hierarchy (following Jakobson and Halle 1956).

Phonological knowledge, of course, includes more than segments and features. A standard model of higher-level phonological structures is shown in Figure 1.6.

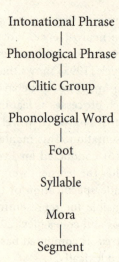

Figure 1.6. Levels in the prosodic hierarchy
SOURCE: Based on Nespor and Vogel (1986)

It is commonly assumed that this hierarchy is universal, though see Özçelik (2017b) for counterarguments.

1.5.4 Phonology as Cognition

What this all means is that phonology is viewed as cognition, best understood by the research practices associated with cognitive science. Phonology is not merely the physical properties of the interface with the motoric system. Although many researchers adopt this stance (Bale and Reiss 2018; Burton Roberts, Carr, and Docherty 2000), it is also fair to note that within Generative Approaches to Second Language Acquisition (GenSLA), phonology holds a much less prominent position than morphology, syntax, semantics, or processing. As recently as 2020 whole books have even been written with the title *Second Language Acquisition* which have failed to include a chapter on phonology. What I hope to demonstrate in this book is that GenSLA must take seriously the notion of phonology as cognition.

2

Phonological Grammars

2.1 INTRODUCTION

L2 learners, then, have phonological *grammars* whose properties we can investigate. Traditional questions such as *what is the initial state? what is the final state? do they respect UG principles?* are all just as valid for phonology as they are for other domains such as morphology or syntax. So, let us turn to some general questions regarding L2 phonological grammars.

2.1.1 The Deficit Hypothesis

Elsewhere in the field of second language acquisition (SLA), we have witnessed a debate between those who argue that certain linguistic properties (e.g. some functional category features) may be impossible for adult speakers to acquire (e.g. Hawkins and Chan 1997; Hawkins and Hattori 2006) and those (such as White 2003) who argue that adult learners *are* able to acquire these features. The first line of thought is what we can call the deficit hypothesis, which holds that if element x is not found in the first language then it will be unlearnable in adult second language acquisition. So, from a deficit perspective, if a speaker's L1 lacks a [tense] feature then it will be impossible for that learner to acquire the feature [tense] in an L2. The opposing view would hold that the lack of surface inflection in production does not entail the lack of the appropriate linguistic feature in the grammar. Lardiere (2007) argues that a Chinese L1 subject who is consistently omitting tense markers in her English L2 production also shows evidence of having acquired the abstract feature related to finiteness in her grammar.

Let us return to the field of L2 phonology. In many second language learning scenarios, we find that someone from a given L1 is attempting to acquire an L2 which has some different phonological properties. Perhaps a feature may be lacking, or the onsets don't branch, or the codas don't project moras, or the feet are iambic rather than trochaic. The empirical question is, *will second language learners be able to acquire structures which are not found in their first language?*

Phonology in Multilingual Grammars. John Archibald, Oxford University Press. © John Archibald 2024.
DOI: 10.1093/oso/9780190923334.003.0002

A classic treatment of this question can be found in the influential work of Brown (2000). We will begin our look at L2 features by discussing Brown's model.

2.1.2 Phonological Features

Brown (2000) argues that if featural representations are lacking in the L1, they will be unacquirable in the L2. She looked at the acquisition of English /l/ and /r/ by speakers of Japanese and Mandarin Chinese. Brown follows Maddieson (1984) in classifying 'r' as a voiced, retroflex fricative ([ʐ])—not as a retroflex sonorant. Duanmu[1] points out that all other obstruents in Standard Chinese are voiceless, so it would be phonologically odd to introduce a voiced segment in this series. He also provides a list of minimal pairs (excepting tone) which rely on the /l/-/ɻ/ contrast, thus motivating a phonemic sonorant contrast.

However, in order to present the form of the general argument, I will continue to assume Brown's featural analysis. In Japanese, [l] and [ɾ] are allophones of a single phoneme /ɾ/ as shown in Figure 2.1.

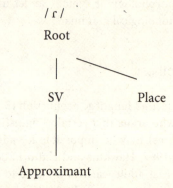

Figure 2.1. Structure of the Japanese/Chinese single liquid
SV = Sonorant Voice

This phoneme may appear only in a simple onset in Japanese. Mandarin Chinese also lacks the contrast (and hence the structure is the same as shown in Figure 2.1). If the *segment* is taken to be the level of explanation (as, say, in the Speech Learning Model, or the Perceptual Assimilation Model), then we might predict that both Mandarin and Japanese speakers should be unable to acoustically discriminate /l/ from /r/ (given their L1 feature geometries).

Brown reports on the overall performance of the subjects on an auditory discrimination task. Such a task demands that a listener hear two stimuli (e.g. 'rip/lip' or 'lip/lip') and judge whether they are the same or different (known as an AX discrimination task, in which listeners are asked whether the sound X (as in the variable *x*) matches the given sound (A)).

---

1. Thanks to Darin Flynn for discussion of these facts.

Her study demonstrated that the Japanese speakers were unable to discriminate /l/ from /r/ in an acoustic task (under 30% accuracy in onset position), whereas the Chinese speakers discriminated the contrast in a manner not significantly different from native speakers, shown in Figure 2.2.

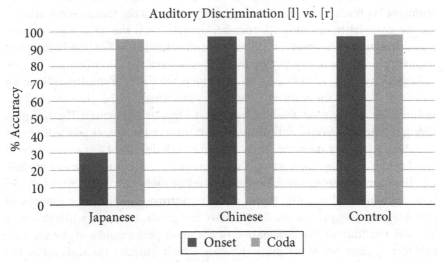

Figure 2.2. Brown's discrimination results
SOURCE: Adapted from Brown (2000)

The same results were obtained in a task which demanded that the subjects access lexical representations (i.e. they saw a picture of a *rake* and of a *lake* and, when hearing a single word, had to point out the picture of the word that they heard). The results are shown in Figure 2.3.

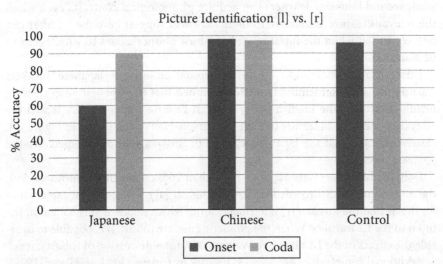

Figure 2.3. Brown's lexical selection results
SOURCE: Adapted from Brown (2000)

The initial hypothesis that speakers of both languages would be unable to perceive the /l/-/r/ distinction because one of the members of the contrast is an L1 *phoneme* is not supported by the Chinese subjects. So what aspect of the L1 could account for this difference? Brown suggests that a speaker may be able to perceive a non-native contrast if the *feature* that distinguishes the two segments is present in the L1 feature geometry (even if the feature is not utilized for the contrast in question). Under her analysis, it is the feature [CORONAL] that distinguishes /l/ from /r/. Chinese requires the [CORONAL] node for some segments in the inventory, but Japanese does not utilize it anywhere.

Regardless, then, of the L1 liquid inventory, the Chinese speaker will have a representation for the feature [CORONAL] somewhere in the phonological inventory (i.e. to contrast alveolar from post-alveolar segments). The Japanese inventory, however, does not contrast any CORONAL phonemes and will, therefore, lack a [CORONAL] node. Thus, Brown concludes that L2 speakers cannot build representations for segments which require features not present in their L1. They can, however, combine the features of their L1 in new ways to yield new segments. Admittedly, there is some controversy about her analysis of Chinese phonology (Duanmu 2000), as we saw above. However, while that may affect the validity of her explanation of the good performance of the Chinese subjects, it does not undermine the data which indicate the difficulties the Japanese learners face.

2.1.3 Robust Cues

There may be reason to believe, however, that this deficit model is too strong. There are a number of studies that suggest under certain circumstances that adult second language learners *can* acquire phonological contrasts even when the relevant feature is inactive in their L1. I will suggest here the L1 filter can be overridden when the input provides robust phonetic cues to what needs to be acquired.

Larson-Hall (2004) looks at the perceptual abilities of Japanese speakers learning Russian. Remember that Brown argued that the Japanese subjects were unable to acquire the English [l]/[r] contrast in onsets because they lacked the relevant phonological feature in their L1. Larson-Hall's data, shown in Figure 2.4, clearly indicates that the Japanese learners of Russian were able to perceive the contrast successfully.

Even the beginners were accurate more than 70% of the time (contrasted with the 30% accuracy of Brown's learners of English [ɹ]). One possible explanation for this is that the Russian [r] is a trilled sound, which makes it very salient in the input to the L2 learners. When the phonetic cues are robust, it is possible to override the effects of the L1 filter (see Wright 2004, for a discussion of robust cues).

Additional complexities are revealed in work by Curtin, Goad, and Pater (1998). They document a case study where English speakers learning Thai are able to acquire a feature that is not present in their L1. The property in question is aspiration, which is usually represented by the feature [spread glottis]. English does not make

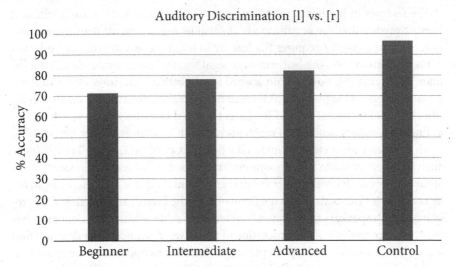

Figure 2.4. Japanese learners of Russian
SOURCE: Adapted from Larson-Hall (2004)

use of the phonetic feature of aspiration contrastively in its lexical items. Ignoring some complexities, suffice it to say that English has aspirated stops at the beginning of stressed syllables (e.g. 'top' [tʰɑp]) but lacks aspiration after an [s] (e.g. 'stop' [stɑp]). Aspiration, then, in English is predictable from the phonetic context and does not have to be memorized as part of the word. Thai, on the contrary, utilizes aspiration contrastively. For example, the word [pet] means 'duck' and the word [pʰet] means 'spicy'. English speakers learning Thai, then, would have to learn how to store the feature of aspiration as part of the lexical entry. Curtin, Goad, and Pater (1998) argue that English speakers *did* show the ability over time to lexicalize this phonological feature. That is to say that although their initial structures were transferred from the L1, they *were* able to trigger new knowledge.

LaCharité and Prévost (1999) propose a refinement of Brown's model. In looking at French speakers acquiring English, they present a hierarchy of difficulty for new sounds. Whereas Brown asserted that if a feature was lacking from the L1 then any contrast dependent on that feature could not be acquired, LaCharité and Prévost argue that a missing articulator node would be more difficult to acquire than a missing terminal node. French learners of English have to acquire the sounds [h] and [θ]. They propose the representations of Figure 2.5 for these sounds:

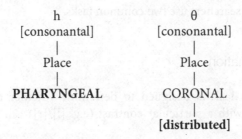

Figure 2.5. Articulator vs. terminal nodes in English

The features in boldface are absent from the French inventory. LaCharité and Prévost predict that the acquisition of /h/ will be more difficult than the acquisition of /θ/ because /h/ requires the learner to trigger a new articulator node. On a discrimination task, the learners were significantly less accurate identifying [h] than identifying [θ]; however, on a word identification task (involving lexical access) there was no significant difference between the performance on [h] versus [θ]. Mah (2003) conducted an ERP (Event-Related Potential) study which looked at English speakers acquiring French and Spanish 'r' sounds. Under her analysis, English lacks a PHARYNGEAL node (/h/ being LARYNGEAL), while French /ʁ/ is analysed as PHARYNGEAL. The notational convention is that features in SMALL CAPS are articulator nodes while other features are placed in square brackets. Spanish /r/, by contrast, is CORONAL. The acquisition of both the French and Spanish 'r' will require English speakers to activate a new terminal node, which Mah defines as [vibrant]. In her analysis of the processing of these two 'r' sounds, Mah does not find any differences between the perception of a French 'r' as opposed to the Spanish 'r'. This is an argument against the LaCharité and Prévost position. There is more to pursue in the phonological question of what is easy and what is difficult to learn.

2.2 METHODOLOGICAL ISSUES

To probe these questions of learning, one of the basic questions of L2 phonological research is to determine whether an individual has acquired a particular structural representation in the L2. The methodological question which immediately arises is how to do so. Production measures are an obvious choice in that it seems suggestive that a subject who is not producing an L2 contrast (e.g. [l]/[r]) has not acquired the necessary representations. However, it may be the case that inaccurate production does not automatically signal inaccurate perception. Perhaps subjects have acquired the correct representations but there are certain environmental factors (e.g. complex sentence structure) which lead to inaccurate production. Therefore, perception (much less under conscious control) may be a better window into grammatical knowledge. Flege (e.g. 1995) has done many studies which demonstrate that inaccurate production is the result of inaccurate perception. Therefore, when we ask ourselves the question, *why are they getting it wrong?* we have to ask whether they are perceiving a contrast accurately and producing it inaccurately, or whether they are perceiving it inaccurately and producing their internal representation accurately. In an attempt to tease these scenarios apart, researchers use two common tasks.

2.2.1 Discrimination

A discrimination task is designed to determine whether a subject who is having difficulty with a particular contrast (e.g. [l]/[r]) can actually perceive the contrast in a non-linguistic context. There are several versions of this sort of task, but one of the most basic is to use what is called an AXB task in which the subject hears three distinct stimuli and has to determine whether the second is identical to the first or the third. So a subject might hear [l], [r], [r], and the targetlike response would be that the second sound was identical to the third. If subjects succeed on this sort of task and yet demonstrate difficulty in production measures, we can conclude that the production difficulties do not arise from basic auditory difficulties.

2.2.2 Lexical Selection

The lexical selection tasks are designed to determine whether the L2 subjects can acquire targetlike lexical representations. Under this paradigm a participant may look at two pictures while they are given instructions like 'point to the *rake*' (i.e. not the *lake*). If subjects have not acquired targetlike representations, then we may assume their performance to be at chance level.

2.3 L2 EMPIRICAL STUDIES

Let us turn to a discussion of some key empirical studies which shed light on these psycholinguistic and acquisition questions.

2.3.1 Features

González Poot (2011) also provides evidence of a situation where L2 learners are able to acquire a contrast based on a feature absent from their L1. He looks at the acquisition of Yucatec Maya ejectives by Spanish speakers. Spanish lacks the [constricted glottis] feature required for the phonological structure of ejectives. Ejectives are a manner of articulation characterized by a forceful release burst on voiceless consonants made by first raising the larynx to increase the supralaryngeal pressure. He conducted both an auditory discrimination task and a forced-choice picture selection task. The results of the auditory discrimination task are shown in Figure 2.6.

In the onset position, the Spanish speakers were not performing significantly differently than the native Yucatec Maya speakers; they were able to acquire the contrast. In the coda position, however, they were not behaving in a nativelike range. One explanation for this goes back to the notion of robust phonetic cues. The transitional cue from the ejective in onset position to the vowel is much more robust than the phonetic cue found when an ejective is at the end of a word. Learners appear to be sensitive to such distinctions. A word-final ejective displays much subtler acoustic cues, and it is much more difficult to recover the place and

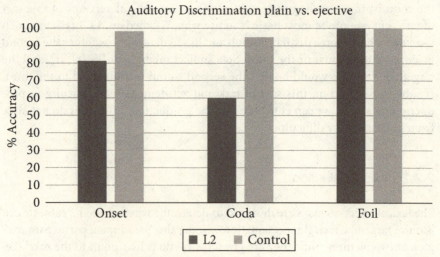

Figure 2.6. Spanish acquisition of Yucatec Maya ejectives
SOURCE: Adapted from González Poot (2011)

manner of the final consonant. This is also true of final palatal stops in Czech (Atkey 2001) and final palatalized consonants in Russian (Kulikov 2010).

2.3.2 Non-robust Cues

Mah, Goad, and Steinhauer (2016) provide data that show the problematic nature of cues which are not robust to the listener. They look at native speakers of French acquiring an English /h/.

They show that subjects accurately perceive [h] in non-linguistic tasks but fail to perceive it accurately in auditory discrimination tasks with lexical items (as determined by the Mis-matched Negativity paradigm in ERP studies). Under this paradigm, subjects are exposed to a majority of a given stimulus (e.g. [p]) and somewhere in the experimental trial an oddball sound (e.g. [b]) is introduced. If a subject detects a difference in the input tokens, a particular electrical signal is generated. However, if the distinction is not perceived, then this can also be read off the electroencephalogram. Thus, Mah's work shows that it is not that the subjects fail to perceive the [h] at an auditory level but rather that they fail to process it when linguistic representations are invoked.

Furthermore, ERP data show that the non-native speaker (NNS) subjects fail to invoke an N400 response to lexical items like 'hair' and 'air'. The N400 response in ERP studies is triggered during the processing of a semantic anomaly. If a native English-speaking subject is exposed to sentences such as 'The pizza is too hot to eat' and 'The pizza is too hot to drink', the latter sentence will trigger a negative electrical pattern 400 ms after the onset of the anomaly (i.e. *drink*).

This suggests that the L1 French subjects' lexical representations are impoverished, as their inaccurate response is on a lexical task, not a discrimination task.

I would argue that these results demonstrate that it is the subtle acoustic properties of the [h]/[θ] contrast which make it difficult for French learners of English to acquire. It is not that the contrast is impossible to acquire but merely that the input cues in the speech signal are more difficult for the learners to perceive and hence more difficult to process. Following Vanderweide (2005), the more robust input strings will be processed and parsed before the less robust strings. As a result, the more robust strings will be grammatically encoded before the less robust strings.

2.3.3 Syllables

Now let us look more closely at the acquisition of consonant clusters. Most of the consonant clusters in the world's languages obey what is known as the Sonority Sequencing Principle (SSP), which captures the fact that the nucleus of a syllable is the most sonorous element, and sonority diminishes towards the edges, as shown in Figure 2.7.

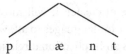

Figure 2.7. The Sonority Sequencing Principle

There are, however, sequences of consonants that violate this generalization, and they tend to involve the phoneme /s/.

In English some s-clusters violate the Sonority Sequencing Principle (e.g. 'st' since the fricative [s] is more sonorous than the stop [t]) while some do not (e.g. 'sn' where the fricative [s] is less sonorous than the nasal [n]).

The analysis of the structure of s-clusters is a complex and problematic area of phonological theory, and I will not go into the details here (but will return to it in Chapter 3, Section 3.7). Many researchers argue that [s] is not really part of the syllable but somehow outside it (attaching at a higher prosodic level). The interesting fact, bringing all this back to second language acquisition, is that L2 learners are aware of this.

2.3.3.1 MARKEDNESS

There is a vast literature in SLA on the role of *markedness* in explaining the behaviour of L2 learners. Since the early 1900s, linguistics has tried to capture somehow the notion of what was 'natural', or common, in language when it came to such patterns involving phonetic inventories, syllable structures, or phonological processes. In the Prague Circle (see Jakobson 1941/1968), for units in contrast there would be an *unmarked* and a *marked* member of the contrast. For example, if a language had a /b/ versus /p/ contrast, then the voiceless /p/ might be unmarked while the voiced /b/ would be marked. In a syllable, the CV structure would be unmarked while the CVC would be marked, hence implying that the presence of onsets was unmarked while the presence of codas was marked. And, with respect to processes, devoicing in coda position might have been unmarked (compared with devoicing in onsets), and voicing intervocalically might have been also unmarked (compared with devoicing intervocalically) thus illustrating the context-sensitivity of markedness.

Markedness is not always viewed as a binary construct, however. Many phenomena can be classified as being either *more* or *less* marked. Take a language that allows onset consonant clusters. Not all clusters are equally likely, and the nested (implicational) relationships are described along a markedness *scale*. So, we might find the pattern shown in Figure 2.8.

$$pj > pl > pn$$

less marked--------more marked

Figure 2.8. Markedness and consonant clusters

If a language has one type of cluster, it will most likely be [pj], as this is the least marked cluster. It is rarer for languages to allow the more marked [pn] onset cluster. Furthermore, there is an implicational relationship inherent in the markedness scale in which the presence of the more marked members ([pn]) implies the presence of the less marked members ([pj]). As we will see, this has implications for the structure of interlanguage grammars as well. Eckman (1991) argues in his Structural Conformity Hypothesis that interlanguage grammars respect the typological universals evident in primary languages. Before looking at those specific claims, let us take a step back to discuss the nature of universals.

2.3.3.2 TYPOLOGICAL UNIVERSALS

Ever since Greenberg (1963) there has been a well-documented difference in the description of language universals. On the one hand are the approaches which we can call *UG-based*, while on the other hand are the *typological*.

A UG-based approach would focus on properties of the grammar, or more accurately, the *I-language*. Such things as structure dependency, or c-command, or vowels projecting moras would be viewed as universal properties of the human language faculty. UG-based approaches seek to explain the universal properties of the mental representation of a grammar.

Typological approaches focus on properties of the data, or more accurately, the *E-language*. The patterns found in the data are analysed, and the following types of patterns might be noted:

- x is more frequent than y.
- Children acquire x before y.
- The presence of y in the data implies the presence of x in the data.

From these observations, a statement of the form 'x is less marked than y' might result. Thus, the unmarked form would be more common, acquired early, and more likely to be present in an interlanguage than the marked form. The work of Carlisle (2001) illustrates this type of perspective, demonstrating that L2 learners modify CCC (i.e. marked) clusters more often than they modify CC (i.e. unmarked) clusters. Eckman (1991) in the same vein shows that all interlanguage grammars which license $C_1C_2C_3$ also allow C_1C_2 and C_2C_3.

The literature is relatively consistent in showing that a construct of markedness may, indeed, be adequate for *describing* L2 learner behaviour on a variety of tasks. But this is not sufficient when it comes to *explaining* the L2 behaviour or explaining the reason the grammar is structured the way it is. In Archibald (1998), I put forward the view that markedness provides us with data which need to be accounted for but do not provide us with an explanation. To quote Kevin Gregg (1993), it is the *explanandum*, not the *explanans*. Saying that CCC clusters are modified more than CC clusters because they are more marked does not *explain* that behavioural pattern.

Eckman (2008: 104) criticises Archibald (as well as Gass and Selinker 2001) for misconstruing the explanation side of markedness. His claim is that both Archibald and Gass and Selinker miss that

there are *levels* of scientific explanations, where the levels correspond to the generality of the laws invoked. To debate whether a generalization is a description or an explanation is to debate the level of the explanation, not whether an explanation has been given. And to reject a hypothesis because it pushes the problem of explanation back one step misses the point that *all* hypotheses push the problem of explanation back one step—indeed, such 'pushing back' is necessary if one is to proceed to a higher level of explanation.

Eckman concludes by noting (2008: 107) that 'typological universals are laws that subsume phenomena under a generalization, make predictions, and thus constitute an explanation'.

I agree with much of what Eckman says. A theory of markedness does make predictions based on the hypothesized general laws. The predictions can be in domains as varied as SLA, child language acquisition, diachronic change, language attrition, or language processing. This is, of course, a property of a good theory.

However, I maintain his critique does *not* address the crucial distinction between I-language and E-language. Put another way, he does not consider the consequences of representational realism; grammar is a mental representation, not a statistical regularity in utterances. Carroll (2001) illustrates this nicely when she gives an example of a purported pattern which might be described as saying 'x happens at the end of a word'. Now, this kind of shorthand (that one might use in teaching Introductory Linguistics) may be a good rule of thumb for describing a pattern. Where does German /d/ turn to [t]? At the end of a word. Crucially, though, she points out that 'the end of a word' is not a representational unit in our mental grammar. So, while markedness makes testable predictions about the behaviours of L2 learners in production or perception tasks, say, it does *not* provide us with an account of the representation of the underlying knowledge. This is where I think Eckman's analogy to the Derived Environment Constraint (from Eckman and Iverson 1997) fails. I believe I am being fair in summarizing his argument along these lines. L2 learner behaviour is consistent with the Derived Environment Constraint in which certain phonological operations apply only across morpheme boundaries (i.e. in derived environments). He argues that this statement *explains* their behaviour because it refers to a more general law (the DEC). He suggests, furthermore, that the Archibald and the Gass and Selinker critiques are akin to saying, 'So why does the Derived Environment Constraint exist? You're not explaining L2 learner behaviour unless you can explain the DEC.' I accept that pushing back the explanation one level can be completely appropriate. However, we need to have, at some level, a description of what the learners know about the DEC. It may not be the L2 researchers who have to provide it; it may be the phonologist (e.g. Kiparsky 1982), but somebody has to take it on. Consider the analogy with illusory vowels that I will discuss more fully in Chapter 3, Section 3.7, or the discussion of differential substitution in Chapter 3, Section 3.3. Why do some subjects hear CC sequences as CəC? Why do some subjects replace a [θ] with a [s] while others replace it with a [t]? The L2 researcher might say that the subjects are behaving as if their lexical entries looked like *x*, *y*, or *z*. Perhaps they have an accurate underlying representation of a CC sequence or of a [θ] or perhaps they have non-targetlike representations. Essentially, that pushes the behavioural explanation back to the level of the lexical entry. But I would say that that is *not* an explanation until we can account for why the lexical entries look the way they do. And this we do by probing the acquisition of phonological features which build the representations of the contrastive phonemes.

After that brief discursus on the scientific method, let us return to some empirical discussion.

2.3.4 Differing Repair Strategies

Broselow (1992) shows that Arabic speakers treat s-clusters that violate the Sonority Sequencing Principle differently than those that do not, as shown in (1):

(1) sweater → [siwɛtar]   study → [istadi]
     slide → [silayd]   ski → [iski]

Singh (1985) demonstrates the same pattern for Hindi speakers shown in (2):

(2) fruit → [fɪrut]   school → [ɪskul]
     please → [pɪlɪz]   spelling → [ɪspɛlɪŋ]

L2 Empirical Studies

Samarajiwa and Abeysekera (1964) show the same pattern by native speakers of Sinhalese speaking Sanskrit, given in (3).

(3) Sanskrit   Sinhalese
     tyage →   [tiyage]   'gift'
     sriyavə →   [siriyavə]   'grace'
     stri →   [istiri]   'woman'

These data suggest that L2 learners have full access to the principles of Sonority Sequencing regardless of their L1 experience.

Papers by Cardoso (2007) and Cardoso, John, and French (2009) also address this issue. They look at English speakers learning Brazilian Portuguese. Brazilian Portuguese lacks onset clusters, and they investigate two hypotheses as to the developmental path that the learners will follow in acquiring L2 English clusters. Hypothesis A is that the learners will acquire the less marked clusters (e.g. [sl]) before the more marked clusters (e.g. [st]). Hypothesis B is that the learners will acquire the clusters which are most frequent in the input ([st]) before the clusters which are less frequent ([sl]). This is an interesting paradigm for two reasons. One is that we want to ask whether speakers who have no sC clusters in their L1 will have knowledge of the universal markedness scale regarding those clusters. If they do, it can't be coming from their L1 but would have to be coming from UG. The second reason is that this provides an interesting natural experiment to tease apart two variables which are usually confounded. For many phenomena, the less marked structure is also the most frequent, thus making it difficult to determine whether accuracy is the result of markedness or frequency. However, in this experimental design, the most frequent cluster is the most marked [st]. If markedness predicted the order of acquisition, we would see the order in (4):

(4) sl > sn > st

If frequency predicted the order of acquisition we would see the order in (5):

(5) st > sl > sn

How do the researchers determine frequency? They are looking at two ESL classes in Brazil that were taught by the same teacher. The classes were recorded in their entirety for two months, yielding 30 hours of data. All instances of sC clusters were coded in student-directed teacher speech. The frequencies shown in Table 2.1 were reported.

Table 2.1. CONSONANT CLUSTER FREQUENCY

Type of sC cluster	Total: 837
st	731 (87.4%)
sl	54 (6.4%)
sn	52 (6.2%)

Clearly, the most frequent string in the input is [st]. This frequency count is consistent with other corpora as shown in Table 2.2.

Table 2.2. THE DISTRIBUTION OF sC CLUSTERS ACROSS DIFFERENT CORPORA

Corpora	Total (N)	sC-initial words (%)		
		st	sl	sn
L2 textbook: written	140	90.7	5.7	3.8
Brown corpus: written (Kucera and Francis 1967)	10,900	87.9	9.3	2.7
ALERT corpus: L2 oral (Collins et al. 2006)	1,020	90.7	5.7	3.8

In analysing the production (from a picture-naming task) of his subjects, Cardoso (2007) demonstrates that the Portuguese learners followed the path predicted by markedness. Even though the [st] clusters were *much* more frequent in the input to the learners, they still acquired the [sl] cluster before the [st] cluster. The production results are shown in Figure 2.9.

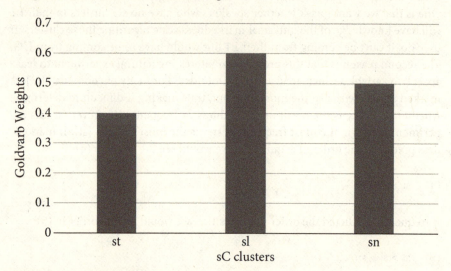

Figure 2.9. Production accuracy by cluster type
SOURCE: Adapted from Cardoso (2007)

What this graph shows is that the [sl] variable accounted for more accurate production, then the [sn] variable, and finally the [st] variable. Note that this is the developmental sequence predicted by markedness, not the sequence predicted by frequency.

But now let us turn to perception data. Cardoso, John, and French (2009) look at the results of a perception task (a forced-choice phone identification task where the subjects had to indicate whether a word began with either an [s] or a vowel), shown in Figure 2.10.

L2 Empirical Studies

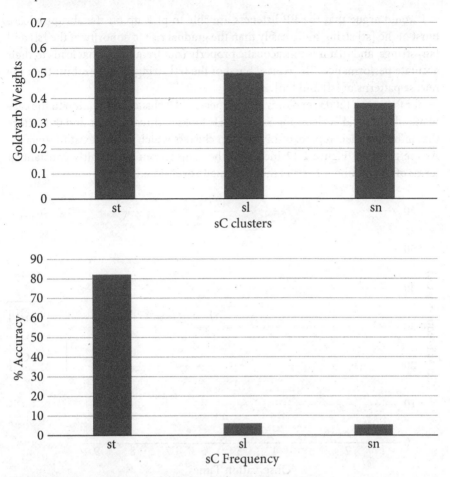

Figure 2.10. Perception accuracy and input frequency
SOURCE: Adapted from Cardoso, John, and French (2009)

The above graphs reveal that, unlike the production data, the subjects were the most accurate on the most frequent [st] string, while showing no difference in performance on [sl] versus [sn]. Cardoso, John, and French point to the role of frequency in explaining the behaviour; however, I think there is another factor to be considered: robust cues of release burst. The waveforms of the input stimuli in Figure 2.11 clearly show a difference.

Figure 2.11. Transition bursts in consonant clusters
SOURCE: Adapted from Cardoso, John, and French (2009)

I would argue that the BP listeners are able to pick up on the abrupt release burst of the [st] string more easily than the gradual rise in sonority of the [sl] and [sn] strings, and that it is this acoustic property (not frequency) that leads to their accurate performance. The release burst of the [st] string is more robust than the release patterns of [sl] and [sn].

Abrahamsson (2003) explores other aspects of L2 cluster production in the case of Mandarin speakers learning Swedish. He looks at three subjects and the factors that influence their repairs of L2 Swedish clusters which do not exist in their L1. As the graph in Figure 2.12 indicates, the subjects remained fairly constant in terms of the number of errors that they made over time.

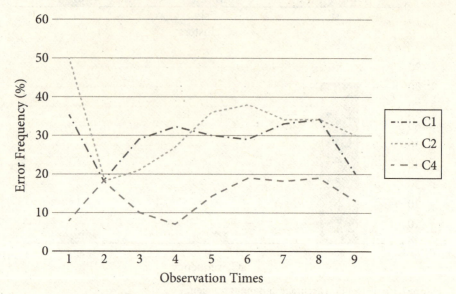

Figure 2.12. Overall error frequencies (deletion + epenthesis), development over time
SOURCE: Adapted from Abrahamsson (2003)

However, what the graph above fails to reveal is that over time the type of error changed, as can be noted in Figure 2.13.

What this graph reveals is that, as the subjects gained in proficiency, the number of epenthesis repairs (compared to deletion repairs) increases. Abrahamsson suggests that the learners adopt an epenthesis repair strategy because they are following a *Recoverability* principle in which they are seeking to make the job of the listener easier; it is easier for the listener to recover the intended lexical item when the speaker epenthesizes compared with when the speaker deletes. While we will explore a structural account in Chapter 4, Section 4.6, these data are certainly consistent with the discussion we will see in Chapter 3, Section 3.7, on Persian and Arabic epenthesis.

I would like briefly to present some related results from Lin (2001), who also looks at factors which influence type of repair strategy. In a study of L1 Chinese (bilingual Mandarin/Taiwanese) learners of English, she finds that on four tasks

L2 Empirical Studies

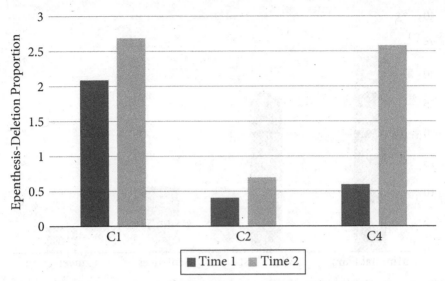

Figure 2.13. Proportion of epenthesis to deletion errors, development over time
SOURCE: Adapted from Abrahamsson (2003)

(minimal pairs, word list reading, sentence reading, and conversation), the number of errors did not vary significantly. The results are shown in Figure 2.14.

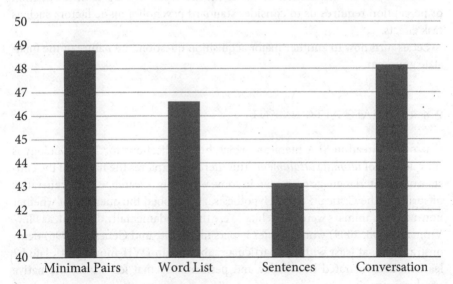

Figure 2.14. Number of errors by task type
SOURCE: Adapted from Lin (2001)

However, what the overall numbers do not reveal are the task effects, as shown in Figure 2.15.

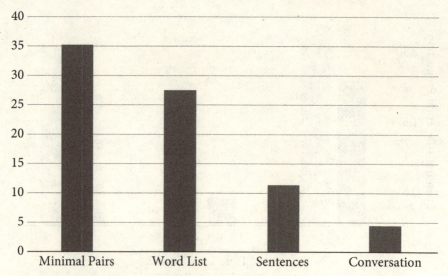

Figure 2.15. Number of epenthesis errors by task type
SOURCE: Adapted from Lin (2001)

The subjects were much more likely to epenthesize in the more formal tasks.

This section has served as a reminder that probing questions such as ease or difficulty in L2 acquisition or the nature of repair strategies in production or perception requires us to consider standard psycholinguistic factors such as task effects.

Let us turn now to another major acquisition question, the nature of the final-state grammar.

2.4 ULTIMATE ATTAINMENT

One other thread in SLA literature which has implications for L2 phonology is the question of *ultimate attainment*. This literature explores the nature of the end-state of the interlanguage grammar. In some ways, this research was the generative offspring of the Critical Period Hypothesis, as it probed the question of whether non-native grammars were nativelike. Were they fundamentally different, as Bley-Vroman (1990, 2009) would argue? Papers like White and Genesee (1996) demonstrate that, at least within a particular sub-domain (WH-movement), late L2 learners demonstrated knowledge and performance that fell within the native speaker range.

Much of the research at the 'sound' end of the spectrum has tended to focus on nativelikeness as viewed through a lens of pronunciation (which is, of course, not the same as phonology). The research program of intelligibility and comprehensibility represented by Munro and Derwing (1995) is a body of work with clear applied implications (Munro and Derwing 2015). Rather than focussing on nativelikeness, intelligibility is a measure of successful communication, and comprehensibility is a measure of necessary effort on the part of the listener to recover the message. As Munro (2008: 194) says, 'native pronunciation in the L2 is not only uncommon but unnecessary.' Other researchers (e.g. Abrahamsson and Hyltenstam 2009; Hyltenstam and Abrahamsson 2000) use phonetic analyses of native versus non-native production of such things as voice onset time to see whether non-native speakers' production could fall within native speaker range. They also explore the extra-linguistic traits (e.g. Age of Acquisition (AoA), aptitude) which are correlated with nativelike performance. The issue of assessing bilingual production is a complex one which, again, is beyond my scope in this book. Kupisch and Rothman (2016) probe these issues deftly in studies of heritage learners, making the case for comparing heritage learners' performance to other bilinguals' performance, not to monolinguals'.

Age effects in second language pronunciation are well documented. Figure 2.16 shows graphs (from Munro, Flege, and Mackay 1996) for the vowels [i] and [ɪ] where the *y* axis indicates the number of subjects who fall within the nativelike range, and the *x* axis indicates Age of Acquisition. It is undeniable that if we know something about the Age of Acquisition, we have a good shot at predicting nativelike vowel production; late acquisition is highly correlated with non-nativelike production. Figure 2.16 reveals this clearly when we look at the descending slopes from left to right.

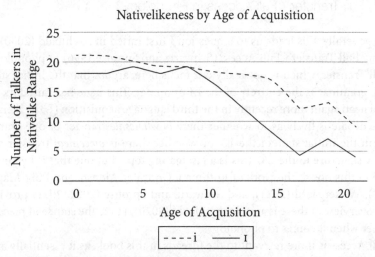

Figure 2.16. Nativelike vowel production by Age of Acquisition of the vowels [i] and [ɪ]
SOURCE: Adapted from Munro, Flege, and Mackay (1996)

However, as Figure 2.17 indicates, nativelikeness is not the only game in town. In this graph, the *x* axis still indicates Age of Acquisition, but the *y* axis now indicates the number of tokens native speakers correctly identified. In other words, the graphs represent the *intelligibility* of the L2 speech.

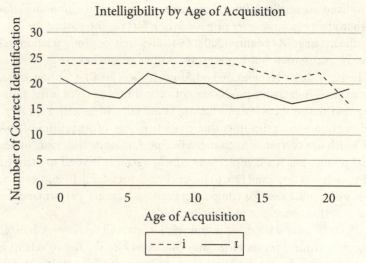

Figure 2.17. Intelligibility by Age of Acquisition for the vowels [i] and [ɪ]
SOURCE: Adapted from Munro, Flege, and Mackay (1996)

Note how the age effects disappear; the slopes are basically horizontal.

2.4.1 Full Transfer / Full Access in Phonology?

More generally, this leads us to a question I first raised in Archibald (2000) concerning Full Transfer / Full Access (Schwartz and Sprouse 1996) in phonology.

Full Transfer, which is not really our focus here, argues that the initial state of the IL grammar is the entirety of the L1 grammar. This issue has raised its theoretical head again more recently in the third language acquisition (L3A) literature, where debate is lively as to whether there is *wholesale* transfer of one grammar to form the initial state of the L3, or whether there is *piecemeal* transfer structure by structure to the L3. This is a fascinating topic but one that is beyond our scope in this book. The work of Rothman, González Alonso, and Puig-Mayenco (2019), Westergaard (2021), and Schwartz and Sprouse (2020, 2021) provides a good overview of these issues. In Archibald (2020), I take the stance of piecemeal transfer when it comes to phonology.

Full Access is more relevant to the threads in this book, as it essentially argues that interlanguage grammars are natural languages and that the hypothesis space considered by L2 learners is constrained by the options UG makes available. Seminal works such as Schwartz and Sprouse (1996), White (2003), Dekydtspotter (2001), and Dekydtspotter, Sprouse, and Swanson (2001) explore these issues in syntax and semantics. In L2 phonology, Major (2001) has explored the question in his construct of universals, as had a body of work looking at markedness effects represented by the approach taken by Carlisle (2001). Representational approaches began to emerge with the research of James (1988) and Young-Scholten (1993).

Note that the question of *ultimate attainment* is distinct from *full access*. It would be logically possible for the end state of an IL grammar to be non-nativelike *and* constrained by UG. Even in cases where the IL grammar is not governed solely by L1 properties, it can still be a natural language.

To bring this back to the issue of ultimate attainment, I turn to some work by David Birdsong. Birdsong (1992) is a study which nicely brings together the questions of learnability and ultimate attainment, working in the tradition of Coppieters (1987), which addresses the challenge perhaps first posed by Long (1990) to see whether any 'late' L2 learners could achieve nativelike proficiency. Birdsong recruited several near-native speakers and subjected them to analysis in a number of domains.

Subject Number	Performance Domain						
	Vowel Length	VOT	Liaison	Global Accent	Se	ECM	Null Object
1		√	√-			√	
2						√	
3		√	√			√	
4			√				
5						√	
6	√	√	√-	√	√	√	
7	√	√		√		√	√
8	√	√	√-			√	
9		√				√	
10	√-					√	
11		√	√			√	
12			√		√	√	
13						√	
14		√				√	
15		√-	√-			√	
16		√	√				
17			√-	√		√	
18		√-	√-		√	√	
19						√	
20			√			√	
21						√	√
22	√-	??		√	√	√	√

Figure 2.18. Summary of Birdsong's near-native speaker findings
SOURCE: Adapted from Birdsong (1992)

Figure 2.18 shows the performance of 22 near-native speakers on four measures of speech, as well as three measures of morphosyntax (reflexives, exceptional case marking (ECM), and null objects) which I will not discuss. The four measures of pronunciation are vowel length, voice onset time (VOT), liaison, and global accent. A check mark in the chart indicates that the near-native speaker's performance fell within the range of native speaker performance. Two clear patterns emerge from the chart: (1) there is not a single row which has check marks in all the cells, and (2) there is not a single column without a check mark. What this means is that Birdsong finds no exemplars of across-the-board near-nativeness; no subject was nativelike in all domains. However, just as interestingly, there was no linguistic domain in which no subjects achieved nativelikeness. This is what led him to propose his universal learnability hypothesis (which we find in the epigraph of this volume): everything is learnable by somebody. As I am not pursuing the issue of age effects in any depth in this book, let me just say that the existence of age effects in second language learning is undeniable. However, from a representational realism point of view, the interesting question is whether there are structural elements which are unlearnable once a particular age is passed, and the answer to that question seems to be *no*.

2.5 ACCESSING GRAMMARS

What I hope to demonstrate in the present section reinforces the necessity of distinguishing between representation and processing. Under extreme conditions, some learners may have difficulty processing a certain phonological construct not found in their L1, but this does not mean that those subjects cannot acquire said construct. Let us probe one such construct in depth.

2.5.1 Deficits Revisited

In the domain of potential barriers to SLA, let us turn to an issue which has received considerable attention in the literature, the phenomenon which has come to be known as *stress deafness*. This literature predicts that speakers of certain languages are doomed to never be able to figure out the stress properties of the language(s) they are learning. Ultimately, I will argue that both the theoretical underpinnings and interpretation of these studies should be reassessed.

2.5.2 Stress Deafness

In a series of studies, Dupoux and colleagues have looked at the processing of stress in second language speakers (L2ers). Their conclusions are that certain L1 groups have difficulty discriminating contrastive stress in a variety of tasks, even into advanced proficiency levels. They catalogue languages as shown in (6) with respect to their ability to 'hear' English stress:

(6)   Totally deaf: French, Finnish, Hungarian
      Partially deaf: Polish
      Not deaf: Spanish

Their analysis is that Spanish has what they call lexical stress while French, Finnish, Hungarian, and Polish do not (Peperkamp and Dupoux 2002).

2.5.2.1 LITERATURE REVIEW

In 1997, Dupoux, Pallier, Sebastián, and Mehler argued that French L1 speakers were impaired in their ability to discriminate stimuli which differed only in the position of stress. This phenomenon, which they dubbed *stress deafness*, was found in tasks which used high phonetic variability and memory load but not in cognitively less demanding tasks such as AX discrimination. Dupoux, Sebastián-Galles, Navarrete, and Peperkamp (2008) probe whether this is a perceptual problem or whether monolingual French speakers might simply lack a 'metalinguistic representation of contrastive stress', which would impair them in memory tasks. They conclude that 'stress "deafness" is better interpreted as a lasting processing problem resulting from the impossibility for French speakers to encode contrastive stress in their phonological representations' (682).

2.5.2.2 ACOUSTIC PROPERTIES OF STRESS

Dupoux and colleagues look at the three acoustic cues for stress: F0, duration, and intensity. None of these is used in French to signal a phonological contrast. French may have allophonic length, where vowels can be predictably lengthened before certain consonants, and has phrase-final accent. There are no minimal pairs relying solely on stress in French.

2.5.2.3 TASKS

Let me begin by looking at some of the tasks which were used.

- AX, low phonetic variability
- ABX, high phonetic variability (HPV)

These discrimination tasks adopted minimal pair nonce forms which differed by either a single phone or stress position (e.g. [muki]/[muti]; [númi]/[numí]).

- Sequence recall, low phonetic variability
- Sequence recall, high phonetic variability

These tasks will be described more below but basically involved subjects listening to a string of five nonce forms (of the type given above) and having to recall the correct order of the string, for example, [númi] [númi] [númi] [numí] [numí].

In the ABX tasks the French subjects made 19% stress errors (compared to 4% by the Spanish subjects). In the recall task the French subjects made 53% stress errors compared to 20% by the Spanish subjects. Thus, they argue that the French subjects are significantly worse on these tasks than the Spanish subjects.

The Dupoux and colleagues (2008: 686) paper suggests that 'perhaps French listeners are not impaired in their phonological representation of contrastive stress, but rather have difficulty with the *metalinguistic* access to this contrast'. So they look at late, instructed learners of Spanish who they suggest would 'surely have metalinguistic knowledge of Spanish stress' to see whether they would show the same limitation as French monolinguals. If these subjects have problems, then it must be a processing deficit, not a metalinguistic deficit.

The first task was a modified version of the sequence recall task with high phonetic variability (stimuli produced by several talkers) from Dupoux, Peperkamp, and Sebastián-Galles (2001). The second is a lexical decision task using word-nonword minimal pairs that vary only in stress position. Thirty-nine late learners of Spanish were compared to 20 native speaker (NS) controls.

In the first experiment, the HPV sequence recall task was administered. The stimuli were either minimal pairs which involved a consonantal contrast (e.g. /fiku/-/fitu/) or a stress contrast (e.g. /númi/-/numí/). They were recorded by native speakers of French who were 'trained to produce Spanish stress patterns' (Dupoux et al. 2008: 691). Spanish marks stress by F0 and duration (Ortega-Llebaria 2006). It seems surprising that they had a French speaker do this, but a Spanish phonetician judged the stress placement to be 'unambiguous' (which is certainly not the same as being encoded in a targetlike fashion). Subjects were told that they were going to learn two words in a foreign language. By pressing one computer key, they heard all the tokens of one word (e.g. /fiku/), and by pressing another key they heard all the tokens of the other word (e.g. /fitu/). When they indicated that they were ready to move on, they were trained on a task where they heard a particular stimulus and had to press the appropriate key on the keyboard. Whether the response was correct was indicated on the screen. When a threshold criterion of seven in a row correct was reached, the subjects moved to the experiment which consisted of four warm-up trials and 28 test trials.

The test trial consisted of hearing 'two or four repetitions, respectively, of the two items'. The experimental task was to reproduce each sequence by pressing the appropriate computer keys in the correct order. This was done both for segmental and stress pairs. To trigger the stress pairs, one key was associated with initial stress (/númi/) while the other key was associated with final stress (/numí/).

Both French monolinguals and the late L2 learners had significantly more stress errors than phoneme errors. Thus, they conclude that the late learners, who had the requisite metalinguistic awareness, still performed badly on stress perception which, thus, implicates stress 'deafness' as a 'robust processing limitation which cannot be eliminated with a significant exposure to a language with contrastive stress' (Dupoux et al. 2008: 695).

The second task was designed to look at stress encoding in the lexicon by means of an auditory lexical decision task. A combination of real Spanish words (e.g. górro, 'hat') and nonwords (e.g. gorró) were generated as stimuli. Participants made a speeded lexical decision, and both response time (RT) and accuracy were measured. All test items were word-nonword pairs with the nonword being generated by moving the stress position from the related word. Half the real words had initial stress, and the other half final stress.

Subjects had to indicate whether the strings were Spanish words or not by pressing computer keys for Yes or No. Instructions were given in Spanish. Subjects made more errors on stress items (24%) than on phoneme items (6%). In comparing accuracy on words versus nonwords, they noted that the error rate for words was moderate (24%) while the error rate for nonwords was high

Accessing Grammars 41

(58%), suggesting that the subjects categorized nonwords as words. From this, they conclude that 'the stress "deafness" effect observed with the sequence recall task is not limited to the encoding of stress in short-term memory but extends to lexical access' (Dupoux et al. 2008: 699). They attribute the high error rate to the inability of the late learners to attend to the relevant suprasegmental distinction, or cue.

Peperkamp, Vendelin, and Dupoux (2010) look at how subjects form the L1s Finnish, Hungarian, and Polish (as well as French). Here is what they say about the L1 stress patterns:

Finnish: initial
Hungarian: initial
Polish: penultimate

These descriptions are broadly accurate, though some complexities are missing. There is no mention made of secondary stresses in Hungarian (which are quantity-sensitive) and certain cases of antepenultimate stress in Polish triggered by extrametrical segments. Such complexities reveal that the stress systems of these languages are not quite so straightforward as indicated.

However, given the acoustic correlates of stress (F0 and duration), Peperkamp, Vendelin, and Dupoux (2010) also note that Finnish and Hungarian use duration contrastively for vowels (while French and Polish do not). From this they predict that the French and Polish subjects should 'exhibit strong "deafness"', while Finnish and Hungarian subjects should exhibit 'weak "deafness"'. This is summarized in Table 2.3.

Table 2.3. ACOUSTIC AND PHONOLOGICAL PROPERTIES OF STRESS SYSTEMS

Language	Domain of stress	Lexical use of stress cues	Variability in stress position	Lexical exceptions (%)
Standard French	Phrase	None	No[a]	0
South-eastern French	Phrase	None	Moderate[b]	0
Finnish	Word	Duration	No[c]	0
Hungarian	Word	Duration	No[c]	0
Polish	Word	None	Moderate[d]	0.1
Spanish	Word	Duration, F0, and intensity	High[e]	17

[a] Final.
[b] Last non-schwa syllable.
[c] Initial.
[d] Penultimate in polysyllables and on the only syllable of monosyllables.
[e] One of the last three syllables.

They use a variant of the sequence recall task from Dupoux, Peperkamp, and Sebastián-Galles (2001). Subjects heard stimuli and then heard a random sequence and had to transcribe the sequence by pressing the two computer keys associated with the stimuli. There were phonemic minimal pairs and stress minimal pairs. None of the items was a real word in any of the source languages. The items were recorded by a native speaker of Dutch who exaggerated the acoustic cues associated with prominence. Stressed vowels did continue to be longer than unstressed ones (but only 12.4 ms longer). They also created a stimulus set where the stress difference of duration was removed (leaving only F0 as a reliable cue).

The subjects heard five repetitions of the two items and had to reproduce the sequence. The sequences tested are listed in (7):

(7)   11121, 11211, 11212, 11221, 12111, 12112, 12122, 12211, 12212, 12221, 21112, 21121, 21122, 21211, 21221, 22112, 22121, 22122, 21222, 22212

The same key was never pressed more than three times in a row.

The results in Table 2.4 showed that the Spanish subjects were significantly different from the other groups. The Polish group was significantly different from the French, Finnish, and Hungarian groups.

Table 2.4. ERROR RATES BY LANGUAGE GROUP

	Phoneme		Stress with duration		Stress without duration	
	% error	SE	% error	SE	% error	SE
Standard French	34.2	3.9	77.5	4.4	84.6	22
SE French	45.8	43	85.4	2.0	86.7	23
Finnish	49.6	53	90.0	2.3	87.1	22
Hungarian	45.4	6.0	80.4	4.3	85.4	3.9
Polish	42.5	6.4	592	7.9	65.4	8.0
Spanish	47.5	5.6	47.1	5.4	48.8	7.4

SOURCE: Adapted from Peperkamp, Vendelin, and Dupoux (2010)
NOTE: Mean error rates and standard errors for the Standard French, South-eastern French, Finnish, Hungarian, Polish, and Spanish participants for the phoneme contrast and the two versions of the stress contrast.

From this, they conclude that speakers of languages with 'predictable stress' (i.e. French, Finnish, and Hungarian) exhibit strong stress deafness. Polish subjects exhibit an intermediate pattern between the French and the Spanish subjects.

While, as we will see below, I am not convinced this is really tapping into *stress* at all, even if we accept these results, there are some more recent studies which we need to consider as well.

White, Muradás-Taylor, and Hellmuth (2016) present some of their own findings but also report on Taylor and Hellmuth (2012). Furthermore, they cite Correia, Butler, Vigário, and Frota (2015), who argue that Portuguese L1 subjects exhibit stress deafness. All of these papers demonstrate deafness from naive listeners whose L1s have non-predictable stress. Remember this is the trait which was supposed to predict performance success on the Dupoux tasks. Both the Portuguese and English subjects had difficulty with the tasks when the stimuli had no unstressed vowel reduction (but only cues like F0 or duration). Taylor and Hellmuth (2012) look at English speakers (who were predicted to exhibit stress deafness) because of their assumption that English stress, being only 'partially predictable', must therefore be encoded in lexical representation. However, they note that English subjects have trouble with L2 stress. Kijak (2009) shows that English learners of Polish perform only slightly better than French subjects on a task of stress identification. English learners of Japanese have difficulty learning the pitch accent patterns of Japanese words (Taylor 2011). Their question was whether performance on the stress deafness suite of tasks is affected by the phonetic realization of stress given that English speakers rely on vowel quality as a signal of stress/unstress (Cutler 2012).

It seems to me that many of the stress deafness studies are confounding the notion of *variable* with *unpredictable*. English stress is assigned in consultation with various parameters (quantity-sensitivity, grammatical category, etc.), but this does not entail that it is lexically stored.

Taylor and Hellmuth (2012) use both an AX task and a sequence recall task with phoneme contrast and stress contrast conditions (like Dupoux et al. 1997). In addition, they introduced three phonetic realizations of stress: melody (M) only (pitch), melodic and dynamic (MD) cues (duration and intensity), and melodic plus dynamic cues and vowel reduction (MDV). As Figure 2.19 shows, the performance of the English speakers was affected by the acoustic cues.

In the M (melodic only) cue condition, the subjects were worst in both the AX and sentence recall task. In the MDV condition, there was no evidence of stress deafness at all. From this, they conclude that the subjects' difficulty is not with the 'encoding' of stress but with the way prominence was encoded in the stimuli. When it was encoded only with melodic cues, the English subjects had difficulty discriminating stress.

White, Muradás-Taylor, and Hellmuth (2016) build on this foundation by examining subjects who had acquired advanced proficiency in L2 Spanish (a language without unstressed vowel reduction) to see whether what they term *cue-dependent stress deafness* is persistent. They looked at 15 advanced L2 Spanish learners and gave them an AX task and a sequence recall task. They were tested under three prominence cue sets: (a) pseudo-English (pitch, intensity, duration, and vowel reduction), (b) pseudo-Spanish (pitch, intensity, and duration), or (c) pseudo-Japanese (pitch only). Like Dupoux and colleagues (2008) a stress deafness index was calculated by subtracting the score on the phoneme tasks from the score on the stress tasks. Unsurprisingly, the subjects were error-free on the

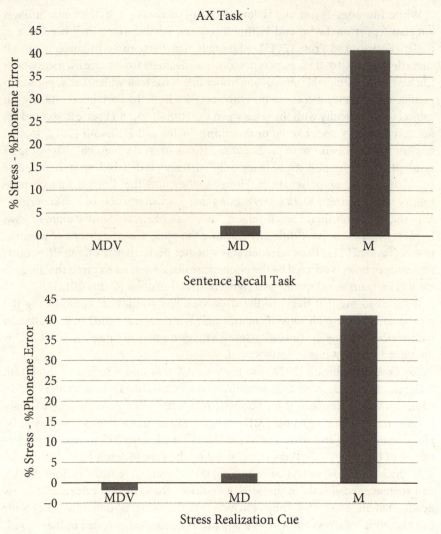

Figure 2.19. Discrimination results by acoustic cue
SOURCE: Adapted from Taylor and Hellmuth (2012)

English condition and showed little signs of trouble with pseudo-Spanish (4%/0% on AX and recall), which confirms that cue-dependent stress deafness is nonpersistent. However, they also performed reasonably well on pseudo-Japanese (16%/15%)—compared with the native listeners of Taylor and Hellmuth (2012), who had 48%/44% stress deafness index scores.

Correia and colleagues (2015) look at monolingual speakers of Portuguese listening to nonsense words. They were given an ABX task. Interstimulus Interval (ISI) for items within a trial was 500 ms. The number of stress errors was significantly higher than the number of phoneme errors. The mean error rate for these European Portuguese (EP) subjects (21%) is comparable to the mean error rate in Dupoux and colleagues (1997) in the ABX task. Correia and colleagues also did a sequence recall task where the stimuli lacked vowel reduction in unstressed positions. In this condition, the subjects were told to 'recall sequences of words of a foreign language'. The test sequences consisted of five tokens, each of which the subjects had to recall. As shown in Figure 2.20, there were significantly more errors in the stress condition than in the phoneme condition. Thus, EP subjects show a similar stress deafness profile as speakers of French. In their third experiment they added vowel reduction to the unstressed items in the recall task. (Note in nuclear position (NP) stress has pitch and duration cues while in post-nuclear (PN) position it has only duration).

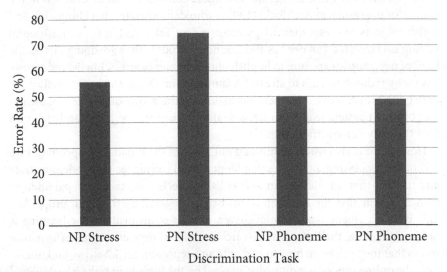

Figure 2.20. Error rates for stress vs. phoneme contrasts
SOURCE: Adapted from Correia et al. (2015)

In the PN position (duration only cueing stress), the stress errors were significantly higher than the phoneme errors, but in the NP position (pitch and duration cueing stress) there was no difference between the stress and phoneme conditions. So, when there was vowel reduction in the unstressed syllable and duration and pitch in the stressed syllable, the EP subjects exhibited no stress deafness effects. The error rates here for stress and phoneme in the NP condition (55%/50%) were comparable to the phoneme errors in the Spanish subjects in Dupoux and colleagues (1997) and Peperkamp, Vendelin, and Dupoux (2010): 56%/48%. Once again, the cue of vowel reduction is critical (and remember that EP, unlike Spanish, has reduced vowels in unstressed syllables).

Thus, they argue, it is not the 'fixed stress' of the L1s which is causing the perceptual problems but the absence of critical cues to stress. Both stress cues and rules of stress placement are language specific, and they both influence so-called stress deafness phenomena.

To wrap up this extended discussion of the processing of stress, the behavioural results are interesting but do not, I think, reveal a representational deficit in, say, French learners of English stress. Both English and French stress are predictable and, hence, computed. However, there are differences between the two languages. As we have seen, English stress applies at the word level while French stress applies at the phrase level. In addition, there are many rules of English segmental phonology which refer to stress, while this is not true of French. A good example would be flapping in English. Note that the /t/ of English becomes a flap after a stressed syllable (e.g. 'city' with a [ɾ], vs. 'attack' with a [t]).

2.5.2.4 WHAT ABOUT REPRESENTATION?

But let us consider these results and the whole construct of stress deafness in the context of the results of Archibald (1993a) who demonstrates that Hungarian and Polish subjects *can* reset their L1 parameters (see Table 2.5) in the acquisition of L2 English stress (cf. van der Pas and Zonneveld 2004). They are doing this on the basis of naturalistic exposure to English phonetic cues to stress. English, of course, has many redundant cues to stress: F0, duration, intensity, and vowel quality. So, perhaps the success of the learners has to do with the nature of the *cue*, not the nature of the L1 system leading to stress deafness. The work of Taylor and Helmuth (2012) clearly demonstrates this.

However, it is also worth reminding ourselves of the broader perspective: if we accept the processing difficulties that Dupoux and colleagues (1997) demonstrate *and* the fact that the Hungarian and Polish subjects can reset their parameters, then it is clear that the resetting is not being triggered by the input properties. This is an argument against input-driven models of acquisition; the learning is not just reflecting the input. The research on both competence and performance shows that they can learn how to compute and represent the L2 stress, and, therefore, the online processing difficulty invoked by the high-load tasks is orthogonal to that question.

This should not be a surprise. There is a growing literature on input processing and cue reweighting in SLA which shows that L2 learners are able to attend to different input cues to be more nativelike, even for contrasts which can be difficult for them to acquire. For example, Yuan and Archibald (2022), Ylinen and colleagues (2009), Shinohara and Iverson (2018), Grenon, Kubota, and Sheppard (2019); and Cheng and colleagues (2019) all look at how L2 learners who do not have a tense/lax vowel contrast in their L1s can learn to attend to not only the durational contrasts of vowels like [i/ɪ] but also spectral contrasts. Such empirical evidence shows that Bohn's (1995) demonstration of learners being 'desensitized' to spectral differences can be overcome.

I believe that what this tells us is that the term *stress deafness* is inappropriate, as it suggests both that learners are unable to arrive at targetlike representations in the L2 and that they are unable to learn to attend to the L2 cues to stress.

2.5.2.5 LINGUISTIC ASSUMPTIONS

A number of papers have addressed the question of L2 learners acquiring stress. Let's step back to ask the basic question, *what is stress?* Phonetically, we can look to identify the acoustic correlates of stress prominence (such as intensity, duration,

Accessing Grammars

pitch, and vowel quality). However, this does not address the question of what the rules of stress placement are in a particular language. Let us consider three hypotheses:

(a) Stress is a property of an individual vowel. Under this assumption, the learner needs to store which vowel is stressed in a word such as *aróma*. One might then expect stress errors to vary considerably from word to word, as the task of the learner is to acquire the correct lexical representation (which includes stress).

(b) Stress is a relative phenomenon. Under this assumption, stress is not viewed as an intrinsic component of the vowel but rather the result of what is called metrical foot structure (e.g. iambic vs. trochaic feet), shown in (8). In this model, stress signals the relative prominence of a *syllable*. The task of the L2 learner then would be to acquire the target foot type. Learners of French would acquire *iambic* (strong on the right) feet, while learners of English would acquire *trochaic* (strong on the left) feet.

(8)

Trochaic Feet	Iambic Foot
/\ /\	/\
S W S W	W S
M à n i t ó b a	c h e v á l

c) Stress assignment is governed by a range of what are known in generative linguistics as *parameters*. While the most complex model, this parametric view (Dresher and Kaye 1990) captures the phonological reality that stress assignment relies on a range of properties such as (a) whether a syllable is light (ending in a vowel) or heavy (closed by a consonant), or (b) whether secondary stresses are allowed. The task of the L2 learner would be to acquire the L2 parameter settings, two of which are listed below as an illustration:

P1: The foot is strong on the [left/right].

English feet are strong on the left; French feet are strong on the right.

P5: Feet are quantity-sensitive (QS) [yes/no].

In QS languages (like English) syllables closed by a consonant (i.e. heavy) are stressed. Compare the stress placement in *agénda* as opposed to *cínema*. If there is a heavy syllable, it gets stressed; if there is none, we see initial stress, as in *cinema*. French is not QS.

Table 2.5 illustrates how languages may differ in their parameter settings.

PHONOLOGICAL GRAMMARS

Table 2.5. CROSS-LINGUISTIC METRICAL PARAMETERS

	Spanish	Polish	Hungarian	English
P1 (word tree)	right	right	left	right
P2 (foot type)	binary	binary	binary	binary
P3 (strong on)	right	right	left	right
P4 (built from)	left	left	left	left
P5 (quantity-sensitive)	yes	no	yes	no
P6 (sensitive to)	rhyme	N/A	nucleus	rhyme
P8 (extrametrical)	yes	no	no	yes
P8A (extrametrical on)	right	N/A	N/A	right

When the parameter settings are different in the first and the second language, we have the potential for transfer. Often, the L1 parameter settings transfer into the L2.

Archibald (1993a) showed that L2 learners were able to reset their existing parameters to new values. In other words, if your L1 is quantity-sensitive to the nucleus (i.e. a long vowel attracts stress), as Hungarian is, you will be able to acquire the English setting of having your stress system sensitive to the rhyme (where a closed syllable can also attract stress). What this study revealed was that a simplistic view of stress assignment is not supported. A simple proposal would follow these lines: Hungarian has a rule of initial stress assignment which will transfer into English; Polish has a rule of penultimate stress assignment which will transfer into English. Interestingly, Özçelik (2021) looks at a case (a mirror image to the Hungarian/English study of Archibald 1993a) where the L1 (English) is quantity-sensitive to both the nucleus and the rhyme but the L2 (Khalkha Mongolian) is quantity-sensitive to only the nucleus. He finds that the learners reset their parameters, demonstrating 'stage-like behavior where each step exhibits the parameters settings employed by a natural language'. Archibald's (1993a, 1993b) studies are also some of the first to demonstrate that the acquisition patterns of metrical properties could also be studied via perception tasks, and not just production tasks. Perception tasks often tap into grammar without the motoric confounds of production studies, and properties such as quantity-sensitivity were shown to affect perception as well. Such work reminds us that, as multilinguals, we listen with an accent too (Archibald 2021).

The adoption of such a parameter-setting analysis reveals that both what transfers into the interlanguage grammar and the nature of the interlanguage grammar is much subtler than a simple rule of stress. Phonological representations must include constructs like quantity-sensitivity, extrametricality, and the like.

However, we must also ask whether subjects whose first languages did not have stress but rather had tone or pitch accent were able to trigger these metrical representations. Archibald (1997a) argues that Chinese and Japanese subjects learning English do not compute metrical representations but rather store stress placement for each lexical item. Ou and Ota (2004) argue that Chinese learners of English show sensitivity to syllable weight in a perception test of English words and hence that these subjects are able to engage in a computational process to generate stress placement. This would be further evidence that second language learners are able to create new representations that are not found in their L1. Similarly, Kawagoe (2003) argues that Japanese learners of English *are* able to acquire a computational system for English metrical properties building on their L1 system of loanword phonology adaptation. Japanese is a pitch accent language (Kawahara 2015) where we find minimal pairs distinguished by the placement of accent, as shown in (9).

(9) /ame+ga/ (unaccented) 'candy+nominative'
     /áme+ga/ (accented) 'rain+nominative'

Kubozono (2006) probes the principles which underlie accent placement in both native Japanese words and in loanwords. He proposes the loanword accent rule given in (10).

(10) Put an accent on the syllable containing the antepenultimate mora, or the third mora from the end of the word.

This is also the rule necessary to account for accent placement on native words as well. He notes (2006: 1143) that the pattern 'resembles the Latin-type accent rule that governs a variety of languages' (i.e. like English). He goes on to observe (2006: 1155), 'the accent rule of Tokyo Japanese is fundamentally similar to the accent rule of Latin and English as far as accented nouns are concerned.' This is another example of how L1 knowledge in one phonological domain can be redeployed to acquire new knowledge in an L2.

Now, let us probe the linguistic assumptions underlying the causal claims. It could be argued their results do show difficulty in processing but not necessarily deficient representations (as is indicated perhaps by the term *deafness*). As the work of Lardiere (2007) demonstrates, problems in surface processing of a feature may arise even when there is accurate underlying representation.

There are some concerns with the theoretical assumptions about linguistic stress in the stress deafness literature. Linguistic theory definitely has a part to play here. The work seems to assume a pre-theoretical, diacritic notion of what they call 'lexical stress'. Three of the languages considered to exhibit stress deafness (French, Finnish, and Hungarian) all exhibit certain fixed stress patterns. French stresses toward the right edge of phonological strings, while Finnish and Hungarian stress toward the left edge of strings (specifically word-initially). Polish, which exhibits partial deafness, has primarily penultimate stress. Spanish, which does not show deafness, has, like English, variable stress placement.

The problem with the causal connection proposed in this literature is that the stress placement of all of these languages is the product of a set of complex factors or principles (see Dresher and Kaye 1990), not a primitive diacritic. Archibald (1993a, 1993b) has looked at the production and perception abilities of native speakers of Hungarian and Spanish and Polish. I have argued that stress is not a primitive of linguistic representation but rather a complex system of knowledge which L2ers must and, evidently, *can* acquire.

Pater (1997a) contends that French L1 subjects are able acquire English trochaic feet but not the quantity-sensitivity of English. Furthermore, Tremblay (2008) demonstrates that only those learners who had acquired English stress settings could use stress as a tool for lexical access. Once again, it is crucial to distinguish between representation and process. Ultimately, what all this shows us is that the studies reveal something about processing but are not a direct window onto representation.

2.5.3 Acquiring Stress

In a number of projects, I have addressed the question of L2 learners acquiring stress. My broad conclusions suggest (a) that adult interlanguages do not violate metrical universals, and (b) that adults are capable of resetting their parameters to the L2 setting. The subjects were quite good at putting English stress on the right syllable. Thus, their interlanguages are a combination of UG principles, correct L2 parameter settings (from resetting), and incorrect L1 parameter settings (from transfer).

Table 2.5 above illustrates how languages may differ in their parameter settings. When the parameter settings are different in the first and the second language, we have the potential for transfer. Often, the L1 parameter settings transfer into the L2.

The studies that I have done (e.g. Archibald 1993a, 1993b) show that L2 learners were able to reset their existing parameters to new values. However, it was less clear whether subjects whose first languages did not have stress but rather had tone were able to trigger these metrical representations. Archibald (1997a) argues that Chinese and Japanese subjects learning English did not compute metrical representations but rather stored stress placement for each lexical item. Ou and Ota (2004) argue that Chinese learners of English show sensitivity to syllable weight in a perception test of English words and hence that these subjects are able to engage in a computational process to generate stress placement. This would be further evidence that second language learners are able to create new representations that are not found in their L1.

2.5.3.1 CHINESE AND JAPANESE AND STRESS DEAFNESS

In the context of stress deafness, one would be tempted to think that an L1 which lacked stress entirely could certainly be argued to lack contrastive stress and would be likely candidates for stress deafness. Ou and Ota's (2004) data along with Kawagoe (2003) argue convincingly that these subjects *are* able to acquire L2 stress. Kawagoe (2003) maintains that Japanese learners of English can develop a computation system for English stress by modifying their native loanword accentuation system. This system happens to be quite similar to the English system in that:

- there is no final stress (trochaic);
- heavy penults are stressed (quantity-sensitive); and
- if penult is light, then the antepenult is stressed (like *cínema*).

Accessing Grammars 51

And if we apply her constraints to English L2 forms, we would generate the forms shown in Table 2.6 (a and b) with the optimal form indicated by the ☞ symbol.

Table 2.6a. JAPANESE LOANWORD STRESS APPLIED TO
THE ENGLISH WORD *AGENDA*

agenda		Nonfinal	Accent head	Rightmost
a.	a.(gen).da			**!
☞b.	a.(gén).da			*
c.	a.(gen).dá	*!		

NOTE: * marks a constraint violation; ! marks a fatal violation.

Table 2.6b. JAPANESE LOANWORD STRESS APPLIED TO
THE ENGLISH WORD *VENISON*

venison		Nonfinal	Accent head	Rightmost
☞a.	(vé.ni)(son)			**
b.	(ve.ní)(son)		*!	*
c.	(ve.ni)(són)	*!		

NOTE: * marks a constraint violation; ! marks a fatal violation.

I recognize that I have not introduced the machinery of Optimality Theory tableaux (and will not draw on it heavily in this book). What the individual tables reveal is that the Japanese rules will choose as the optimal candidate the form which is identical to actual English stress placement.

Ou and Ota (2004) also explore the question of the computation of stress. Remember that Archibald (1997) argued that speakers of non-stress languages might *store* stress rather than compute it. Kawagoe (2003) demonstrates that Japanese (L1 pitch accent) learners can *compute* English L2 stress. Similarly, Ou and Ota argue that Chinese learners can do so too. They look at the stress patterns on monomorphemic words by Chinese learners of English. They adopt Duanmu's (2007) position that Mandarin has trochaic feet. The constraints they propose are given in (11):

(11)   *Trochee*: The stress occurs on the left side of the foot.
       Parse-syllable: Syllables must be footed.
       Weight-to-Stress Principle (WSP): Stress is placed on heavy syllables.
       Nonfinality: The final syllable must not be footed.

For consistency in my writing, I will refer to the WSP as quantity-sensitivity (QS) for the rest of this section. The ranking would be as in (12):

(12)   *Trochee, Parse-syllable >> QS, Nonfinality*

In Mandarin the ranking would be *Parse-syllable* >> *QS, Nonfinality*, while in English the ranking would be *QS, Nonfinality* >> *Parse-syllable*. Thus, the subjects have to rerank their L1 constraints to arrive at the L2 grammar. In a production experiment involving 450 pseudo-words, which were placed in carrier sentences to reveal the grammatical category (noun or verb), 20 advanced L2 learners of English were recorded. Eight subjects were sensitive to syllable weight and extrametricality, while 11 subjects were sensitive to extrametricality but not syllable weight. Only 1 subject was sensitive to neither (and thus was in the L1 state). However, all the other subjects showed that they were moving through developmental stages by reranking constraints which show sensitivity to the computation of stress. The 8 more advanced subjects also showed some fine-grained distinctions within the quantity-sensitivity domain, as sonorant codas tended to attract stress more than obstruent codas (an L1 property).

The Kawagoe and Ou and Ota studies show that the L2 learners are able to engage in the computation of L2 English stress. Regardless of their purported stress deafness, these findings about their grammatical development with respect to the computational system of English stress are, for me, central and striking.

The results of Schwab, Giroud, Meyer, and Dellwo (2020) are also highly informative. They looked at native speakers of French (a fixed-stress language) learning Spanish (a variable-stress language). They found that the French listeners were able to improve their ability to discriminate stress contrasts in Spanish after only four hours of training.

I want to conclude this section with a brief discussion of a study done by Özçelik (2017c). The study looks at L1 English and L1 French learners of L2 Turkish. Özçelik argues that both French and Turkish are footless languages. In analysing the results of his production study, though, he builds the case that the English L1 subjects are unable to expunge the foot from their IL Turkish grammars (even though they do get stress placement correct eventually). This claim has broad implications for the nature of bilingual architecture that I am not going to get into here. But we would have to explore what it means for a structure to *not* be expunged, and we would have to explore whether there are other structures at different levels of phonology, or indeed different levels of grammar, which cannot be expunged. Taken uncritically, which is not what Özçelik does, the model seems to assume that each interlanguage grammar becomes some sort of superset grammar. Would the non-target-appropriate features have to be suppressed by executive control somehow? As I say, ignoring these questions, for me the take-home message of the Özçelik study is the centrality of an abstract structural unit like *foot* to the understanding of the L2 Turkish grammar.

2.6 INDIVIDUAL DIFFERENCES

It is worth acknowledging that up until now, and frankly for the rest of the book, I am focussing my attention on the core properties of the language module, the linguistic environment, and their interaction. I am not spending much time on how other cognitive traits might influence the rapidity or success of the acquisition of the linguistic property in question. There is, of course, a rich psycholinguistic literature which looks at the effect of such factors as empathy, motivation, attitude, aptitude, working memory, and the like on both language acquisition and language performance.

In the L2 literature this kind of issue is usually phrased in the form of a question: does x make the learner better at SLA? To answer, we need to be very explicit about three questions: (1) what is x? (2) what does it mean to be *better*? and (3) which aspects of SLA are we referring to? For many of the affective factors discussed in the literature, there is not a straightforward definition of x. Nor is it always easy to determine what being better at a particular aspect of language entails.

In fact, the whole notion of what it could mean to be 'better' at phonology is something I address in a chapter in a collection on advanced proficiency (Archibald 2018). How should we define the construct of 'advanced' in the domain of L2 phonology? Given what we know about the separate components of linguistic competence, and the separate components of proficiency (or communicative competence), it is clear that there is no straightforward correlation between, say, a high score on a standardized proficiency test and a reduced foreign accent. There are many cases of highly proficient L2ers with strong accents (Greta Thunberg, Javier Bardem, Joseph Conrad). Conversely, we may be able to achieve by mimicry quite nativelike speech for isolated phrases in a language we do not even understand. How would we identify the locus of advanced phonology? There, I argue that there is no single hallmark of 'advanced' L2 phonology. Pursuing the articulation of such a construct, however, has the benefit of revealing that, while L2 accents are ubiquitous, there are no phonological features or structures which are blocked from acquisition. Not all speakers may be advanced, but all *can* advance.

As a first step in formalizing the notion of advanced phonology, consider the common distinction between *knowledge* and *skill*. Knowledge is a relatively stable trait in an individual. You either have the knowledge (i.e. mental representation) of the English words *cat* or *quodlibet*, or you do not. Native speakers of English know that /l/ and /r/ are contrastive in English, while native speakers of Japanese know that they are not in Japanese. Native speakers of French know that [p] and [b] are contrastive, while native speakers of Thai know that [pʰ], [p], and [b] are all contrastive. However, as with all aspects of human knowledge, our ability to access or implement that knowledge varies under certain real-world conditions. We thus invoke a construct such as proficiency or fluency to try to capture the notion of skill or ability in using a second language. Under this approach then, what does it mean to have 'advanced' phonology: advanced knowledge or advanced skill?

Finally, to return to the question of linking extralinguistic factors with linguistic knowledge, we often cannot articulate a clear causal link between the affective trait and the linguistic property. Should risk taking affect stress assignment more than inflectional morphology? If so, why? If not, why not? Such psycholinguistic literature controls for such factors to add to our understanding of the broader model of SLA. However, in my view, there has been a paucity of work in L2 phonology from this perspective. Work has certainly been done on L2 sentence processing (see Archibald 2017a for a summary). There has also been work (Abrahamsson and Hyltenstam 2008; Bongaerts et al. 1997; Flege 2018) on individual variation in aspects such as nativelikeness of accent and what factors influence it (Age of Acquisition, aptitude, input, etc.). Very few researchers combine an interest in phonological theory with an interest in general cognition. One glaring exception would be Darcy, Park, and Yang (2015), who tested working memory, attention control, and processing speed to see whether there were correlations with phonological processing in domains such as phonetic categorization, complex onsets, and word stress.

2.6.1 Working Memory

The working hypothesis is that greater working memory would give subjects longer access to the L2 input and, hence, better ability to process it. It might assist what Lidz and Gagliardi (2015) refer to as the inference engine which compares input to hypotheses generated by the grammar. Darcy, Park, and Yang (2015) assessed working memory in the L1 of subjects (30 Korean learners of English). They first gave a Simple Span Task which consisted of forward digit, backward digit, forward nonword, and backward nonword recall tasks. Series length increased from 3 to 10 items. Perfect recall would be scored at 208. There was also a complex span task which consisted of a sentence repetition task. Then they were given a paired-associates learning task (learning to associate two stimuli).

The working hypothesis here is that higher processing speed would help prevent processing overload in the subjects as the speech input comes in. They assessed processing speed with a speeded naming task in which subjects had to name the sizes, colours, and shapes of as many items (out of 20) as possible in 30 seconds.

Table 2.7 shows the results of the working memory tasks for both the non-native speakers of English and a control group of native speakers.

Table 2.7. WORKING MEMORY TASKS IN L1

		N	Mean	SD	Min.	Max.	CI (95%)
Digit forward + backward L1(max.: 208)	Inexp.	15	822	23.9	36	146	13.25
	Experienced	15	1013	27.3	68	153	15.10
	NE	15	79.1	29.8	38	147	16.50
Nonword forward + backward L1 (max.: 208)	Inexp.	15	31.1	12.1	15	62	6.68
	Experienced	15	295	10.6	14	46	5.88
	NE	15	21.1	16.3	10	76	9.01
Complex span sentence recall L1 (max.: 54)	Inexp.	15	312	6.2	25	44	3.45
	Experienced	15	30.9	7.1	22	44	3.92
	NE	15	41.7	6.1	30	52	3.39

NOTE: Inexp. = inexperienced learners; CI = confidence interval; Experienced = experienced learners; NE = native English speakers; SD = standard deviation.

2.6.2 Phonological Processing

Darcy, Park, and Yang (2015) administered three tests to assess phonological processing.

(1) To assess segmental processing, they used a speeded segmental categorization task via an ABX procedure.
(2) To assess suprasegmental (stress) processing they used the Dupoux stress deaf sequence recall task which was discussed earlier in Section 2.5.2.3.
(3) To assess phonotactic knowledge, they utilized an auditory lexical decision task.

Figure 2.21 summarizes the results of some of the phonological tasks.

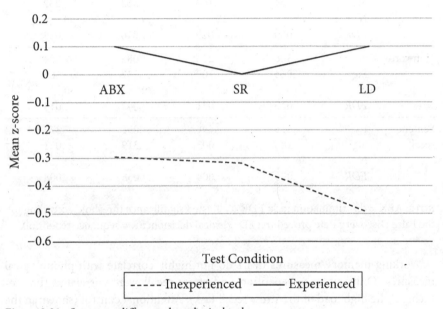

Figure 2.21. Scores on different phonological tasks
SOURCE: Adapted from Darcy et al. (2015)
NOTE: ABX = discrimination; SR - sequence repetition; LD = lexical decision.

So, the question is, is there a correlation between behaviour on the phonological tasks with general cognitive factors?

Their hypothesis is that individuals with larger storage of a larger span or better-quality processing will show more robust phonological representations in the L2 which might result in 'reduced inhibition from the L1 during processing' and hence more nativelike performance on the phonological tasks. While not pursuing the issue, I do wonder what it means for one representation to be more 'robust' than another. I am reminded of Reiss's (2017: 431/432) amusing note in motivating their 'substance-free' phonology that because the 'mental representation of a mouse is not smaller than that of an elephant; the mental representation of a brick is not heavier than that of a feather; the mental representation of the diameter of an atom is not smaller than the mental representation of the diameter of the Milky Way; and even if we demonstrate that producing [p'] is more physically challenging than producing [p], it does not follow that the mental representation of the former is more complex than that of the latter'. I can imagine that robustness might be a construct which could make a representation more resistant to attrition or faster to access, but that does seem to be more a processing issue than a representational issue.

As Table 2.8 shows, there is, in fact, not much correlation with working memory.

Table 2.8. WORKING MEMORY AND PHONOLOGY SCORES

		Segmentals (ABX)	Stress (SR)	Phonotactics (LD)	Phonological score
Digits	r	.021	.188	−.069	.139
	Sig.	.459	.164	.362	.232
	N	26	29	29	30
	FDR	.050	.029	.046	.033
Nonwords	r	.306	.236	.082	.284
	Sig.	.064	.109	.337	.064
	N	26	29	29	30
	FDR	.013	.021	.042	.013
Sentence recall	r	.215	.494	.091	.375
	Sig.	.146	.003	.319	.021
	N	26	29	29	30
	FDR	.025	.004	.038	.008

NOTE: ABX = discrimination task; FDR = adjusted significance threshold according to the False Discovery Rate procedure; LD = lexical decision; SR = sequence repetition.

Working memory measures in L1 do not highly correlate with phonological measures. Only sentence repetition and stress recall were correlated (but remember the high load of the stress recall task). Attentional control (shown in the 'nonwords' row) did not correlate significantly with phonological measures. The only correlation with processing speed was the stress task (which I have raised questions about in Section 2.5.2.3), as shown in Table 2.9.

Table 2.9. PROCESSING SPEED AND DIFFERENT TASKS

		Segmentals (ABX)	Stress (SR)	Phonotactics (LD)	Phonological score
Processing speed	r	.370	.427	.023	317
	Sig.	.032	.011	.453	.044
	N	26	29	29	30
	FDR	.025	.013	.050	.038

NOTE: ABX = discrimination task; FDR = adjusted significance threshold according to the False Discovery Rate procedure; LD = lexical decision; SR = sequence repetition.

Individual Differences

The main significance was between complex span (sentence repetition) and a composite score they generated called overall *phonological score*. It is this score which concerns me most. They administered the three tasks for phonological knowledge: the ABX segment discrimination, the stress sequence repetition, and the onset cluster lexical decision task. In the first stage of their analysis, they 'computed a z-score for each participant for each task using the mean and standard deviation of the entire sample ($N = 45$)' (Darcy, Park, and Yang 2015: 67). A linear mixed effects model on these z-scores revealed there was no significant effect of task. In the second stage of their analysis, 'an overall z-score was computed for each participant by averaging across the z-scores obtained for the test condition on each task to examine the effects for phonological development' (Darcy, Park, and Yang 2015: 68). So this 'phonological score' is an average of the results across three very diverse tasks. We need to question what this tells us. I recognize that there was not a significant task effect, but it does strike me as decidedly odd epistemologically to merge these scores in this fashion to, in effect, reify a *phonological processing aptitude*.

Remember that in a computational theory of mind (Pylyshyn 1984) processes act upon representations to produce other representations. I believe it is cognitively incoherent to note a correlation between a particular trait and an amalgam score which is not analogous to any mental representation. I am willing to grant a charitable interpretation to these results. To some extent, I consider the search for the role of isolable cognitive factors in L2 phonology to be parallel to situations we have seen before in the history of science. Many researchers have posited elements which had not been empirically verified. Hippocrates proposed the four humours (blood, yellow bile, black bile, and phlegm). Galen suggested there were four personality types (sanguine, choleric, melancholic, and phlegmatic). More recently, there have been proposals for different blood types (A, O, etc.), as well as such entities as genes, strings, gravitational waves, flavours of quarks, and the Higgs boson. Sometimes, science demonstrates the physical reality of the theoretical proposals (e.g. genes, gravitational waves), but sometimes it does not (humours). The question remaining to be answered is whether the various cognitive factors being proposed are more like humours or more like genes. And, of course, only time will tell.

There is a burgeoning literature on individual variation in second language speech (see Munro 2021). As always, when it comes to explaining the representational properties of interlanguage grammars, we face the dual challenges of what Rice and Avery (1995) call *global uniformity* and *local variation*. How do we explain the commonalities across a group of learners (global uniformity), and the differences between them (local variation). Variation in itself, however, is to be expected and is not a problem for a representational theory. As Dresher (1999) shows, even deterministic parsers come to decision points, and learners may take different paths. Clear evidence for this is seen in child language acquisition; Fikkert (1994) and Bohn and Santos (2018) show that different children take different routes to arrive at the adult target grammar, yet all stages are possible grammars. Özçelik (2017a) discusses these issues with respect to L2 phonology in his *Prosodic Acquisition Path Hypothesis*. For example, if the learner determines that the target language is footed, then new options become available (head-direction, weight-sensitivity, extrametricality, boundedness, etc.). If the learner determines that the feet are bounded, then new options become available (binarity, iterativity, direction of construction, etc.). Özçelik (2017a) shows that all of the choices made by the learners yield UG-sanctioned grammars.

In the next section, I explore a case study which looks at how transfer can be more complex than just a straight copy from the L1 to the L2.

2.7 PRESERVING L1 FEATURES IN AN L2: A LOOK AT CHAIN SHIFT

Jesney (2005, 2007) argues that it is not just the L1 features but the L1 feature *combinations* that are relevant to the initial state of SLA. She demonstrates this by looking at a phenomenon known as chain shift. An example from child phonology known as the 'Puzzle, Puddle, Pickle' problem illustrates the basic phenomenon (Figure 2.22).

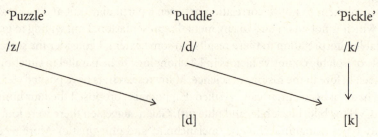

Figure 2.22. The 'Puzzle, Puddle, Pickle' problem
SOURCE: Adapted from Jesney (2005)

Notice that underlying /z/ sounds are produced as [d] by the child. Underlying /d/ and /k/ sounds both surface as [k]. Jesney explains this is via the mechanism of *preferential feature preservation*. Graphically, this can be illustrated as in Figure 2.23.

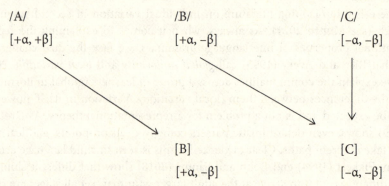

Figure 2.23. Preferential feature preservation
SOURCE: Adapted from Jesney (2005)

What this means is that when the features [+α] and [+ß] co-occur, it is preferential in the language to preserve the [+α] value, but the value of the [ß] feature can change. Let us look at a concrete example in Figure 2.24.

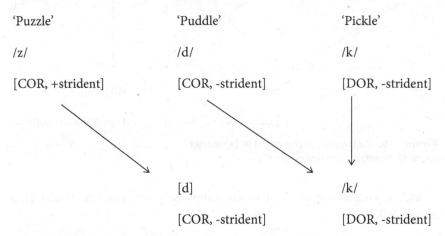

Figure 2.24. Preferential preservation of [COR]
SOURCE: Adapted from Jesney (2005)

In this instance, the child is faced with a combination of the features CORONAL and [+ strident]. Under these circumstances, the child wants to preserve the CORONAL feature even if it means changing the value of the [strident] feature. However, when the co-occurring features are CORONAL and [-strident], the CORONAL feature does not have to be preserved. Jesney (2007) provides acoustic and typological justification for these claims.

Let us now investigate how this applies to second language learning. Lee (2000) documents that Korean learners of English exhibit a type of chain shift in which underlying /θ/ surfaces as [s], underlying /s/ becomes [ʃ] before an [i], and underlying /ʃ/ becomes [ʃ]. Graphically we can illustrate this as in Figure 2.25.

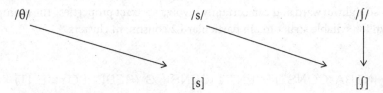

Figure 2.25. Korean L2 chain shift
SOURCE: Adapted from Jesney (2005)

Korean learners prefer to maintain the [anterior] value of a feature in the combination [+anterior, −strident]. When the combination is [+anterior, +strident], then the value of anterior can change, as shown in Figure 2.26.

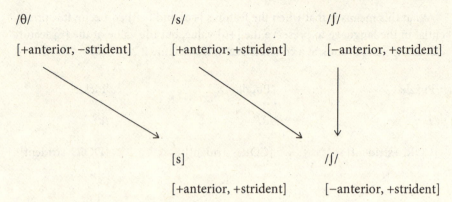

Figure 2.26. Preferential preservation of [+anterior]
SOURCE: Adapted from Jesney (2005)

Such a pattern would result in the following pronunciations (taken from Jesney 2005).

θ→s→ʃ chain shift of subject15 in L2 English (Lee 2000: 198–199)

a. /θ/→[s]   b. /s/→[ʃ]   c. /ʃ/→[ʃ]
   [s] 'thing'   [ʃ] 'sing'   [ʃ] 'ship'
   [s] 'think'   [ʃ] 'sit'   [ʃ] 'she'
   [s] 'thick'   [ʃ] 'sink'   [ʃ] 'shoes'
   [s] 'thin'   [ʃ] 'sick'   [ʃ] 'shell'

Evidence for this preferential feature combination comes from the grammar of the L1, which in this case is Korean. Other examples are found in Japanese and some Latin American dialects of Spanish (Eckman, Elreyes, and Iverson 2003). It is this property of preferential feature preservation which is transferring from the L1 and influencing the character of the L2 speech. Sometimes the properties of the L2 system are not the result of a deficit but rather of properties of the L1 which may be quite subtle and may be related to *combinations* of features.

The next case study I turn to is also designed to reveal that transfer is not always straightforward and can certainly involve abstract properties. The example is drawn for syllable structure, in particular L2 consonant clusters.

2.8 INTRA-CONSTITUENT LICENSING (REDEPLOYMENT)

Here I want to recapitulate the argument made in Archibald (2003) about transfer viewed within a model of Government Phonology (Kaye, Lowenstamm, and Vergnaud 1990).

While I am not wedded to the model of Government Phonology (GP), I use it here to further my argument that abstract representations help us to understand and explain learner behaviour.

Intra-constituent Licensing (Redeployment)

Under GP, phonological strings are grouped in hierarchical constituents with heads. Typically, heads can license a greater range of contrasts than non-heads. I will give the minimum information about the theory necessary to demonstrate the form of the argument.

(1) All phonological constituents consist minimally of a head.
(2) The rhyme is the head of the syllable, and, therefore, the onset is a non-head. Onsets themselves, though, are headed.
(3) Constituents are maximally binary branching.

GP does not sanction codas, but I will refer to them graphically in order to be parsimonious as to the theoretical machinery I introduce (but nothing crucially hinges on whether I refer here to codas or to the standard GP term *Onsets of Empty-Headed Syllables*). In Figure 2.27, note the following graphical conventions:

(1) Heads are underlined.
(2) Mapping to heads is shown with a vertical line, while mapping to non-heads is shown with an oblique line.
(3) The arrows indicate a construct known as *intra-constituent licensing* that is how a head can license a dependent within a constituent (the necessary details of which will be spelled out later).

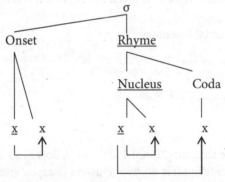

Figure 2.27. Intra-constituent syllabic licensing

What such a model will reveal is that it is structural *relations* which transfer, and this explains L2 behaviour.

Let us consider data from two different languages (Finnish and Korean) which share the property of not allowing consonant clusters within a syllable. I will probe how the notion of a phonological parser can account for the different behaviours that learners from these two languages display in acquiring English consonantal sequences and provide an analysis for these differences.

2.8.1 Korean Phonology

The first group to consider is speakers of Korean. The Korean segmental inventory is given in (13) (from Lee 1998).

(13) Korean segmental inventory:

p	t	c	k	
p'	t'	c'	k'	
p^h	t^h	c^h	k^h	
s				h
s'				
m	n		ŋ	
	r	j	w	

Turning to constraints on syllable structure, Korean does allow final codas [p, t, k, m, n, ŋ, l], but the distinctions among stops observed in onsets are neutralized to voiceless unaspirated. Lee (1998) argues that glides in prevocalic position are part of light diphthongs, and that Korean does not allow either branching onsets or branching nuclei.

2.8.2 Finnish Phonology

The Finnish segmental inventory is given in (14) (from Hakulinen 1961).

(14) Finnish segmental inventory:

p	t	k	
	d		
v	s		h
	l, r, j		
m	n	ŋ	

Concerning syllable structure, Finnish does not allow branching onsets. It does allow coda consonants but has no final clusters (Ringen and Heinämäki 1999). Only dentals [t, s, n, r, l] are permitted word-finally. In word-internal codas [t, s, n, r, l, s, t, h] and the first part of geminates are found. These observations indicate that codas can only license unmarked ([CORONAL] or placeless) elements in Finnish.

In sum, then, both Finnish and Korean allow some coda consonants, but neither language allows initial or final consonant clusters. As a result of these similarities across the two languages, if we simply looked at surface strings, we might be tempted to predict that Finnish and Korean speakers would acquire English consonant clusters in the same way. I hope to demonstrate that this is not the case.

2.8.3 L2 Data

Broselow and Finer (1991) have presented data on the production of onset clusters from Korean learners of English. These data show that Korean subjects have greater difficulty producing some English clusters than others. The Korean error rates for onset clusters are given in (15).

(15)   Korean error rates: Onset clusters

pr	br	fr
2/383	16/384	21/382
(.5%)	(4.1%)	(5.5%)

Broselow and Finer argue that a phonetically based minimal sonority distance (MSD) parameter can account for the differences in accuracy. I will not discuss the differential across cluster types but, rather, will investigate the difficulty that the Korean subjects have compared to the Finnish subjects. I believe that the two groups are comparable in that all subjects were residing in North America, had received English instruction in their home countries, and ranged in proficiency from high intermediate to advanced. Eckman and Iverson (1994) demonstrate that Korean subjects also have difficulty with coda clusters, producing 187 errors on 1,096 opportunities, an error rate of 17.1%.

Finnish subjects, on the contrary, do not seem to have difficulty either with onset clusters or with coda clusters. Archibald (2003) found the accuracy rates in spontaneous production tasks (an informal conversation) shown in Table 2.10.

Table 2.10. FINNISH ERROR RATES

Subject number	Onset cluster accuracy	Coda cluster accuracy
1	42/42 (100%)	113/113 (100%)
2	24/24 (100%)	47/49 (95.9%)
3	26/29 (89.7%)	32/37 (86.5%)
4	72/72 (100%)	94/94 (100%)
Total	164/167 (98.2%)	286/293 (97.6%)

I argue that the behaviour of the second language learners can be accounted for by appealing to certain segmental properties of their first languages ultimately having to do with the featural representation of the liquid inventory. Archibald (1998) argues that the presence of obstruent + liquid onset clusters in a language implies the presence of an /l/-/r/ contrast in the segmental inventory, but not vice versa. I will briefly outline the typological support for this claim.

Maddieson (1984) lists 14 languages (Korean, Japanese, Dan, Dagbani, Senadi, Akan, Lelemi, Beembe, Teke, Vietnamese, Tagalog, Hawaiian, Mandarin, and Zoque) with a single liquid, and none of them shows robust evidence of having consonant clusters at all, and no evidence of allowing obstruent plus liquid clusters. There is also support for this claim in such typologically diverse languages as Sanuma

(Borgman 1990), Kikuyu (Armstrong 1940), Ganda (Cole 1967), Nkore-Kiga (Taylor 1985), and Cayuga (Dyck, personal communication, citing Chafe 1977). Historically, there also seems to be a connection between these two structures in that when older languages had more than one liquid (e.g. Proto-Austronesian), they allowed clusters, but their descendants (Japanese, Chinese, Korean, Vietnamese) that have one liquid have no clusters (Baldi 1991). Similarly, Proto-Aztecan had no liquids and no clusters. One descendant (Huichol) has one liquid and no clusters, while another descendant (Nahuatl) has two liquids and allows clusters (Suárez 1983). There is also a connection between children acquiring the liquid contrast in English and their acquisition of clusters (see Gierut and O'Connor 2002).

2.8.4 Finnish Borrowings

Finnish treatment of loanwords helps to shed some light on what we see in the L2 phonology of Finnish speakers. The inventory in (12) reveals that it has two liquids, and remember it allows no consonant clusters. Older loanwords respect the absence of clusters. Hakulinen (1961) reports that borrowings from Germanic languages which begin with an initial cluster are reduced in Finnish, such that only the last consonant is retained, as was the case in Proto-Finnic as well. Examples of this pattern are given in (16).

(16)   Older loanwords:
       Swedish   Finnish
       strand   ranta   'waterfront'
       stol   tuoli   'chair'
       klister   liisteri   'paste'

However, more recent borrowings from English seem to retain their clusters, as shown in (17).

(17)   Recent loanwords:
       English   Finnish
       stress   stressi
       strategy   strategia

There appears to be something about Finnish which allows it to borrow words into the language and retain the clusters, and which allows Finnish speakers to acquire clusters when they are not sanctioned by the L1.

2.8.5 Sonorant Voice Structure

Young-Scholten and Archibald (2000) argue that there is a derived sonority argument to be made for the connection between these seemingly unrelated

Intra-constituent Licensing (Redeployment)

phenomena of having a liquid contrast in the segmental inventory and the ability to acquire L2 consonant clusters. I will not go through the argument in detail here. The basic idea is that by having a liquid contrast, the L1 has enough segmental structure to maintain a contrast between two segments in an onset or coda. Following Rice (1992), Young-Scholten and Archibald (2000) view sonority as a property reflected in the amount of structure under a Sonorant Voice (SV) node. English has an expanded SV node because it contrasts nasals and two liquids. Minimal sonority distance, under this model, refers to the relative amount of SV structure in two adjacent segments. However, because Korean *lacks* a liquid contrast in its segmental inventory, it consequently lacks the relevant structure for arriving at the English minimal sonority distance to license a cluster. The degree of SV structure permitted in each language is shown in (18) (based on Rice 1992).

(18)

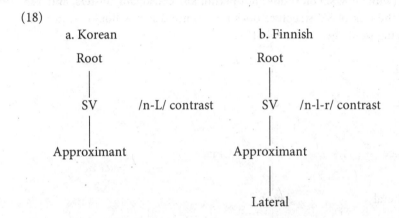

In Korean (18a), the feature approximant distinguishes liquids from nasals (which would be specified by a bare SV node). The lack of a distinction among liquids, symbolized by /L/, is reflected through the absence of the feature [lateral], in contrast to Finnish (18b). In short, a language like Finnish which maintains a phonemic liquid contrast has more structure under the SV node. A language like Korean which does not make this contrast does not have the sonorancy representations to consult when dealing with questions about minimal sonority distance.

Under such a model, the traditional phonetic construct of minimal sonority distance would be reconceived as a structural relationship, as shown in (19).

(19) Minimal sonority parameter
Parameter: SV government requires that the governor must have at least x more nodes than the governee
Settings: $x = 1, 2,$ or 3
Default: $x = 3$

The English setting would be $x = 2$ (allowing stop + liquid clusters), while Korean and Finnish would have a setting of $x = 3$ (prohibiting onset clusters). The Korean string would be as shown in (20).

(20)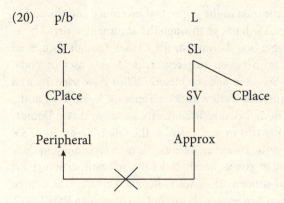

Korean (with an MSD of 3) does not permit any consonant clusters, and, furthermore, the lack of SV structure does not license a stop + liquid cluster. The Finnish string would be as shown in (21).

(21)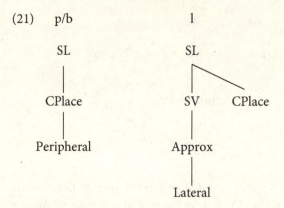

In comparing Finnish and Korean learners of English, Finnish learners have the relevant segmental structures in their L1 (as shown in (19)) and simply have to learn to 'redeploy' these structures. Learners from an L1 such as Korean have to acquire both a new feature structure (as shown in 16a) *and* a new parameter setting. This added demand on the second group of learners appears to be more difficult and results in more errors. I would maintain that the data from the Finnish subjects in Table 2.9 support my claim that it is easier for Finnish speakers to acquire English consonant clusters than it is for Korean speakers because of the L1 liquid inventory.

2.8.6 A Parsing Comparison

Let us bring these components together by looking at the parsing of consonantal sequences in English by speakers of the two L1s in question. The first steps are given in (22).

Intra-constituent Licensing (Redeployment)

(22)

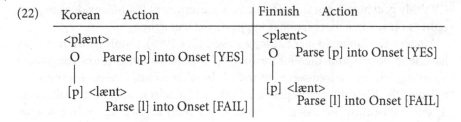

Now let us consider what happens at this point of parsing failure in the two languages. As others have noted (Fodor 1998a), parsing failures are opportunities for learning. Recall that neither L1 allows onset clusters, so the attempt to parse [l] into the onset after [p] will fail. Some change must be made to the L2 grammar. As a result, the action shown in (23) will be taken by both languages.

(23)   Korean   Action | Finnish   Action
      O   License a dependent | O   License a dependent
  /\   in the Onset. | /\   in the Onset.
[p] <lænt> | [p] <lænt>

The inductive process that will lead to this step is less obvious for the Korean learners than for the Finnish learners because the evidence for intra-constituent licensing is less robust in Korean than in Finnish. To demonstrate why this is the case, consider the intra-constituent licensing strength scale, shown in (24), which I propose reflects the ease with which head/dependent relations can be redeployed to new positions within the syllable.

(24)   Intra-constituent licensing strength scale:

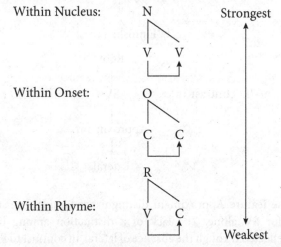

Such a scale is basically seeking to account for the typological patterns of syllable type where CVC is less marked than CCV, and CCV is less marked than

CVV. My goal here is not to articulate how Government Phonology does this but rather to cast it in a more familiar implicational hierarchy.

Modern Korean no longer has long vowels (Lee 1998). Finnish, however, does have long vowels and therefore a robust L1 instantiation of intra-constituent licensing that can be transferred to the L2. In other words, Finnish speakers can redeploy the licensing of a dependent in their L1 nuclei to acquire a weaker case of intra-constituent licensing (an onset dependent) in their L2. While Korean sanctions codas (rhyme-internal dependents), it appears that the L1 property of licensing a dependent in a weaker position on the scale does not allow the redeployment of the property to acquire a more robust position (an onset dependent) in the L2. Korean speakers will therefore have to rely on their inductive reasoning to make the necessary adjustment to their grammar. Let us nevertheless assume that the necessary change occurs in both the Korean and Finnish interlanguage grammars and that both are in the same state, as shown earlier in (21). We come now to the question of determining which segments can be licensed in the new dependent position. Here, again, the two languages differ. Let us consider the question that the algorithm asks at this point: *can the next element [l] be assigned to the onset?* Having arrived at a grammar which sanctions branching onsets, the parser must now determine which segments can be licensed in that new position. The relationship between the members of an onset cluster have been described in various ways that refer to voice, place, and manner (see Dresher and van der Hulst 1998; Rice 1992; Steriade 1982). The central question is this: is the element under focus different enough (with respect to some property (e.g. sonority) or feature (e.g. derived sonority)) to be parsed into the onset? Under the analysis that has been built up to this point, the Korean learners do not have the knowledge to answer that question as, recall, their L1 does not have a liquid contrast. The degree of SV structure permitted in each language is shown in (25) (based on Rice 1992).

(25) SV structure:

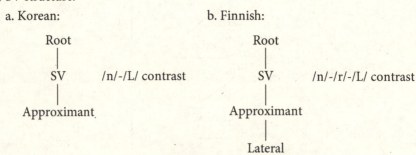

In Korean (25a), the feature Approximant distinguishes liquids from nasals, which are specified for SV alone. The lack of a distinction among liquids, symbolized by /L/, is reflected through the absence of lateral, in contrast to Finnish (25b). In short, a language like Finnish which maintains a phonemic liquid contrast has more structure under the SV node. A language like Korean which does not make this contrast does not have the sonorancy representations to consult when dealing with questions about minimal sonority distance.

Let us return to the current state of our parser, which is asking, *can the next element [l] be assigned to the onset?* The Korean parser is forced to answer [?] while the Finnish parser returns an answer of [Yes]. Again, the Korean learners will have to invoke changes to their grammar via induction, as opposed to the Finnish learners, who are able to redeploy their existing L1 representations and resources (I-learning). The current state of the parser is now as in (26).

(26)

Korean	Action	Finnish	Action
O ╱╲ [p] [l]<ænt>	Can the [1] be assigned to the Onset? [?]	O ╱╲ [p] [1]<ænt>	Can the [1] be assigned to the Onset? [YES]

Blending some steps together, the parser arrives at the next state, as shown in (27).

(27)

Korean	Action	Finnish	Action
O N C ╱╲ │ │ [p] [l][æ][n]<t>	Assign the [æ] to the Nucleus; assign the [n] to the Coda (the L1 allows this).	O N C ╱╲ │ │ [p] [1][æ][n]<t>	Assign the [æ] to the Nucleus; assign the [n] to the Coda (the L1 allows this).

The remaining task is to consider the parsing of the final [t]. Both L1s, as seen in Sections 2.8.1 and 2.8.2, sanction a [t] in the coda, but neither L1 allows coda clusters. For the sake of brevity, I would like to suggest that exactly the same arguments that we have just gone through for onsets hold for the acquisition of English coda clusters by speakers of Korean and Finnish, but I will not go through the details (see Archibald 2003, 2004, for an in-depth discussion).

In this section, I have investigated a number of broad questions related to the acquisition of consonant clusters in a second language. Drawing on the structural relations and phonological principles of Government Phonology, I have argued that the behaviour of second language learners can be accounted for by a top-down, left-to-right phonological parser, similar in design to that proposed by Phillips (1996) for syntax. Invoking the cognitive architecture of Carroll (2001), I have demonstrated that we can account for the different behaviours of speakers of languages that share the trait of lacking tautosyllabic clusters (Korean and Finnish) when they learn a language which allows such clusters (English). Properties of the L1 segmental inventory and a licensing strength scale were proposed to explain why Finnish learners had less trouble than Korean learners when acquiring English clusters.

In this way, considering the contributions of the parser allows us to describe and explain the behaviour of the L2ers when it comes to the production of consonant clusters.

2.9 PHONOLOGICAL PARSING

When second language learners whose L1 does not contain consonantal sequences are exposed to such sequences in their L2, the appropriate prosodic structures must be acquired. Specifically, learners must assign segments to particular prosodic positions. To investigate how this takes place, we turn to a discussion of phonological parsing. Archibald (2003) presents the basics of a model of phonological parsing in which phonological structure is assigned on the basis of a left-to-right parse (unlike approaches to syllabification discussed in Broselow (1992). In this domain, a phonological parser would assemble a string of segments into a syllabic hierarchy. This is analogous to a syntactic parser (see Berwick and Stabler 2019) which assembles a string of lexical items into a phrasal hierarchy. The phonological parser is consistent with Phillips (1996), which assumes that *parsing is grammar*. Such a stance is also reminiscent of Lightfoot (2020) and, indeed, Dresher (1999), who both argue that the grammar is the parser. Such an approach is preferable in terms of parsimony.

Structures are built from left to right in a deterministic fashion following certain *economy* conditions which are not directly relevant here (see also Chomsky 2015, for a discussion of economy cast as Minimal Search). These approaches can be argued to better model actual learner parsing (where the input does come in sequentially) and also to be simpler even though a certain amount of look-ahead has to be built in to avoid backtracking. While a syntactic parse is successful if the sentence is interpretable at logical form (LF), we must ask what the phonological analogue of this would be. At the word level, my assumption is that the parse succeeds if lexical access (or activation) takes place. Second language learners whose L1 does not license certain consonantal sequences are exposed to certain sequences in the L2 input and must learn to parse them (i.e. assign the segments to a hierarchical syllabic structure). Let us begin by going through a parse of the string *trip* by a native English speaker.

Step 1: Link segmental content to the lowest prosodic node.

Step 2: Can the first element be assigned to the onset? [Y/N]
   [Yes] → Assign it to the onset

Onset
|
[t] <rip>

At this stage [t] has been parsed (indicated by square brackets) while <rip> remain unparsed (represented by angle brackets).

Step 3: Can the next element be assigned to the onset? [Y/N]
    [Yes] → Assign it to the onset

Onset

[t] [r] <i p>

Step 4: Can the next element be assigned to the onset? [Y/N]
    [No] → Assign it to the nucleus

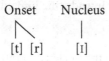

Onset   Nucleus

[t] [r]   [ɪ]

Step 5: Can the next element be assigned to the nucleus? [Y/N]
    [No] → Assign it to the coda

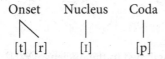

Onset   Nucleus   Coda

[t] [r]   [ɪ]   [p]

Step 6: Lexical activation

Drawing on the data of Broselow (1992), we look at the SLA of English by native speakers of Arabic whose L1 does not sanction branching onsets.

Step 1: Can the first element be assigned to the onset? [Y/N]
    [Yes] → Assign it to the onset

Onset
|
[t] <rip>

Step 2: Can the next element be assigned to the onset? [Y/N]
    [No; L1 setting] → Assign it to the nucleus <FAIL>
    Is the string consistent with the SSP? [Y/N]
    [Yes] → Leave the current element unparsed.

Onset
|
[t] <r> <ip>

Drawing on Holland and colleagues (1986), we adopt a version of a condition-action rule. The general form of the type of rule is:

> If condition C holds, then perform operation O.

Specifically for parsing, we adopt the following rules of parsing:

> IF consistent with SSP, THEN leave element unparsed.
> IF inconsistent with SSP, THEN delink element.

This type of algorithm allows us to parse without introducing limited look-ahead. Returning to the parsing of *trip*, we are at Step 3.

> Step 3: Can the next element be assigned to the nucleus? [Y/N]
>   [Yes] → Assign it to the nucleus.

```
Onset      Nucleus
  |          |
[t] <r>    [ɪ] <p>
```

> Step 4: Can the next element be assigned to the nucleus? [Y/N]
>   [No] → Assign it to the Coda.

```
Onset    Nucleus   Coda
  |         |        |
[t] <r>    [ɪ]      [p]
```

Note that this parse will fail because not all segmental material has been licensed by a higher level of prosodic structure. This illicit structure must be repaired. What is the repair strategy? The learner must fix the parse by projecting new prosodic structure (in this case a syllabic nucleus). The new nucleus goes to the left of the unparsed element.

[t] [i] <r> [i p]

In this way, examining the behaviour of the parser allows us to explain the site of epenthesis.

Parsing is the process by which input is mapped onto representation, and, as such, it is a necessary part of any learning theory (see Fodor 1998a, 1998b). We do, however, need to address what, on the surface, appears to be a conundrum. I will illustrate with the question of epenthetic vowels: if a second language learner produces a vowel where there is none in the target form, are they (a) accurately producing a non-nativelike lexical representation, or (b) inaccurately

Phonological Parsing

producing a nativelike lexical representation? The apparently paradoxical answer is *both*, depending on the L1. The Japanese parser when processing an L2 English s-cluster *triggers* a phantom vowel and, as a result (following Brown and Matthews 2004: 24), lexicalize that vowel:

> The learner perceives illusory segments that are not present in the acoustic signal. When attempting to store a representation for an L2 target form that contains a segmental sequence not sanctioned by the native language phonology, he or she will encode in that representation the material perceived as L2 intake. It is therefore highly unlikely that second language learners store L2 forms, particularly during the early stages of acquisition, that are identical to representations posited for native-speakers. Yet, this is the predominant assumption adopted in studies of L2 phonological acquisition.
>
> Theoretical analyses that attempt to account for systematic differences between non-native realizations of L2 forms and their target realizations have traditionally assumed native-like representations that are then subjected to rules, processes, or constraints transferred from the L1 phonology. Such assumptions presuppose accurate alignment of L2 intake with L2 input that cannot be maintained in the context of the perceptual illusions that have been shown to occur. We would claim then that the role of a learner's L1 phonology in the acquisition of an L2 has its primary influence in the perception of L2 input rather than in the production of L2 targets.

Hence, their production of an epenthetic vowel is the result of accurately producing a non-targetlike representation. But another language may behave in a different way. We will delve into this more deeply in the next chapter, but consider the behaviour of L1 Persian (and Saudi Arabic) subjects. The Persian parser, unlike the Japanese parser, when processing an L2 English s-cluster does *not* trigger a phantom vowel (because of certain properties of Persian phonology, in particular, syllable structure), and, as a result, their production of the epenthetic vowel is result of inaccurately producing a targetlike representation.

At this stage of proficiency, the learner is parsing the input (which includes a consonant cluster) and ends up inserting the epenthetic vowel. The result is that the learner's underlying representations are non-nativelike in that they include the epenthetic vowel. Later on in development, the learner will be able to take advantage of a variety of cues (orthography, inductive reasoning, metalinguistic knowledge, etc.), and the underlying representation will change from the non-nativelike /tirip/ to the native /trip/. This is consistent with Abrahamsson (2003), who proposes that learners proceed through the following stages when acquiring consonant clusters in an L2: (1) deletion of the illicit consonant, (2) epenthesis of a vowel to repair syllable structure, and (3) acquisition of the consonant in the appropriate position. The view espoused here proposes that, at early stages in acquisition, learners have incorrect underlying representations. Evidence that early representations are indeed inaccurate has been provided by Dehaene-Lambertz, Dupoux, and Gout (2000), who demonstrate via behavioural tasks and ERP analysis that Japanese speakers hear an epenthetic vowel between the two consonants in a string like [ebzo] (which is illicit in Japanese). The epenthetic vowel is not inserted late in a production routine; speakers actually hear it even when it is not present in the input. That is, even when there is no lexical entry available (i.e. for nonce forms), speakers perceive a vowel. Following from this, when setting up an underlying representation for a lexical item, the learner's initial assumption will be that the underlying representation is the same as the perceived surface form (consistent with Lexicon Optimization; van Oostendorp 2016. But this is only the beginning stage when it comes to acquiring an underlying form. Learners will come to know that their initial hypotheses may have been incorrect. They may discover that something they thought was predictable was in fact unpredictable, that is, that the status of a sound is recategorized from allophone to phoneme. This has been explored in detail in, for example, Eckman and Iverson (1997) and Eckman, Elreyes, and Iverson (2003).

It would go beyond the scope of this book to delve deeply into the nature of production/perception asymmetries. Suffice it to say that while the empirical examples recently discussed might suggest that these are issues related to specific languages, this is also an issue fundamental to the architecture of phonology (Flemming 2021; Lassetre and Donegan 1998; Pinget, Kager, and Van de Velde 2020; Tessier and Jesney 2014; Van de Weijer 2019).

This is, of course, central to theories of acquisition and is something that has been addressed under different guises in the work of Dresher, particularly Dresher and van der Hulst (1995), where the notion of *global determinacy* is introduced. What they point out is that the environmental cues to a particular phonological structure are not always local. For example, an English voiced obstruent may be cued more reliably by preceding vowel length than actual vocal fold vibration (*bead/beat*). Vowel harmony may happen productively but be blocked in certain environments. In short, as has been noted in the study of L2 morphosyntax for years, interlanguage grammars get restructured as the developmental path unfolds. This is true for phonological grammars and lexical representations as well.

For a word containing a target cluster, the learner will thereby posit an epenthetic vowel as part of the stored form. At a later stage of proficiency, the learner will realize (through induction) that this vowel is not, in fact, in the underlying string, and the parse will fail. There are a few possible sources for this type of knowledge. One would be the existence of minimal pairs or near-minimal pairs related to the target CVC sequence. Examples of such pairs are given in (28).

(28) train/terrain   trade/tirade
      claps/collapse   plate/palate
      clean/Colleen   plot/pilot
      dress/duress   plow/pillow
      drive/derive   sting/sitting

If the learner becomes aware of such pairs (and some of these—like [stíŋ] and [sítíŋ]—would have stress differences as well that would serve as an additional cue), then there will be an impetus to realize that the pronunciation of 'drive' with an epenthetic vowel between [d] and [r] cannot be correct. It is also plausible to assume that literacy facts and orthography in languages like English play a role in making learners aware that their L1 parsing strategies are failing in the parsing of onset clusters.

Our understanding of production/comprehension differences is enhanced by Blanco-Elorrieta and Pylkkänen (2015, 2016). These studies are not on L2 phonology but rather on language switching, yet I consider them relevant. The studies utilize magnetoencephalography (MEG) techniques to see what happens when bilinguals either produce or perceive switching between their two languages. In language *production* there is a close relationship between language control and general cognitive control, but this is not the case in *comprehension*. Language control in production recruits domain-general regions (dorsolateral prefrontal regions bilaterally). These regions are also implicated in *non-language* switching tasks. Comprehension, by contrast, recruits language-specific regions (anterior cingulate cortex) which are not implicated in a non-language switching task. In this light, we see that the perceptual illusions of the Japanese listeners are part of *grammar*. The produced epenthetic vowels, however, are under cognitive executive control.

2.10 REPRESENTATIONAL REALISM

Much work has been done on the SLA of syllable structure (see Young-Scholten and Archibald 2000, for a summary). The focus has tended to be on the acquisition of consonantal sequences in the L2 which are not licensed in the L1. But a more fundamental question has also been posed, and that is whether we need models of an abstract syllable at all. It has been proposed (Coté 2000; Steriade 2009) that we can explain the behavioural data with reference only to linear strings with the necessity of adding more complex hierarchical models of syllable structure.

We must ask whether there are data which would lead us to prefer one model over the other. Kabak and Idsardi (2007) present just such a study when they look at the SLA of English consonant clusters. Their goal is to assess explanations for a commonly noted phenomenon in L2 speech: epenthesis to repair illicit consonantal sequences. It has long been known that Japanese L1 subjects insert epenthetic vowels when producing English clusters, as evidenced in examples such as (29):

(29) 'strike' → [su.to.ɾa.i.kɯ]

Dupoux and colleagues (2008) demonstrate that Japanese L1 subjects actually *perceive* these epenthetic vowels in environments which violate the L1 grammar even when no actual vowel is physically present. A Japanese subject presented with the input string [ebzo] would hear [ebuzo] because that is what the L1 grammar leads the listener to expect. Japanese has restrictions on which consonants can appear in coda position. Licit coda consonants are (a) nasals and (b) geminate obstruents, as shown in (30), where the · represents a syllable boundary:

(30) kap·pa   'a legendary being'
      gak·koo   'school'
      tom·bo   'dragonfly'
      kaŋ·gae 'thought'

The items in (31) would be illicit sequences:

(31) *kap·ta
      *tog·ba

In these sequences, as in [ebzo], Japanese subjects perceive an epenthetic vowel. The question which Kabak and Idsardi pose is, *what is the locus of explanation for this pattern?* Dupoux and colleagues (2008) use stimuli which have both illicit sequences *and* illicit codas. Thus, a confound arises between determining whether the faulty perception occurs because of consonantal contact restrictions (e.g. because [b·z] is impossible) or because of coda conditions (e.g. [b] cannot be a coda consonant). Is there any way for us to tease apart Kabak and Idsardi's hypotheses shown in (32) to determine whether we need the construct of 'coda' in our grammar?

(32) *Consonantal Contact Hypothesis: L2 listeners will apply perceptual epenthesis to all consonantal sequences which are illicit in the L1.*

      Coda Condition Hypothesis: L2 listeners will apply perceptual epenthesis only when there is a syllable structure violation concerning the coda consonant.

The Japanese examples cited above do not allow us to test between these two hypotheses, but Korean data provide just the test case we are looking for. In Korean, there are constraints on syllable structure summarized in (33):

(33) | Initial | Medial | Final |
      |---------|----------|--------|
      | *km- | *-pkm- | *-pk |
      | *mr- | *-kmr- | *-km |
      | *mw- | *-tnw- | *-tn |

At times, morphological concatenation will create such a banned sequence, and phonological adjustments take place as a result. Two rules are of interest here: (a) Nasalization and (b) Lateralization.

The rule of Nasalization takes a C + N sequence and transforms it into a N + N sequence, as shown in (34).

(34) puək^h + mun ⇒ puəŋ + mun   'kitchen door'

Representational Realism

The rule of Lateralization takes a L + N sequence and transforms it into an L + L sequence, as shown in (35).

(35)   tal + nala $\Rightarrow$ tal – la · ɾa   'moon country'

These rules are crucial when it comes to assessing the two hypotheses given above in (28).

Kabak and Idsardi (2007) give three reasons why a $C_1 \cdot C_2$ sequence might be repaired:

(1) C_1 is a licit coda; C_2 is a licit onset *but* the sequence is illicit.
(2) C_1 is an illicit coda (e.g. [c], [h], etc.).
(3) C_2 is an illicit onset (this is not critical here).

The question is whether both types of illicit structures trigger perceptual epenthesis. To answer this question, they conducted an AX (same/different) discrimination task with nonce words. The stimuli were constructed to contain illicit sequences either with epenthetic vowels or not. The appropriate Korean epenthetic vowel was used ([ɪ] after palatals, [ʊ] elsewhere). The experimental design is summarized in Table 2.11.

Table 2.11. KABAK AND IDSARDI RESEARCH DESIGN

			C_2	
			Oral stop (e.g. [tʰ])	Nasal (e.g. [n], [m])
	Licit	[k]	Licit	Illicit
C_1		[l]	Licit	Illicit
	Illicit	[c]	Illicit	Illicit
		[j]	Illicit	Illicit
		[g]	Illicit	Illicit

There was a 1,500 ms ISI. The data (from 25 NNS and 25 NS controls) were analysed with both d' and A' scores, but the A' are the most relevant here.

Hypothesis A: Under the Consonantal Contact Hypothesis, all cases of illicit contact should trigger epenthesis (e.g. [k.m], [l.n], [c.m], [c.tʰ]).
Hypothesis B: Under the Coda Condition Hypothesis, permissible coda sequences should not trigger epenthesis (e.g. [k.m], [l.n]).

2.10.1 Results

The d' scores (and their non-parametric analogue A') are calculated to take into account both discrimination ability and response bias in subjects. We might think that a subject who scored 100% on identifying all different stimuli as different (i.e. *hits*) would be doing so because they had the perceptual acuity to distinguish the stimuli. But what if they were pressing Yes all the time? Even when the stimuli were the same, they would press Yes. These would result in *false alarms* (erroneous distinctions) and suggest that we need to take the response bias of the subject into account. How many *misses* (erroneous identification) and how many false alarms do we find? The d' and A' scores take into account the misses and false alarms in calculating the subject's ability to discriminate, as summarized in Table 2.12.

Table 2.12. POSSIBLE RESPONSES IN A DISCRIMINATION TASK

	Response: (Different) yes	Response: (Same) no
Stimuli: (Different) yes	Hit	Miss
Stimuli: (Same) no	False alarm	Correct rejection

Kabak and Idsardi (2007) report on A' scores. The different sequences seemed to fall into three groups when the A' scores were ranked. The highest A' scores were for [lt], [ln], and [kt], in the middle were [gm], [km], and [gt], while the lowest A' scores were for [cm], [jm], [jt], and [ct]. To find out whether the middle group was behaving more like the high group or the low group, a cluster analysis (mixed effects) was run, and it was clear that the data clustered as shown in Table 2.13.

Table 2.13. DISCRIMINATION ACCURACY
OF DIFFERENT CONSONANTAL SEQUENCES

Sequence	Type	Mean A'
ln	Bad contact	0.95
kt^h	OK	0.94
lt^h	OK	0.94
gt^h	Bad contact	0.85
km	Bad contact	0.82
gm	Bad contact	0.74
ct^h	Bad coda	0.61
jt^h	Bad coda	0.51
cm	Bad coda	0.50
jm	Bad coda	0.49

2.10.2 Summary

What this shows is that it is the bad coda condition behaves differently than the bad contact condition. These results, then, demonstrate the validity of the construct of a coda and, more generally, of abstract, hierarchical syllabic representations in the interlanguage phonological grammars. This is not just linear adjacency; we need hierarchical structure.

Conclusion

2.11 CONCLUSION

In this chapter, I have set the context of the study of L2 phonology within frameworks of language learnability where phonology is viewed as a type of knowledge, a type of cognition, not merely motoric routines. Under these models we look for such familiar components as environmental effects, parsing strategies, and descriptions of the initial and final states of knowledge, as well as accounts of the transitional stages. This perspective gives us insight into what the architecture of an L2 phonological grammar looks like. It consists of rich, hierarchical representations in the domains of features, syllables, and higher prosodic levels such as metrical feet. They are not representations which are merely 'noticed' in the input.

With this background in place, let us turn to our discussion of the first phonological interface: phonology and phonetics.

The Phonetics/Phonology Interface

3

3.1 INTRODUCTION

There is a long history of trying to draw the line between phonetics and phonology. Ladd (2014) provides a valuable summary of this (and other) issues. I will adopt the position he articulates: 'I start from the assumption . . . that the categories manipulated by the phonology are abstractions over a lot of phonetic variation that can be adequately described only in quantitative terms' (99). However, my view is that we need to incorporate such gradient phonetic effects into our processing and learning theories and not into our representational models (as Laboratory Phonology and Exemplar Theory would suggest).

A central goal of the book, then, is to unify the different strands of generative approaches to second language acquisition (GenSLA) that have become unravelled. When dealing with something as complex as human language, it is understandable that sub-domains develop complex, internally consistent theories. Whether we are delving into Montague semantics, minimalist syntax, Distributed Morphology, Laboratory Phonology, or linear mixed effects modelling, explaining the core issues to an outsider may be challenging. This book can be viewed either as a thought experiment or an exercise in the philosophy of science to see what the consequences of an internally consistent model of L2 phonology would look like when we take into account interfaces with phonetics, morphology, and syntax.

3.2 ABSTRACT REPRESENTATIONS

From at least the time of Sapir (2008/1933) we have sought and found evidence for the necessity of abstract representations such as the phoneme. More recently, Phillips and colleagues (2000) conducted a magnetoencephalographic (MEG) study which relies on the brain's ability to detect deviant stimuli as revealed through a Mismatched Negativity signal. The study showed that non-matching items (oddballs) are identified at a phonemic level, thus demonstrating that constructs such as the

Phonology in Multilingual Grammars. John Archibald, Oxford University Press. © John Archibald 2024.
DOI: 10.1093/oso/9780190923334.003.0003

phoneme are quite real in terms of cognitive neuroscience. Work in the school of Dresher's (2009) Contrastive Hierarchy also shows the need of abstract phonological features. For example, Dyck (1995) shows that languages which represent a feature such as [+high] on an [i] vowel behave differently than languages which do not have this feature present on [i] (in terms of such processes as feature spreading or assimilation). It is, therefore, *not* the acoustic signal properties of the [i] vowel which predict its behaviour but rather the mental representation. And this mental representation is abstract. This is consistent with work in disparate frameworks (Archibald 2023; Pulleyblank 2006) which argue that the mapping of features to segments is a *learning* problem. This mapping is provided by neither Universal Grammar (UG) nor something that needs to be 'noticed' in the input (see Carroll 2001; Rast 2008).

Evidence for abstract representations in L2 learners also can be found in Archibald (1993a, 2005). In these works, I show that such prosodic constructs as extrametricality and foot structure, as well as the construct of derived sonority, explain the properties of L2 grammars. None of them can be read directly off the input signal. Weber (2014) shows that foot structure (not segmental properties) is critical to understanding the differential effects on intelligibility of different kinds of stress errors. Finally, there is compelling evidence in González Poot (2011) that is problematic for exemplar theory. González Poot looked at the acquisition of Yucatec Mayan ejectives by native speakers of Spanish. Spanish lacks the distinctive feature [constricted glottis] necessary to represent this class of sound. In looking at the discrimination abilities of his subjects he noticed two things: (1) in onset position the non-native subjects were indistinguishable from the native speakers, and (2) there was a definite pattern when it came to accuracy scores: k'/p' > t'/tʃ' > ts'. That is to say, non-strident consonants were perceived most accurately, and strident consonants were perceived least accurately. In the coda position, the pattern was (roughly) the reverse, with strident ejectives being most accurately perceived and non-strident ones being least accurately perceived. What these data reveal are (1) that non-native speakers *can* acquire new features, and (2) that their behaviour cannot be explained simply by having them store each exemplar of ejectives they hear, as their accuracy is highly correlated with acoustic saliency factors (such as cue robustness, following Wright 2004). A lesson to be drawn from this study is that the input influences the learning path and is not part of the representation. Note that not *all* exemplars of the feature [constricted glottis] are parsed at the same time. In onset position, non-strident stops are processed more accurately while in coda position strident stops are. These connections are not stipulations as they are grounded typologically and phonetically. What we see in this study is that perceptual accuracy paves the way for grammatical restructuring and the *phonologization* of the feature [constricted glottis].

3.2.1 Background

The acquisition of the sound system of a second language is a complex, well-studied phenomenon (Bohn and Munro 2007; Hansen and Zampini 2008). One of the questions which receives much attention (Archibald 2005; Levy 2004; McAllister 2007) is whether a subject is able to acquire an L2 structure which is absent from the first language (L1). There are many factors that can influence this development (L1 transfer, level of proficiency, etc.). However, there is also considerable evidence (Strange and Shafer 2008) that many L2 sounds can be misperceived by L2 learners. Many (e.g. Flege 1995) have argued that inaccurate perception underlies accented production. The basic point is this: if an L2 learner is observed to produce a sound in a non-nativelike way, we are unsure whether they have a nativelike representation that they are failing to produce accurately, or whether they have a non-nativelike representation. If they do have nativelike representation but are producing it in a non-targetlike fashion, this presents a learning problem which is often tackled as having to rerank constraints in Optimality Theory. If, however, we see evidence of inaccurate perception, we can be quite confident that the L2 learner does not have a nativelike phonological representation. Therefore, perceptual measures can be taken as good windows into L2 phonological competence. The wealth of literature on L2 perception makes it clear that we are dealing with a complex phenomenon but that not all new sounds are equally difficult to acquire. This is the basis of Flege's (1995) Speech Learning Model (SLM), which maintains that L2 sounds which are perceptually distant from L1 sounds (i.e. *new* sounds) will be more easily acquired than L2 sounds which are perceptually close to an L1 sound (i.e. *similar* sounds). It is also central to Rast (2008), who categorizes sounds as either 'distant' or 'close' when comparing phonemic inventories. What we lack is a synthesis of the role of phonology and its interfaces to look at these questions.

3.3 PERCEPTIBILITY

We begin our empirical discussion of the phonetics/phonology interface by considering the role of perception in the acquisition of L2 phonology. There is clearly a wide literature on cross-linguistics perception (Best and Tyler 2007; Flege 1995; Strange 1995; Van Leussen and Escudero 2015) which is often much more at home in the phonetics world than the phonology world.

To appreciate the role of perception in acquisition, let us ask a familiar question from the study of both first and second language acquisition. Imagine that a speaker produces a non-targetlike form. So, instead of saying [blu] for 'blue', the speaker says [bju], or instead of saying [bɪt] for 'bit', the speaker says [bit]. Immediately, the question arises as to whether the learners are producing the non-targetlike form (a) because they can't *hear* the difference, or (b) because they can't *articulate* the distinction. To phrase this another way, do they have inaccurate representations like /bju/ and /bit/ which they are producing faithfully, or conversely, do they have accurate representations like /blu/ and /bɪt/ which they are producing inaccurately? Of course, an individual's representation can change over time; learning can happen. It seems to have been a common experience for many people who took introductory phonetics to have heard their instructor say

Perceptibility 83

something like, 'Some languages make a distinction between *x* and *y*', where whatever distinction under discussion was imperceptible to the student (so it sounds to them like the instructor said, 'Some languages make a distinction between *x* and *x*'). Less anecdotally, Rochet (1995) presents a wonderful data set where he documents the differential perception of a French high, front, rounded vowel [ü]. English speakers tend to hear and produce it as [u] (a high, back, rounded vowel) while Portuguese speakers tend to hear and produce it as [i] (a high, front, unrounded vowel); both populations get two out of the three features correct. These are examples of what is known as *differential substitution*, where a single target sound, say [θ], may be produced as [t] or [s] or [f] by different learners with different L1s (though as Munro (2021) reminds us not all speakers from a given L1 behave in the same fashion). And there is even the case of two dialects of French substituting either [s] for [θ] (European French), or [t] for [θ] (Quebec French). A non-technical response would be to say that each language chooses the sound which is 'closest' to the target sound. Alas, the devil being in the details, we need a way to measure proximity. I turn to that shortly when discussing the work of Brannen (2011).

But, starting more simply, one of the most common stances taken in L2 speech is that the earliest acquired elements are those which are deemed easiest to hear. Let's unpack the assumptions underlying such a simple-sounding statement. In Flege's SLM terms, L2 sounds which are *different* from L1 sounds will be easier to hear and thus will allow the setting up of a new phonetic category. Similar sounds are more likely to be classed as equivalent to the L1 phonetic categories. However, we need to look behind the notion of equivalence classification to the learning algorithm particularly with respect to feature mapping and ask, *what are the* cues *to trigger the setting up of a new category?*

There is, of course, a rich literature on cross-linguistic speech perception which investigates the processing and categorization of the speech signal. One way of distinguishing stances within this literature is the question of how much the model relies on abstract symbolic representation. There are some approaches (e.g. Ohala 1983) which would minimize the need for abstract representation while others (e.g. Raimy and Cairns 2009) argue for phonology as cognition. And then there are the arguments about the actual form of phonological representations, ranging from a view which holds that fine phonetic detail is part of the representation (Pierrehumbert, Beckman, and Ladd 2000; Steriade 2009) to a view that representations are very abstract (Kaye 1990) to a view that the representations are 'substance free' (Reiss 2017).

I raise these issues in this section because the notion of perceptibility can be used in an attempt to explain the order of acquisition (in either first or second language acquisition) along the lines of *segment* x *is acquired before segment* y *because it is more perceptible*. Taking an example from first language acquisition (FLA), Vanderweide (2005) looks at the acquisition of prevocalic consonantal sequences by Dutch-speaking children. She argues that children acquire segments in the context of greatest perceptibility. Children will acquire a particular consonantal segment when it precedes a vowel (e.g. [so]) before they acquire the same segment in the environment preceding a sonorant (e.g. [sn]) and before they acquire it preceding an obstruent (e.g. [st]). My position is that the properties of the signal affect not the representation but the learning. Following Wright (2001), what makes a signal more or less perceptible has to do with the robustness of the associated phonetic cues. He refers to internal cues (such as formant structure) and contextual cues (such as release burst) when defining robustness. As we will see in Section 3.5 on intake frequency, the robustness of acoustic cue determines when input becomes intake to the processor. More robust cues are processed before less robust cues; not all information becomes available at the same time (thus allowing us to develop a transition theory). Therefore, acquisition is gradual. Later, we will turn to an extended discussion of this issue with a case study of the acquisition of Yucatec Maya ejectives by native speakers of Spanish (González Poot 2011, 2014).

Let us consider one brief case study here on the acquisition of various L2 laryngeal features to illustrate the point. Wright (2004: 35) defines a perceptual cue as 'information in the acoustic signal that allows the listener to apprehend the existence of a phonological contrast'. A number of recent studies show that L2 learners are initially more sensitive to transitional release cues than to internal cues in the acquisition of sounds which are not built on L1 features. The processing of these robust cues sets the stage for the developmental paths observed in the acquisition by delimiting the set of sounds which become intake to the processor. González Poot's study of L2 ejectives reveals a differing pattern of discrimination accuracy in onsets as opposed to codas. This is shown in (36):

(36)   Onset: p' > k' > t', tʃ' > ts'
       Coda: tʃ' > ts' > k' > p' > t'

We see that in onset position the release burst of the ejective stop is more perceptible than the glottalized release from the strident affricate. Figure 3.1 shows the release from an ejective compared to a plain stop in prevocalic position. Note the spike in the waveform for the ejective [p'].

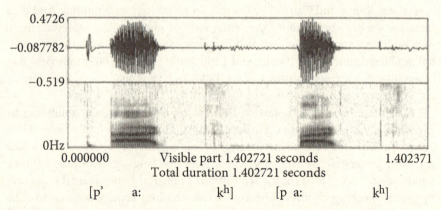

Figure 3.1. Different release bursts
SOURCE: Adapted from González Poot (2011)

Jackson (2009) shows that both English and French L1 subjects were especially sensitive to Hindi voiced aspirated stops. The release burst (transitional) and murmured voicing (internal) cues, shown in Figure 3.2, were attended to by the L2 listeners, and yet they were *not* attending to closure voicing (a cue which is important for native Hindi listeners).

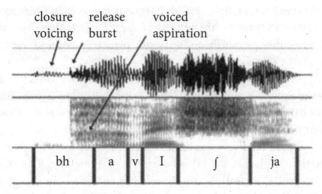

Figure 3.2. Consonant to vowel recovery cues
SOURCE: Adapted from Jackson (2009)

Finally, a suite of experiments by Cardoso (2007) demonstrates the unexpected, for him, sensitivity that Brazilian Portuguese speakers have to the English [st] cluster (compared to [sn] and [sl]). One explanation for this sensitivity is the profile of the release burst of the stop following the [s], compared with the lack of burst in the [sn] or [sl] clusters as seen in Figure 3.3.

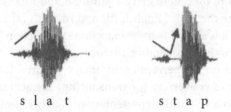

Figure 3.3. Transition to sonorant vs. obstruent
SOURCE: Adapted from Cardoso, John, and French (2009)

All this is to say that there are properties of the acoustic signal capable of influencing which sounds are processed earlier in the developmental path.

So, to explore the role of perception, let us begin with an overview of the work of Brannen (2011). The basic question is a familiar one: how do we map target sounds onto internal representations? She proposes the *Auditory Distance Model*. She assumes that the L2 learner has direct access to all the *phonetic* features provided by UG. An auditory distance algorithm will compare the target intake features with those encoded on L1 segments. In this way, the IL phonological representations are determined. There is much to be commended in the insights and mechanisms of Brannen's approach. However, as we shall see, it faces empirical challenges. Nonetheless, I consider it worth discussing at length, as its failures result from the direct realist architecture and provide motivation for the indirect realist approach we take here. Where I believe the problem lies (a problem shared in the Bayesian approach discussed later in Chapter 6) is in the assumption of direct perception and hence representation of phonetic features. Following Nearey (1990, 1992) and Ohala (1986), I argue that this is an untenable position. As Nearey (1992: 153) notes, 'the objects of speech perception (and production) are viewed as neither primarily auditory nor primarily gestural; rather, they are abstract, symbolic elements.'

Brannen's proposed algorithm for measuring auditory distance determines whether features match and their relative weight. Feature enhancement (to be discussed shortly) can add to the relative weight of a given feature. Now, as we are talking about features, it behooves us to say something about her use of the term *feature*. She adopts a relatively standard model of feature use where we might represent a particular phone, say [s], as a matrix of something like [CORONAL, +continuant, −voice, −nasal]. Similarly, when it comes to phonological features, she makes the relatively standard assumption that phonological representations may not include all the information that phonetic representations do. For example, in the preceding example, it may be redundant to specify that a consonant which is [−voice] is also [−nasal], so the phoneme may not include the [−nasal] feature. In this respect, she adopts a model of phonological underspecification where only contrastive features are specified (Rice and Avery 1995). This is what is to be acquired. However, she argues that *non-contrastive* features play a role in transfer. In this model, the input to the learner is a fully specified phonetic matrix (the surface form of the L2 target). She looks at the well-studied (e.g. Hancin-Bhatt 1994) literature on differential substitution and focusses on why speakers of some L1s replace the target English /θ/ and /ð/ with [s] and [z] while others choose [t] and [d]. It is argued that the inaccurate production is caused by inaccurate perception. How is this operationalized?

Transfer is based on the perception of 'intake features' for Brannen. For her, *intake* is the result of converting (or transducing) the acoustic signal (which is non-linguistic) into a linguistic representation. Acoustic features which are not relevant will be stripped from the intake representation.

3.3.1 Calculating Auditory Distance

The intake form is compared to stored representations. Features in the intake which are not found in the stored representation are noted, and the 'distances' of those features from the targets are calculated. The intake form is then mapped onto the stored representation which is the 'closest'. This is reminiscent of the goodness-of-fit models of Best (1995) and, indeed, equivalence classification models like Flege (1995). In Brannen's model, the mismatches are assigned a cost. A violation which is more easily perceived (i.e. more salient) is more costly. Auditory distance is measured by how far the mismatched feature in the native representation is from the corresponding intake feature. Differential costs of mismatches are well documented in the literature (Goad and White 2019; Howe and Pulleyblank 2004; Pater 1997b). Many models try to incorporate notions such as 'make minimal changes' or 'preserve important contrasts'. Brannen adopts an auditory distance scale, as shown in Figure 3.4.

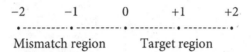

Figure 3.4. Auditory distance scale
SOURCE: Adapted from Brannen (2011)

To understand the scale, we need to consider her theory of feature *weighting*. And to understand the feature weighting, we need to take into account the notion of *enhancement*. Enhancement is a construct introduced by Keyser and Stevens (2006) in which they note that certain combinations of phonetic features helped to make segmental contrasts more distinct. For example, a [s]/[ʃ] contrast can be subtle but if, as in English, the [ʃ] sound is produced with lip rounding (i.e. [+round]), then the contrast for the [ʃ] is phonetically enhanced. The rounding on [ʃ] (−anterior) serves to enhance the contrast with [s] (+anterior). The [anterior] feature is implemented by low spectral prominence on F3 but [ʃ] has weak F3 levels. Therefore, lip rounding added to [ʃ] will boost F3 levels and enhance the contrast. The converse of this is when a particular feature combination *mutes* a contrast (i.e. does *not* enhance it), thus making it more subtle.

Feature enhancement, then, is another way to make items prominent and to preserve contrasts. Certain combinations of features enhance our ability to perceive a contrast. Some examples from Keyser and Stevens (2006) are given in (37).

(37) • Rounding enhances back
 • Back enhances lateral

The following are the key enhancement relationships for Brannen:

1. [round] enhances [−anterior]
2. [strident] enhances [continuant]
3. [mellow] enhances [stop]
4. [dental] mutes [strident]
5. [alveolar] enhances [strident]

Within this model, if a feature is enhanced, it receives a boost to its integer value, as shown in Table 3.1.

THE PHONETICS/PHONOLOGY INTERFACE

Table 3.1. FEATURE WEIGHT SCALE

Feature	Inherent weight	Enhanced weight
LAB, COR, DOR	2	N/A
Stop, continuant	1	Mellow enhances stop →2
		Strident enhances continuant →2
Strident, mellow	1	Alveolar, post-alveolar enhance strident →2
Lip, dental, alveolar, post-alveolar	1	Round enhances post-alveolar →2
Laminal, apical	1	N/A
Round, unround	1	N/A

A hypothetical example of how the machinery would work is given in Table 3.2, where *recessive* is indicative of a less salient feature.

Table 3.2. AUDITORY DISTANCE MACHINERY

Intake target form [ts] COR (salient) +2 Stop (recessive) +1 Strident (enhanced) +2 Alveolar (recessive) +1	Evaluation of mismatches	Distance on scale
Candidate #1 [t]	COR (salient) +2	0
	Stop (enhanced) +2	1
	Mellow (recessive) −1	3
	Alveolar (recessive) +1	0
		Total = 4
Candidate #2 [s]	COR (salient) +2	0
	Continuant (enhanced) −2	3
	Strident (enhanced) +2	0
	Alveolar (recessive) +1	0
		Total = 3

Because candidate #2 ([s]) is closer to the input target (with a distance of 3 rather than 4), [s] is predicted to be chosen as the equivalent to [ts], and it is the 'closest'.

3.3.2 Empirical Results

Brannen looked at English target interdentals being acquired by speakers of European French, Quebec French, Japanese, and Russian. The task was an AXB task. I will not go into the details, but it is fair to say that while some of the predicted patterns emerged (thus supporting a perceptual basis for differential

Perceptibility

substitution), many did not. For example (2011: 185), the 'differences between the two dialects of French did not clearly emerge: both EF and QF tended to misperceive the interdental fricative as [f], and for EF, equally as [s]'.

For me, the take-home message is that empirically, while there is some variation, her model shows considerable success in demonstrating that auditory distance and phonetic enhancement play a role in equivalence classification. She demonstrates the value in considering both phonological features (in the stored matrix) and phonetic features (in the input matrix) in the acquisition process. However, I do have some reservations or refinements that I would like to discuss.

3.3.3 Concerns

Brannen's model is a direct realist model (see Best 1995) which ascribes to the learner the ability to read the fully specified phonetic matrix off the auditory input. Brannen refers to this as 'access to UG'. Nearey (1990) sets out the landscape of issues involved and stances taken on this position very well. We need to identify three domains: (1) discrete symbolic elements, (2) continuous articulatory/gestural elements, and (3) continuous auditory/acoustic elements. There are different theoretical postures which relate these three domains where *strong* is to be read as 'simple, robust, and transparent':

(a) Double strong (Blumstein and Stevens 1981). Strong relations between mental symbols and gestures *and* strong relations between symbols and auditory properties.
(b) Strong gestural (Motor Theory (Liberman and Mattingly 1985), Direct Realism (Best 1995)). Strong ties between mental symbol and gesture. Complex and indirect connections between mental symbols and auditory properties.
(c) Strong auditory (Kingston and Diehl 1994). Strong relations between mental symbols and auditory properties. Complex and indirect links between mental symbols and gestures.
(d) Double weak (Nearey 1990, 1992). Calls into question the phonetic bases of phonological universals and points out that the relationships among mental symbols, gestures, and auditory properties are complex and variable.

Nearey's Double-Weak Model reminds us of the problem with the direct realist approach taken by Brannen: phonetic features do not map invariably onto phonological features. Languages can vary in the phonetic cues used to signal stress: some combination of pitch, duration, intensity, and vowel quality. Languages can vary in the phonetic cues which most reliably signal voicing in coda position. In English the most reliable cue is the length of the preceding vowel, while in Polish this is not a reliable cue to consonant voicing (Keating 1990). The work of Dresher (e.g.

2009) on the Contrastive Hierarchy of phonological features also illuminates the fundamental problem. Even if we consider a limited data set such as the features necessary to distinguish a three-vowel system, an immediate interface problem arises: different languages with the same three surface vowels (say, [i, ɑ, u]) may have different feature hierarchies. Consider the two options shown in Figure 3.5.

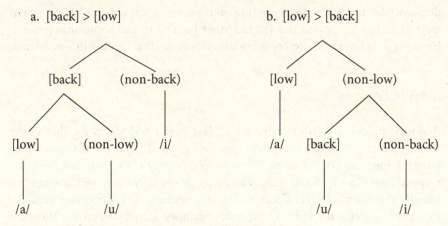

Figure 3.5. Feature hierarchies of two three-vowel systems
SOURCE: Adapted from Cowper and Hall (2019)

In (a), the feature [±low] is contrastive only on back vowels, while in (b), *all* vowels are distinguished by [±low] with [±back] being contrastive only for non-low vowels. Without delving into the phonological details, what this tells us is that the phonological features cannot be read directly and transparently from the acoustic signal. The [a] in (a) sounds exactly the same as the [a] in (b), yet they have different representations. The [a] in (a) has a contrastive [back] feature which might spread, while the [a] in (b) has no contrastive [back] feature and would, thus, not participate in feature spreading. From an acquisition perspective, one does not just *notice* that [a] is [back]; one has to *learn* the phonological representation of /a/.

As Dyck (1995) and Hall (2017) have shown, only phonological features which are contrastive and hence active in the language can be involved in phonological processes. Take a hypothetical example where in one language the phoneme /i/ has a feature [+high] associated with it, while in another language the phoneme /i/ is underspecified for height. The prediction, which is empirically tested and confirmed in Dyck (1995), is that only in the language with the [+high] feature active can there be a process like height spreading. This demonstrates that the value of [high] cannot be directly read off the phonetic input just by hearing an [i]. Dresher (2018) recognizes that it may not be the phonetic features which are innate but, rather, the learning algorithm, which he calls the Successive Division Algorithm. Under this process, the learner will first divide the vowel space with respect to a single feature (say, [+back] and [−back]). Then the next division will be on the basis of, say, [+high] and [−high]. In this way, the phonological space is defined by making serial decisions about the necessary contrasts. I will not explore the implications of this model for SLA here. Archibald (2019) has adopted it to account for an interesting case in third language acquisition where L3 learners of English transferred their L1 Arabic consonants but their L2 French vowels into L3 English. The Contrastive Hierarchy makes it clear why French vowels are 'closer' to English vowels but Arabic consonants are 'closer' to English consonants. Here, though, the main message is that simply hearing an [i] will not tell the learner what type of representation to set up for /i/.

Let us consider the fact of French using the feature [±voice] while English uses the feature [±spread glottis] to implement, say, a [p]/[b] contrast (Iverson and Salmons 1995). Jackson (2009) and Archibald and Jackson (2010) show that native speakers of French were better at perceiving Hindi [voice] contrasts, while native speakers of English were better at perceiving [spread glottis] contrasts (thus confirming the phonological analysis). A child learning French would be exposed to an environmental [p] and store the feature [−voice], while a child learning English would be exposed to an environmental [p] and store the feature [+spread glottis]. I won't solve this learning puzzle here but will use it to note the problem for Brannen: being exposed to a particular sound does not lead to a deterministic process by which a single feature is encoded in a fully specified phonetic matrix.

It is problems such as these that make direct realist models of the phonetics/ phonology interface problematic and lead us to adopt indirect realist models.

While not the central focus of this book, I want to address in this sidebar one surprising critique of indirect realism that was raised by Best (1995). She suggests that indirect realism is incompatible with evolution by natural selection because evolution requires the niche of real objects in the world (not representations) to be adaptable. Clearly, I cannot do justice to the whole evolution of language issue here, but I do want to say a few things. In the arguments of Berwick and Chomsky (2016), we see that the one big difference between *Homo sapiens* and our common ancestors is that modern humans can generate new representations by the Merge operation. It is Merge which groups together individual elements and creates a hierarchical labelled structure. We know that our common ancestors share some of our traits. Even functional approaches to evolution admit that distant relatives like frogs have concepts (or proto-concepts). For example, they act differently in the presence of a fly (shooting their tongues out) than in the presence of a rock (not shooting their tongues out), which suggests some sort of mental distinction between *fly* and *not-fly*. But, as Hurford (2014) suggests, while many animals have internal concepts, only humans are able to talk about them. Pinker and Jackendoff (2005) argue at length that human grammars could have evolved via natural selection over the 300,000 generations since the emergence of *Homo sapiens*. And even if Chomsky and Pinker differ in what the selective advantage of language might have been (Chomsky: thinking; Pinker: communication), the advantage which accrues stems from changes in the state of the organism when it comes to surviving in a particular environmental niche. Miyagawa and colleagues' (2014) Integration Hypothesis suggests that there were *lexical* protolanguages (animal call systems) and *song* protolanguages (found in songbirds and gibbons) but that only humans integrated these existing systems to result in hierarchical structures with componential meaning. Remember that the basic property of recursion is found not only in morphology and syntax but also in phonology (Féry 2010; Hunyadi 2010; Kabak and Revithiadou 2009; van der Hulst 2010). Evolution must account for the emergence of an I-language in the species. Our common ancestors had concepts, plausibly general cognitive concepts such as *action* or *object*. However, very similar to the Bootstrapping Problem in child language acquisition (Pinker 1984), at some point in the species, human minds had to represent *linguistic* or *grammatical* categories, not just cognitive categories. A representational realist account is not incompatible with what we know of evolution.

Let us continue our discussion of segmental phenomena by looking at cross-linguistic substitution patterns when L2 segments are not found in the L1 inventory.

3.3.4 Differential Substitution

Native speakers of Russian and French acquiring English [θ] provide an example of what is known as *differential substitution*. Both Russian and French lack the phoneme /θ/. Both Russian and French have the phonemes /t/, /d/, /s/, and /z/. (Continental) French speakers tend to substitute the fricative [s], while Russian speakers substitute the stop [t]. Different languages substitute different segments. Why? This is, of course, a complex issue as revealed when we expand the data set even slightly. James (1988) shows that Dutch speakers (who also lack /θ/) substitute stops in onsets but fricatives in codas. Brannen (2011) and Lombardi (2003) show that Quebec French speakers substitute stops while Continental French speakers substitute fricatives. The basic point is that all of the subjects are exposed to L2 English input (which includes interdental fricatives), and yet they produce different sounds when the target is a [θ] (or [ð]).

3.4 MECHANISMS OF ACQUISITION

L1 transfer, as noted, can be a key factor in the nature of the interlanguage phonological grammar. Particularly within the domain of speech perception, this phenomenon is often referred to as the L1 *filter*. Brown (2000) provides a nice overview of how we shoehorn the L2 sounds into L1 categories.

This leads us to the situations in which the L1 filter can be overridden. As we saw, Brown (2000) argues that if the L1 phonological feature necessary for a particular L2 contrast was absent, then the developmental prognosis for the L2 learner was bleak. However, as we saw (in Chapter 1, Section 1.6.1) this was too strong a position to take. While the L1 can provide information which influences early categorization, there is nothing which prohibits the categorization from changing.

L2 learners *can* override the L1 filter. In the model I am proposing here, this can happen under two conditions:

(a) The input provides 'robust' cues to the need to set up a new representation for the purpose of contrast.
(b) The L1 grammar provides structures which can be redeployed to set up a new representation.

Let us explore each of these cases separately.

3.5 INTAKE FREQUENCY: ACQUISITION BY PHONETICS

The construct of *intake frequency* is designed to handle questions of phonological representation. More specifically, it is designed to account for the developmental path of the restructuring of phonological representations.

As noted earlier, any theory of language acquisition has to take into account the cognitive representation of the learner, the effect of the linguistic environment, and the output of the linguistic system. Linguistic theory is an attempt to describe and explain the nature of linguistic knowledge. The properties of the environment (input and output) may be directly observed (as evidenced in Behaviourist approaches), but the grammar must be inferred. Similarly, we cannot directly observe which elements of the linguistic environment are attended to first, but rather, we require a *theory* of perception and comprehension, just as we require a theory of production (see Levelt 1989).

The field of SLA has long recognized that a distinction needs to be made between *input* and *intake* (Carroll 2001; Corder 1967; VanPatten 2003). Input, on the one hand, is the sum total of the linguistic environment, or the primary linguistic data (PLD) to which the learner is exposed. Intake, on the other hand, is the subset of the PLD processed by a learner at a given time. Input frequency can be directly measured via such things as type frequency of token frequency in a given corpus. Researchers differ on how this input frequency affects the grammatical representation with some models (usage-based models (Wulff and Ellis 2018)), arguing that the grammar is a stochastic model of the input patterns, while others (e.g. Dresher 2009) do not representationally encode input frequency. The role of frequency in psycholinguistic processing is complex but less controversial. Frequency can influence speed of lexical retrieval, production accuracy, language change, and so on.

The construct of *intake* is designed to account for the fact that learners acquire certain elements earlier than others, and it may be because they are attending to them (Guion and Pederson 2007), or they are processable (Pienemann 1998), or they are more easily perceived (Schmidt 1990). But note the risk of circularity that such a construct confronts, as illustrated in the following dialogue:

Q: Why is this form produced/perceived accurately?
A: Because it was intake.

Q: How do you know it was intake?
A: Because it was produced/perceived accurately.

The *explanandum* in L2 phonology includes behavioural accuracy in production or perception tasks. One of the most basic facts about second language speech is that many L2 learners have difficulty producing or perceiving certain L2 sounds accurately. The reasons for this are myriad but include the following:

- L1 transfer (Trofimovich and Baker 2006)
- Amount of experience (Bohn and Flege 1992)
- Amount of L2 use (Guion et al. 2000)
- Age of learning (Herschensohn 2000)
- Orthography (Escudero and Wanrooi 2010; Hayes-Harb and Masuda 2008)
- Frequency (Davidson 2006)
- Probability (Wilson and Davidson 2013)
- Attention (Guion and Pederson 2007; Schmidt 1990)
- Training (Wang, Jongman, and Sereno 2003)

Clearly, all of these factors affect the learning process, the learning path, and the grammatical representation (and perhaps, even, the final achievable state); they are all empirical questions. If we were to focus on the early stages of SLA, the question could be formulated as, *what's the way to acquire L2 elements?* Possible answers have suggested that elements are acquired early if they are less marked, attended to, more frequent, orthographically encoded, and on and on. The broader question remains: what filters the input? Despite the fact that there is rich environmental information, we don't learn everything at the same time. Why? What is the *explanans*?

There is, of course, a vast literature in cross-linguistic speech perception which I will not survey here (see Colantoni, Steele, and Escudero 2015, for a fine overview; also Hansen Edwards and Zampini 2008). Giving simplistic examples, we know that we may produce a [ü] as [u] if our L1 does not have /ü/, or that we may perceive a [q] as [k] if our L1 does not have /q/. Models such as Flege's Speech Learning Model (SLM) or Best and Tyler's L2 Perceptual Assimilation Model (PAM-L2) provide explanations as to which L2 sounds are mapped onto which L1 categories. These models tend to focus on non-representational aspects of the grammar and generally focus on the acoustic/phonetic space as the locus of explanation (and, indeed, the model of what is to be acquired).

Here, I take the stance that phonology is cognition and not merely physics. However, physics can play a role in explaining the developmental path as we shall see. In Archibald (2013) I explore the idea of gaining insight into the nature of the L1 filter by reverse engineering the elements which came through the filter. The task of the L2 researcher is akin to that of an archaeologist looking at an unknown artefact, or early humans looking at the monolith in Stanley Kubrick's *2001: A Space Odyssey*. We look at the output data (which may be perceptual discrimination or a recording of production) and try to figure out what the system that generated

Intake Frequency: Acquisition by Phonetics

that output looks like. I postulated that there are several components to the black box on our workbench:

- Universal principles
- Markedness
- L1 grammar
- A learning algorithm

To determine what else might be in the box, let us look at some examples of the acquisition of L2 phonological features. The features given in Table 3.3 tend to show accurate performance (González Poot 2011) in a range of L2 studies.

Table 3.3. NEW SEGMENTS BASED ON AN L1 FEATURE

[CORONAL]	L1 Mandarin / L2 English	/l/-/ɹ/
	L1 Japanese / L2 Russian	/l/-/r/
[voice]	L1 Korean / L2 English	/f/-/v/
	L1 Japanese / L2 Russian	/ş/-/z̧/
[continuant]	L1 Korean / L2 English	/p/-/f/
		/b/-/v/
[anterior]	L1 English / L2 Czech	/c/-/t/
		/ɟ/-/d/

In all of these cases, the role of robustness and syllable position is attenuated. By this, I mean that the L2 acquisition appears to occur across the board and is less influenced by such things as the acoustic properties of sub-members of the class (e.g. [t] vs. [d]), or phonological context (e.g. onset vs. coda). The notation in (38) is meant to capture the fact that L1 feature plays the most important role in acquiring a new element. Such constructs as the type of cue to the new contrast or the position in which the new contrast occurs are not so important, where >> is meant to be read as *is produced more accurately than*.

(38)   [L1 feature] >> [cue]/[position]

3.5.1 Inaccuracies on Non-L1 Features

As I have noted, there are also, however, cases of inaccurate perception. Table 3.4 summarizes some instances.

Table 3.4. FEATURES CAUSING INACCURATE PERCEPTION

[CORONAL]	L1 Japanese / L2 English	/l/-/ɹ/
[vibrant]	L1 Japanese / L2 Russian	/l/-/r/
[PHARYNGEAL]	L1 English / L2 French	/ɹ/-/ʀ/

It is worth commenting that some of the results given here were interpreted as being 'inaccurate' performance, but some range between 60% and 80% accuracy; it is important that we take factors such as level of proficiency into account when comparing results. However, without diving deeper into the data to see what factors might be associated with variation in performance, an 80% accuracy rate is quite high!

3.5.2 Accurate Perception of Non-L1 Features

Of most relevance to my argument in this section, however, is the third category, which focusses on the successful acquisition of L2 contrasts based on features which are *not* found in the L1, as shown in Table 3.5.

Table 3.5. Cases of successful acquisition of *new* features

[CORONAL]	L1 Japanese / L2 English codas	/l/-/ɹ/
[vibrant]	L1 Japanese / L2 Russian (advanced)	/l/-/r/
[strident]	L1 Japanese / L2 English	/s/-/θ/
[strident]	L1 French / L2 Japanese	/f/-/ɸ/
[continuant]	L1 French / L2 English	/θ/-/t/

In all of these cases where the new contrast is *not* based on an L1 feature, the roles of robustness and phonological position become more important, as shown in (39).

(39) [cue]/[position] >> [feature]

What we are beginning to see emerge here is a catalogue of elements which pass successfully through the L1 filter, and this is what we can reverse engineer. The list of such items is, so far:

- English liquids for Mandarin learners
- English liquids in coda position for Japanese learners
- Russian [r] for Japanese learners
- English labiodental fricatives for Korean learners
- Russian palatal fricatives for Japanese learners
- Czech palatal stops for English learners
- English interdental fricatives for Japanese learners
- Japanese bilabial fricatives for French learners
- English interdental fricatives for French learners

Elsewhere in the literature, we have seen successful acquisition based on features such as [click] (Best et al. 1988) and [long] (Summerell 2007).

3.5.3 Properties of the Input Signal

Drawing on the work of Wright (2004) and Keyser and Stevens (2006), we can begin to see where the locus of explanation lies. Segments which rely on a feature which is phonetically robust or segments which are found in a position where cues are enhanced are privileged. These privileged segments make it through the L1 filter and become intake to the processor; the phonetic properties make them more accessible to the processor.

According to Wright (2004) three main properties make a cue robust:

1. Transitional burst release
2. Internal formant transitions
3. Resistance to environmental masking

The first two are quite specific acoustic properties, while the third is more of a functional classification. What starts as a property of the signal (and is more likely to survive degradation and to survive 'listener distraction' (such as the L1 filter)) is more likely to be encoded (i.e. become phonologized) in the L2 grammar. These robust cues are what allow the listener to apprehend early on that there is a phonological contrast. A survey of the literature suggests that the following features are universally robust:

- [click]: Best et al. (1988)
- [strident]: Jesney (2005)
- [vibrant]: Larson-Hall (2004)
- [ejection]: González Poot (2014)
- [long]: Summerell (2007)

3.5.4 Intake

Intake frequency is a mechanism which allows us to address Orwell's Problem in SLA. Most coarsely, this says, *in the face of so much evidence, how can we fail to learn?* A more nuanced take would be, *we can learn new elements but they're not all acquired at once; why do some elements override the L1 filter earlier than others?* Wright's (2001) notion of *robust* cues (see also Wilson and Davidson 2013) give us the mechanism we need. According to Wright, a robustly encoded signal is more likely to survive signal degradation; it is more likely to become intake. Clements's (2009) version of robustness theory notes that 'primary' features (such as [sonorant], [continuant], [voice]) provide a stronger auditory response than others. Enhancement is feature based, as it affects *classes* of sounds, not just individual segments (another argument for abstract representations). What starts as a property of the signal becomes a property of the representation and, thus, becomes lexicalized. Each instance of either a robust cue such as [strident], [continuant], [click], or [ejective] (with a double release burst) or a phonetic enhancement feature (following Keyser and Stevens 2006) such as rounding on alveopalatal fricatives will add a boost to an intake frequency counter; certain input is privileged to become intake. Iverson and Evans's (2009) work is also consistent with these cues being part of the processing/learning modules, as they show L2 learners can be trained to attend to different cues. In a Mis-matched Negativity ERP study, they show that Finnish learners started to rely on spectral (rather than durational) cues to English i/ɪ after training. In other words, Finns have the contrast but can *learn* new ways to implement and perceive it.

3.5.5 Philosophical Grounds

On philosophical grounds we should also prefer consistency in the representations across the modules of phonology, morphology, and syntax. Under the neo-empiricist (direct realist) view, phonological representations would be fundamentally different from syntactic ones (with respect to abstraction) and, if Distributed Morphology (DM) is adopted (see McGinnis 2016), then also fundamentally different from morphology. And while it is true that phonology is marked by its connection with the physical system of articulation (e.g. Bromberger and Halle 2000), developing a unified model is desirable given what we know of other areas of cognitive science. The gradient phonetic effects can be attributed to what Pylyshyn (1984) assigns to the 'transducer'. Pierrehumbert, Beckman, and Ladd (2000) argue that DM requires a language-specific categorical (or discrete) component in combination with a universal quantitative (or continuous) phonetics at spell out. From this, they conclude that DM cannot be the correct model of morphological representation. My argument is that we adopt the most parsimonious architecture with the gradiency built into the processing and learning modules. There are, of course, epistemological models which either blur or deny the distinction between grammar and processing (O'Grady 2005; Phillips and Ehrenhofer 2015). There are also models which invoke Bayesian probability (Watanabe and Chien 2015) and the construct of *entropy* in seeking to explain learner behaviour. These are accounts which argue that *knowledge* (or belief) is governed by the same principles as *action*. The change in the state of the current grammar is made to maximize the entropy (Hayes and Wilson 2008) of the system. Adopting this as a model of acquiring phonological representations runs directly into Dresher's (1999) *epistemological problem*. There is still the need for a transducer to get from the vocabulary of the acoustic input to the vocabulary of phonological cognition. These researchers, thus, extend a notion drawn from *knowledge-how* and apply it to *knowledge-that*. Critics of this kind of Bayesian epistemology (Dretske 2003; Pollock 1991, 2006) argue that human beliefs (i.e. knowledge of well formedness of strings) are not gradient in this fashion.

We can see in the study of L2 phonology that phonological representations are categorial, with the level of phonetic detail influencing the *learning* and *processing* of phonological knowledge but not part of the *representation*. This model of phonology is also central to the phonology/morphology interface, as we will see in the next chapter. Drawing on Embick (2010), I show how a local, serial model can account for what we see in L2 morphology as well.

3.5.6 Frequency Redux

My starting point has been that segments which have particular phonetic properties are privileged in the processing (i.e. become intake). The mechanism which I propose for this to occur is *intake frequency*. L2ers can clearly acquire new representations, but everything is not all acquired at once. Some material gets through the L1 filter earlier or faster than other material. The question is, *why?* The answer I propose here is that L2ers can acquire new structure via *phonetic* means. In the "Redeployment" section (3.6), we will look at cases where L2ers can acquire new structure via *phonological* means.

González Poot (2011) looks at the acquisition of Yucatec Mayan ejectives by native speakers of Spanish. Ejectives are represented by the feature [constricted glottis], which Spanish lacks. On the basis of both an auditory discrimination task and a forced choice picture selection task, González Poot demonstrates that the non-native speakers did not perform significantly differently than native speakers in the onset position but did perform significantly differently in the coda position. The results of the discrimination task are shown in Figure 3.6.

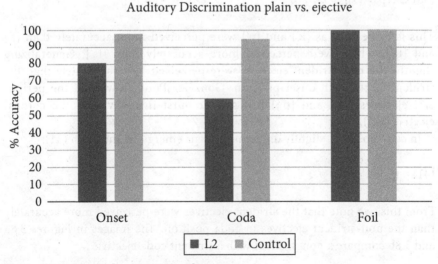

Figure 3.6. Auditory discrimination of L2 ejectives
SOURCE: Adapted from González Poot (2011)

Acoustically, the recoverability cues for ejectives are much subtler in coda position than in onset position. Figure 3.7 compares an ejective stop with a nonejective stop in onset position. Note the release burst in the wave form.

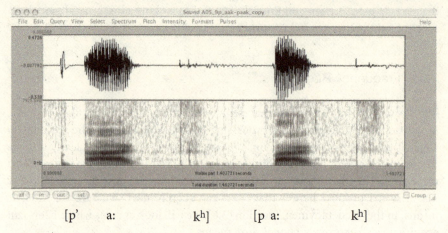

Figure 3.7. Acoustic signature of ejective vs. plain stop
SOURCE: Adapted from González Poot (2011)

The behavioural results indicate that the L2ers can acquire new phonological contrasts, but it was clear that not all contrasts were acquired at the same time. In terms of perception accuracy in onset position, the hierarchy shown in (40) emerges:

(40)   k'/p' > t'/tʃ' > ts'

This is to be read as [k'] and [p'] were perceived more accurately than [t'] and [tʃ'], which were perceived more accurately than [ts']. Generalizing slightly, the non-strident ejectives were perceived more accurately than the strident ejectives in onset position. González Poot shows that the peripheral ejectives ([k'] and [p']) had greater burst intensity than the coronal ejective ([t']).

In coda position, slightly different patterns emerge, as shown in (41):

(41)   tʃ' > ts' > k' > p' > t'

From this, we note that the strident ejectives were perceived more accurately than the non-strident ejectives in coda position. The images in Figures 3.8a and 3.8b compare a non-strident with a strident coda ejective.

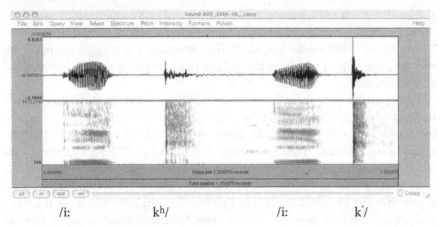

/i: kʰ/   /i: k'/

Figure 3.8a. Non-strident ejectives in coda position
SOURCE: Adapted from González Poot (2011)

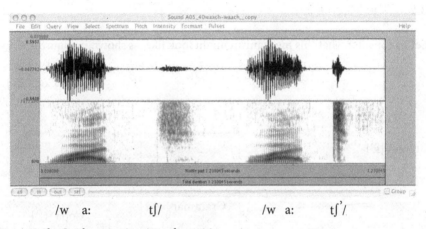

/w   a: tʃ/   /w   a: tʃ'/

Figure 3.8b. Strident ejectives in coda position
SOURCE: Adapted from González Poot (2011)

The recoverability cues to coda strident ejectives are more robust (witness the longer duration of high-frequency energy) than non-strident ejectives in codas. This is also true of final palatal stops in Czech (Atkey 2001) and final palatalized consonants in Russian (Kulikov 2010).

González Poot's work reveals that not all exemplars of [constricted glottis] are processed or acquired at the same time. In onset position, we see that non-strident stops are privileged in terms of becoming intake to the phonological processor. In the coda position, we see that strident stops are privileged in terms of becoming intake to the phonological processor. This privilege is referred to as a boosting intake frequency. Both strident and non-strident stops may have the same input (or environmental) frequency, but it is their phonetic properties which stipulate their intake frequency. This enhanced intake frequency paves the way for grammatical restructuring and the phonologization of the [constricted glottis] feature.

Typologically, Greenberg (1963) notes that there are languages with ejectives in onset and coda position, and languages with ejectives in onsets only, but no languages with ejectives in codas only. Stops are the least marked ejectives, followed by affricates, then sonorants, then fricatives (Kim and Pulleyblank 2009). Having an affricate ejective with strident release at the end of a word compared with a stop ejective provides an extra phonetic cue (stridency) which seems to boost perceptibility. All of this together suggests that these interlanguage grammars are governed by the same typological and phonetic facts as primary grammars.

3.5.7 The Mechanism

Let us consider what this mechanism might look like, as shown in Figure 3.9.

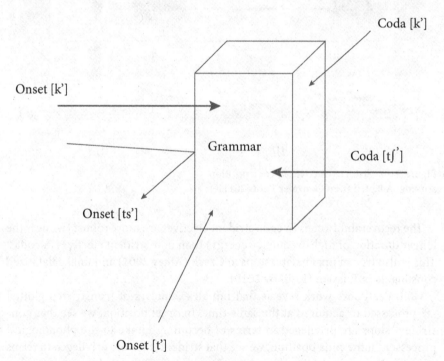

Figure 3.9. The mechanism of intake frequency

An onset [kʼ] and a coda [tʃʼ] would be more likely to become intake than, say, an onset [tsʼ] or a coda [kʼ]. If there is a counter which tracks frequency, then each instance, say, of [h] and each instance of [s] would add one to the counter. However, there are other factors which can boost the intake frequency. For example, the robust [s] would have its intake frequency increased, while the non-robust [h] would not. A segment occurring in a strong metrical position (e.g. stressed or the beginning of a foot) would have its intake frequency augmented, while a segment in a weak position would not. A liquid would have its intake frequency score raised in coda position but not in onset position.

Intake frequency, therefore, is not claiming that onsets are privileged over codas or that codas are privileged over onsets. Rather, some elements have their intake frequency boosted in onsets (say, non-strident ejectives), and some elements have their intake frequency boosted in codas (say, liquid contrasts). Learning is mitigated by intake frequency which, in turn, is modulated by robust phonetic cues. Elements which become intake earlier are represented in the lexical entry (or underlying representation) earlier.

3.6 REDEPLOYMENT: ACQUISITION BY PHONOLOGY

There is a second route to acquire novel L2 structure: acquisition by phonology. Let us look at how this can work. Archibald (2005) briefly outlines an example to illustrate the construct of *redeployment* of L1 knowledge to acquire an L2 structure which was absent from the L1 grammar. The example was of English speakers acquiring Japanese long consonants and long vowels drawing on Summerell (2007).

3.6.1 L2 Acquisition of Length

Summerell looks at the acquisition of Japanese phonemic length contrasts by adult English speakers. Fifty-six subjects were divided into four groups according to their Japanese proficiency: 19 beginners, 13 intermediates, 12 advanced, and 12 native speaker (NS) Japanese controls. All subjects reported normal hearing. Her population is summarized in Table 3.6.

Table 3.6. EXPERIMENTAL POPULATION FOR L2 LENGTH CONTRASTS

	Beginners	Intermediate	Advanced	Control
Number of subjects	19	13	12	12
Mean age at testing	20.3	22.8	31.2	28.6
Mean age of exposure	19.3	19.6	21.9	N/A
Mean months of instruction	5.6	18.6	18.8	N/A
Mean years in Japan	0	0.07	3.75	N/A

Japanese has both a phonemic vowel length and consonant length contrast, as illustrated in (42).

(42) [i]   'stomach'
      [ii]   'good'
      [saka]   'slope'
      [sakka]   'writer'

She considers three hypotheses:

1. L1 English speakers will be unable to acquire either vocalic or consonantal contrasts. L1 English subjects will perceive both short and long vowels, and single and geminate consonants as 'similar' (in the Speech Learning Model sense) since there are no contrasts in their L1.
2. L1 English speakers will be able to acquire vocalic length contrasts since English vowels have quantity contrasts. However, since English lacks consonantal length contrasts, L1 English speakers will perceive both single and geminate consonants as 'similar', and the formation of a new category will likely be hindered.
3. L1 English speakers will be able to acquire both vocalic and consonantal contrasts by redeploying the mora licensing properties from their L1 grammar.

3.6.1.1 TASKS AND STIMULI

The subjects performed three tasks: (1) an auditory discrimination (AXB) task, (2) a lexical knowledge task, and (3) a picture identification task.

3.6.1.2 AXB AUDITORY DISCRIMINATION

Natural speech stimuli were used to test discriminatory ability in word-medial position (since geminates are found only in this position in Japanese). The test items were two-syllable words with either 2 (CVCV) or 3 (CVVCV, CVCCV) moras, and each set shared the same pitch pattern, as shown in (43) in three words which all share a low-high pitch pattern:

(43)   *kite* (CVCV)   'wear'
       kiite (CVVCV)   'listen'
       kitte (CVCCV)   'stamp'

Vowel stimuli included five voiced vowels (i-ii; e-ee; a-aa; u-uu; o-oo) and two voiceless vowels (i̥ and u̥). Consonantal stimuli included stops (p-pp; t-tt; k-kk), fricatives and affricates (s-ss; ʃ-ʃʃ; tʃ-tʃʃ) and nasals (m-mm; n-nn; ŋ-ŋŋ). There were 144 triads recorded by a female speaker of standard Japanese. The stimuli were divided into six sets of 24 trials. Since this test did not require lexical access,

Redeployment: Acquisition by Phonology

nonce words were used to create minimal pairs when required. A 250 ms inter-stimulus interval was used to invoke auditory level perception (Werker and Logan 1985).

3.6.1.3 LEXICAL KNOWLEDGE TASK

The purpose of this task was to allow the results of the picture identification task to be properly interpreted. Therefore, Summerell ensured that the subjects in fact were familiar with all the test words. Before the experiment, subjects were given a list of 39 words (both in the Roman alphabet and Japanese *kana*) along with a drawing of each item and the English translation. The subjects were asked to familiarize themselves with the words. Only subjects who achieved 100% accuracy on Task 2 (lexical knowledge) were allowed to proceed to Task 3 (picture identification). One subject was discarded for not meeting this threshold.

3.6.1.4 PICTURE IDENTIFICATION TASK

This task was designed to see whether subjects could accurately discriminate among items when lexical access was required. The assumption is that accurate identification would signal accurate lexical representation. Since only subjects who achieved 100% accuracy on Task 2 could be given Task 3, any errors were ascribed to incorrect perception or representation rather than lack of lexical knowledge.

On this task, two drawings were paired, with one labelled A and the other B. The drawings were presented on the computer screen accompanied by an aural stimulus of the form shown in (44).

(44) *Watashi-wa   ima* _____ *to   iimashita.*
  I - Topic now   that say –PAST
  'I said _____ just now'

Subjects pressed either A or B to identify which picture they believed to correspond with the lexical item heard in the sentence.

3.6.1.5 RESULTS AND DISCUSSION

The data on Tasks 1 and 3 were analysed using non-parametric statistics. Mean ranks were calculated to determine the relationships between language group (L1 English or Japanese) and Proficiency Group (Beginner, Intermediate, Advanced, NS Control). The mean rank represents the average rankings of each group based on a comparison of the subjects' rank orders. First, the data are ranked according to the numerical test scores. In this case, a correct response was scored as 1 and an incorrect response as 0. Let us look at a hypothetical example. Table 3.7 shows the scores of subjects assigned to two groups (I and II) with four subjects in each group. In this case the highest score out of eight subjects receives the rank of 8 (Subject A).

Table 3.7. INTERPRETING RANKED DATA

Group I

Subject	Total points	Rank	Sum of ranks	Mean rank
A	10	8	24	6
B	6	5.5 (5/6)		
C	8	7		
D	5	3.5 (3/4)		

Group II

Subject	Total points	Rank	Sum of ranks	Mean rank
E	6	5.5 (5/6)	12	3
F	4	2		
G	5	3.5 (5/6)		
H	2	1		

The subject who scored the second highest is given the ranking of 7 (Subject C). Because the third and fourth subjects (B and E) are tied (at 6th and 5th place), they are both given a ranking of 5.5. Subjects D and G are also tied, so they are ranked at 3.5. Subject F is ranked as 2, and Subject H (with the lowest score) at 1. By adding up the ranks of all Group I subjects, we arrive at what is known as the Sum of Ranks which, for Group I is 24. For Group II the Sum of Ranks is 12. The group mean rank is the Sum of Ranks divided by the number of subjects. The Mann-Whitney U test (the non-parametric equivalent of the independent two-sample t-test) was used to compare groups. The results of the auditory discrimination task are shown in Table 3.8.

Table 3.8. AUDITORY DISCRIMINATION RESULTS

Contrast	Group	% Correct	Standard deviation	Mean rank	Mann-Whitney U test	Probability
V vs. VV	L1= E	95.58	10.630	26.5	187.00	.290
	L1 = J	96.88	7.924	33.00		
	mean	95.84	7.792	—		
C vs. CC	L1 = E	95.08	8.322	28.42	223.50	.677
	L1 = J	94.63	8.667	26.32		
	mean	95.33	8.951	—		
Stops	L1 = E	95.87	7.432	28.33	227.50	.718
	L1 = J	94.83	6.992	26.68		
	mean	96.66	7.295	—		
Fricatives	L1 = E	93.53	11.841	28.08	238.50	.929
	L1 = J	93.01	11.123	27.67		
	mean	93.42	11.602	—		
Nasals	L1 = E	95.85	8.063	27.37	238.50	.909
	L1 = J	96.05	7.787	30.05		
	mean	95.89	7.956	—		
	L1 = J	92.68	9.401	24.09		
	mean	94.70	9.432	—		

As shown above, the mean accuracy rates for both L1 English (all groups combined) and L1 Japanese were very high (always over 92%). There was no significant difference (p > .05) between the performance of the native and non-native speakers with respect to their accuracy rates on this task. Notably, the non-native speakers were nativelike in their ability to perceive both long and short consonants and vowels.

When we break the performance down by level of Japanese proficiency, some interesting patterns emerge, as shown in Table 3.9. The Kruskal-Wallis test is the non-parametric analogue of the one-way Analysis of Variance (ANOVA). This was used for a one-way independent group analysis of variance, and no significant difference was observed among groups.

Table 3.9. COMPARISON OF DIFFERENT SUBJECT GROUPS

Contrast	Group	% Correct	Standard deviation	Mean rank	Kruskal-Wallis Test	Probability
V vs. VV	1	93.68	10.530	27.58	1.999	.573
	2	96.70	5.064	27.00		
	3	97.38	3.940	28.33		
	4	96.88	7.924	33.00		
	mean	95.84	7.792	—		
C vs. CC	1	93.00	12.369	28.63	.840	.840
	2	96.43	6.283	25.92		
	3	96.93	4.126	30.79		
	4	94.63	8.667	26.32		
	mean	95.33	8.951	—		
Stops	1	94.33	10.063	27.32	.968	.809
	2	96.69	5.397	27.00		
	3	97.44	3.302	31.38		
	4	94.83	6.992	26.68		
	mean	96.66	7.295	—		
Fricatives	1	91.09	16.067	27.71	.178	.981
	2	95.27	8.622	29.35		
	3	95.51	5.143	27.08		
	4	93.00	11.123	27.91		
	mean	93.43	11.601	—		
Nasals	1	93.59	10.978	24.21	2.190	.534
	2	97.32	4.873	29.15		
	3	97.83	3.933	30.46		
	4	96.05	7.887	30.50		
	mean	95.89	7.956	—		

1 = Beginner; 2 = Intermediate; 3 = Advanced; 4 = Native.

Once again, we note that the non-native speakers were performing indistinguishably from the native speakers when it comes to discriminating length contrast accurately. This is consistent with Muroi (1995).

3.6.1.6 Picture Identification Results

Table 3.10 summarizes the results of the picture identification task.

Table 3.10. Picture identification task results

Contrast	Group	% Correct	Mean rank	Mann-Whitney U test	Probability
V vs. VV	L1 = E	94.96	27.00	137.50	.011*
	L1 = J	100.00	32.00		
	mean	95.99	—		
C vs. CC	L1 = E	89.23	24.66	136.50	.014*
	L1 = J	99.13	38.59		
	mean	93.65	—		

Note that the durational contrasts for both vowels and consonants are significantly different when all of the L1 English speakers are taken as a single group. However, when we break the results down by group (as shown in Table 3.11), an interesting developmental path emerges.

Table 3.11. Performance by proficiency level

Contrast	Group	% Correct	Mean rank	Kruskal-Wallis test	Probability
V vs. VV	1	94.44	24.81	8.113	.044*
	2	97.07	28.69		
	3	92.06	22.00		
	4	100.00	36.50		
	mean	95.99	—		
C vs. CC	1	90.21	20.94	10.641	.014*
	2	95.97	29.73		
	3	92.27	24.75		
	4	99.13	38.59		
	mean	93.65	—		

What this indicates is that there are significant differences between the groups. Closer inspection of the data reveals that the significant differences occur between the Beginner and Control Groups. The Intermediate and Advanced learners are *not* behaving significantly differently from the NS control group.

This clearly demonstrates that learning is possible; the door is not closed. Second language learners get better over time.

3.6.1.7 Why Do They Get Better?

Following Summerell (as well as Mah and Archibald 2003), I would argue that the English speakers are redeploying knowledge from their L1 to acquire new phonemic contrasts in their L2. English has a distinction between tense vowels (like [i]) and lax vowels (like [ɪ]). It is commonly argued that the tense vowels

Redeployment: Acquisition by Phonology

are bimoraic while the lax vowels are monomoraic. Some researchers (e.g. Zec 1995) make a distinction, shown in (45), between strong (μ_s) and weak (μ_w) moras as well.

(45)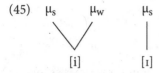

Furthermore, English is a quantity-sensitive language in which heavy syllables attract stress placement. The theoretical device by which we capture syllable weight is moraic structure in the syllable given in (46).

(46)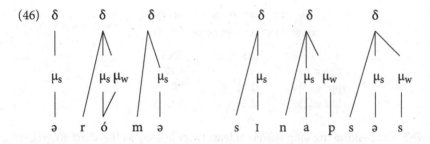

In Japanese, geminate consonants are licensed by a weak mora for the Japanese word for 'cut', as we see in (47).

(47)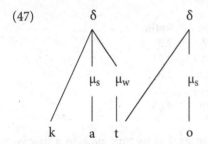

So, while the English grammar does not allow geminate consonants, it does allow a closed (CVC) syllable to be heavy due to the final consonant projecting a weak mora. I am following the analysis of Summerell (2007) here, but I would also note that the argument holds even without a weak/strong mora distinction if English final consonants project a mora, and Japanese geminates are linked to both a mora and an onset. My argument here is that the English speakers can take the weight-bearing mora structure from their L1 and redeploy it to acquire the Japanese geminate consonants. In Summerell (2007) we see that this is true for perception tasks.

A small study reported in Mah and Archibald (2003) shows this to be the case in production as well. The geminate productions of one non-native speaker were recorded. The baselines in (48) were noted for the ratio of short to long consonants in native speakers of Japanese:

(48) /tt/ vs. /t/ /pp/ vs. /p/ /kk/ vs. /k/
Mean Ratio 3.00 2.71 2.80

Roughly speaking, the closure for the geminates are about three times as long as the closure time for singletons. When we compare with the non-native speaker (NNS) production, we see the results in Table 3.12.

The NNS was making much longer closures for geminates. The same was true in vocalic production, as shown in Table 3.13 for our non-native speaker.

Table 3.12. NATIVE VS. NON-NATIVE
CONSONANTAL LENGTH CONTRASTS

	NS	NNS
/tt/ vs. /t/	3.00	3.95
/pp/ vs. /p/	2.71	4.0
/kk/ vs. /k/	2.80	3.87

The NNS was making the long vowels at least twice as long as the short vowels.

The preceding examples have shown us how L2 learners can acquire novel

Table 3.13. NON-NATIVE VOCALIC LENGTH
CONTRASTS

Vowel quality	Duration	Ratio
/a/ vs. /aa/	.118/.295	2.5
/i/ vs. /ii/	.106/.341	3.21
/u/ vs. /uu/	.082/.219	2.67
/e/ vs. /ee/	.114/.351	3.07
/o/ vs. /oo/	.148/.339	2.09

structures by redeploying abstract L1 structures. Let us turn now to a discussion of another area in which abstract representations nicely explain behavioural facts: epenthetic and illusory vowels.

3.7 ILLUSORY VOWELS IN PRODUCTION AND PERCEPTION

Of course, there is much discussion of the addition of epenthetic vowels (i.e. vowels pronounced which are not in the input) in L2 *production* (Carlisle (2001), Abrahamsson (2003), etc.). A Spanish speaker articulating the English word *speak* might well say something like [e]speak. But we know that L1 phonology also affects L2 *perception*. To place this in context, let us refer back to the input/intake distinction (Corder 1967). It is often assumed that intake is a subset of input, specifically, the subset of input which is processed by the learner. However, sometimes intake *exceeds* input. This problem of what could be called *augmented reality* is, following the pattern of terminology such as Orwell's and Plato's Problems, what I will call *Escher's Problem*.

3.7.1 Escher's Problem

M. C. Escher was a Dutch artist (1898–1972) known for his optical illusions (or what he called *impossible constructions*). Consider the piece *Waterfall* (1961), shown in Figure 3.10.

Figure 3.10. Visual illusions by M. C. Escher

If one starts at the bottom of the waterfall, the channel runs to the right, turns left, right and left again, never seeming to flow uphill, and then the water leaves the trough and cascades downward. How is this possible? Clearly it isn't possible in our physical universe. But how are such optical illusions relevant to second language phonology?

3.7.2 Perceptual Illusions

Studies from a number of L1s such as Japanese (Dupoux et al. 1999; Matthews and Brown 2004), Korean (Kabak and Idsardi 2007), and Brazilian Portuguese

(Cardoso 2007) reveal the perception of illusory vowels in the L2. Let us consider some of the relevant data.

Japanese does not allow obstruent consonantal sequences word medially, as shown in (49).

(49) *ac·tor
      *chap·ter

What this signifies is that an English word with a [kt] medial sequence or a [pt] medial sequence violates Japanese phonotactics.

As is evident from both loanword phonology and L2 pronunciation (Matthews and Brown 2004) in production, Japanese speakers insert an epenthetic vowel between such obstruent strings as shown in (50):

(50) 'baseball' → 'basubaru'

However, what is critical for our discussion here is that this happens in *perception* too. When exposed to an illicit Japanese string like [ebzo], the Japanese subjects hear [ebɯzo] whether or not there is a vowel present (Dupoux et al. 1997). This is revealed through a variety of tasks (behavioural, discrimination, ERP, etc.). To give one example, subjects participating in an AXB discrimination task would make a high percentage of errors when faced with stimuli such as those in (51).

(51) ebzo ebɯzo ebzo

Thus, they hear a vowel when none is present in the acoustic input because their *grammar* leads them to believe that one should be there. The grammar dictates the reality.

Matthews and Brown (2004) point out that Thai listeners, however, do *not* hear an illusory vowel in this medial obstruent string environment because Thai, unlike Japanese, *allows* medial obstruent strings. So, a Thai listener when hearing a string like [ebzo] would hear [ebzo]. However, Thai does not allow sC initial clusters. In production, they epenthesize to break up the sC as shown in (52).

(52) spa → [səpa]

Perceptual tasks also caused difficulty, in that the advanced learners made 60% errors on discriminating sC strings from səC strings. Even when accurate in discrimination, there were very long response times; this is a difficult task. And let us remember, they did fine on medial strings like [ebzo].

Kabak and Idsardi (2007), as we saw in Chapter 2, Section 2.10 in an elegant analysis of Korean epenthesis, show that these perceptual illusions are mediated by phonological structure (specifically *coda*) and not just by linear adjacency.

Illusory Vowels in Production and Perception

Remember that not all bad contacts were treated the same; the bad coda condition was significantly worse (as revealed by comparing A' scores) than bad contacts—and some bad contacts (e.g. [ln]) were not that bad at all! Explanation of the occurrence of the epenthetic vowel was based on whether a particular consonant was licensed by a coda node, *not* whether the string was illicit. Grammar dictates reality.

Cardoso (2007; Cardoso, John, and French 2009) has looked at the perception of English sC clusters by Brazilian Portuguese (BP) speakers. BP does not allow sC onsets. It allows obstruent +liquid onsets, and (maximally) singleton coda consonants. The BP subjects had difficulty discriminating accurately between sC and [i]sC strings (where [i] is the BP epenthetic vowel). Beginning-level subjects were performing at chance levels on discrimination tasks, though their performance did get better over time. These results are shown in (53).

(53)   Beginner: 51% accuracy
        Intermediate: 65% accuracy
        Advanced: 79% accuracy

Once again, when the L1 grammar stipulates that an epenthetic vowel should be present, the subjects hear a vowel whether or not there is one in the input.

3.7.3 Redeployment Redux

Let us turn now to a discussion of redeployment at the level of the syllable by looking at the performance of L1 Persian speakers and L1 Arabic speakers who are acquiring L2 English onset clusters.

3.7.3.1 PERSIAN AND ARABIC

Persian, like Japanese, Thai, and Brazilian Portuguese, lacks onset s-clusters. It is well documented that L1 speakers of the last three have difficulty accurately perceiving the English onset clusters. We will see that Persian L1 subjects are able to accurately perceive such initial L2 consonantal sequences in spite of the fact that such sequences are illicit in their L1. To appreciate the significance of this, consider the comparisons shown in Table 3.14.

Table 3.14. PERCEPTION ERRORS CORRELATED WITH LINGUISTIC PROPERTIES

L1	sC onsets	Branching onsets	Branching codas	% Errors
Japanese	No	No	No	72
Thai	No	No	No	60
Brazilian Portuguese	No	Yes	No	50
Persian	No	No	Yes	??

114 THE PHONETICS/PHONOLOGY INTERFACE

What sorts of predictions or hypotheses emerge from this chart? Let us begin by noting that all three L1s have great difficulty with the perception task. The fact that Brazilian Portuguese allows branching onsets (but not sC onsets) does not help these subjects (in fact, they have the lowest accuracy scores). How will the Persian L1 subjects behave? If the relevant factor is presence or absence of sC clusters, then Persian speakers should also have difficulty with this task. If the relevant factor is the presence of branching onsets, then they should not pattern like the Brazilian Portuguese subjects. If the relevant factor is the presence of branching codas, then the Persian subjects should behave differently than the other L1 groups, as shown in Table 3.15.

3.7.3.2 SUBJECTS AND TASKS
Let us look more closely at the research subjects and the tasks they completed.

Table 3.15. PERSIAN AND ARABIC TASKS

L1	Number of subjects	Perception	Production
Persian	15	ABX	Picture naming
		Forced-choice identification	Sentence reading
NA Arabic	8	Nonce word writing	Elicited imitation
HA Arabic	8	Nonce word writing	Elicited imitation

3.7.3.3 DISCRIMINATION
The Persian speakers were asked to discriminate between /s/ and /es/, via an ABX discrimination task. The stimuli were produced by the same female native speaker reading from a list of pseudo-words in the identification task (taken from Cardoso 2007). The words were then cut and pasted using Audacity, with two identical and one variation of each pseudo-word in random order. The inter-stimulus interval between B and X was set to be 800 ms, long enough to favour a phonemic analysis (Werker and Logan 1985). This interval forces hearers to rely on pre-existing mental representations of sounds and avoids comparing the stimuli in auditory sensory memory. This task had 30 items—10 /sl/, 10 /sn/, and 10 /st/ tokens of pseudo-words randomly ordered—and took approximately 10 minutes, including a 3-minute training. Participants had to mark the correct response on their answer sheet.

3.7.3.4 FORCED CHOICE
In the study we administered a forced choice identification experiment adapted from Cardoso (2007). Participants were asked to decide whether the stimuli that they heard began with a consonant (i.e. sC) or with a vowel (i.e. [e]sC). After being asked 'to listen to a set of English words', the participants heard a recording of a female native speaker reading 30 pseudo-words. As Cardoso reports, 'these

pseudowords were created using WordGenerator v. 1.7 (http://billposer.org/Softw are/WordGenerator.html), a program that generates hypothetical words based on specifications such as segmental content and syllable structure, as provided by the researcher.' The 30 items selected included 10 /sl/, 10 /st/, and 10 /sn/ tokens which in turn included 5 /s/ and 5 /es/ combinations. The stimuli were recorded in a soundproof booth in a phonetics lab. The recording was then edited (normalized and cut into single stimuli at 44.1 kHz, 16-bit resolution) using Audacity. At the actual test administration time, the stimuli were played on a Mac, and participants were wearing headphones. Immediately after hearing each stimulus, the participants were asked to mark on the answer sheet the alternative that best described the initial sound that they heard: a vowel ([e]) or an [s]. To avoid random selection, the participants were also given the option of selecting a question mark to indicate uncertainty (e.g. due to distraction, fatigue); however, in only a few cases was this option chosen, seven in total. The task lasted approximately 10 minutes, including a 3-minute demonstration and training session so that the participants could become familiar with the task. A sample question available on the answer sheet is illustrated in (54).

(54)   a. esnip   b. snip   c. ?

The word participants heard: 'snip'. The correct response was b.

3.7.3.5 Sentence Reading
The sentence-reading task was adapted from Boudaoud (2008). Boudaoud's test contained 59 topically unrelated sentences containing the three onset clusters /st/, /sn/, and /sl/. However, results from a pilot study revealed that the length of the test (with 59 sentences) could have affected the results, as the participant reported feeling fatigued by the end of the test. Therefore, only 29 sentences were chosen randomly from the list. Although the reading instrument contained 29 sentences in all, the target clusters /st/, /sn/, and /sl/ actually occur 10 times for each cluster; one sentence, exceptionally, contained two occurrences of these target clusters.

Instructions: Read aloud the following sentences, please:

Dan **slept** *early today.*

3.7.3.6 Picture Naming
To obtain more natural data, the formal task was followed by an informal picture-based interview. This was a friendly conversation between a graduate student and the participants about some pictures containing one of the /sl/, /st/, and /sn/ clusters. This task was adapted from Boudaoud (2008). An example of an [sl] and [st] trigger is given in Figure 3.11.

Figure 3.11. Pictures of *slippers* and *stars* used in the informal production task

3.7.3.7 NONCE WORD WRITING

The writing of pseudo-words was employed as the method to assess the Arabic participants' perception of the same set of English initial sC(C) clusters tested in the production task. Some of the stimuli were taken from the study by Cardoso, John, and French (2009) (i.e. only the items with /st/, /sn/, and /sl/). The rest of the items were created as suggested by McDonough and Trofimovich (2008: 90): 'Nonwords are often created manually by changing one letter in a real word. For example, nonwords *foltow*, *cose*, *rable* were created by substituting one letter in the following English words: *follow*, *case*, and *table*.'

In this task, participants listened to pseudo-words with sC(C) initial clusters in a carrier sentence (i.e. *please write . . . now*). The words were uttered by a native speaker of English. Participants were asked to write their answers on a piece of paper. The scoring did not assess *which* vowel they wrote. However, the task was unambiguous in scoring whether they included a vowel. The aim of this task is to test their perception of the initial sC(C) words. A control group consisting of two native speakers of Canadian English took the same perception task and performed perfectly.

3.7.3.8 ELICITED IMITATION

A repetition task was used to elicit the Arabic participants' production of English initial sC(C) clusters (sentences were partially adopted and modified from Almalki (2014) and Salem (2014)). In this task, participants were asked to listen to a sentence, then immediately repeat it. A total of 20 sentences which included initial sC(C) cluster words was recorded. The procedure involved having participants listen to a sentence uttered by a native speaker of English. Participants were recorded individually repeating the sentence they had just heard. This task was chosen to eliminate any possible orthography effects found in sentence reading tasks.

Elicited imitation (EI) studies have long been used in SLA research. The motivation for the methodology is that the repetition is governed by the learner's grammar; it is not just a mimicking task. Recent studies such as Kim, Tracy-Ventura, and Jung (2016) have shown a strong correlation between EI scores and proficiency and a weak correlation between EI and working memory. Yan and colleagues (2016: 498) in their meta-analysis conclude that 'EI tasks in general have a strong ability to discriminate between speakers across proficiency levels'. In designing the task, the preceding environments (i.e. the final phonemes in words before the cluster) were controlled.[1] The words that came before the clusters ended with a single consonant to eliminate vowels or consonant clusters before the target clusters (e.g. I love my ol**d s**chool a lot). The position of all the target words is in the middle of the sentence.

Table 3.16 adds the Persian subjects' performance.

Table 3.16. PERCEPTION ERRORS CORRELATED WITH LINGUISTIC PROPERTIES REVISED

L1	sC onsets	Branching onsets	Branching codas	% Errors
Japanese	No	No	No	72
Thai	No	No	No	60
Brazilian Portuguese	No	Yes	No	50
Persian	No	No	Yes	16

Clearly, the Persian L1 subjects were not behaving like the other L1 groups which lack sC clusters. Several phonological theories do not sanction branching codas (Kehrein and Golston 2004; Kiparsky 2003; Vaux and Wolfe 2009). As a result, such models of syllable structure invoke right-edge appendices (which attach above the coda level). I adopt a model where Cs which conform to the Sonority Sequencing Principle (SSP) are appendices to the syllable (σ), while SSP-violating Cs are appendices to the foot, as shown in the Persian examples in Figure 3.12.

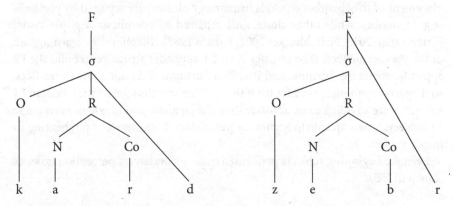

Figure 3.12. Right-edge appendices in Persian at the syllable and foot levels

---

1. There is no reason to believe that the occurrence of a coda cluster in a word would affect onset production; therefore, we did not focus on whether a word ended with a single or double consonant.

English has typologically marked initial sequences (such as [st]) which are also commonly represented not as standard branching onsets (such as [br] or [pl]) but rather as some sort of appendix as well. Some researchers argue that it is a left-edge appendix where the [s] attaches directly to a higher prosodic node (not the onset), but (following Archibald and Yousefi 2018; Goad 2016; Kaye 1992) I will assume that sC clusters have the [s] as the coda of an empty-headed syllable and the [t] as an appendix at the syllable level, as shown below in Figure 3.13.

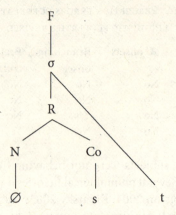

Figure 3.13. Proposed structure of an initial English sC cluster

I recognize that this is a more abstract proposal than some made in the literature (see Goad 2016), but drawing on the arguments in Archibald, Yousefi, and Alhemaid (2022), I adopt that analysis here largely because it explains the placement of the epenthetic vowels insofar as s-clusters are repaired by prothesis (e.g. [e]smoke), while other clusters are repaired by epenthesis (e.g. p[e]lastic) (Fatemi et al. 2012; Fleischhacker 2001; Karimi 1987). Therefore, the learning task of the Persian subjects is to transfer their L1 appendix structure to build the L2 appendix structure. Japanese and Brazilian Portuguese do not allow appendices, so they have nothing to transfer from the L1. This accounts for why the Persian L1 subjects were so much more accurate than the Japanese and Brazilian Portuguese L1 subjects when it came to accurately perceiving sC clusters and not hearing illusory vowels.

Even the beginning subjects performed quite accurately on perception tasks, as shown in (55).

(55) Beginner: 75%
Intermediate: 85%
Advanced: 90%
No significant difference between proficiency levels on accuracy of perception (Kruskal-Wallis test; p = .170)

The performance of the subjects in perception and production across cluster types is shown in Figure 3.14.

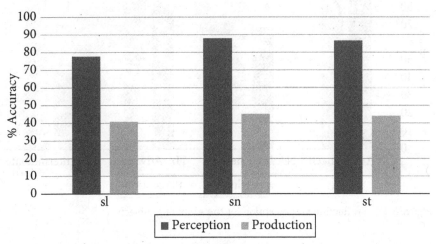

Figure 3.14. Production vs. perception for Persian L1 subjects

Now let us consider the L1 Arabic subjects described in Archibald, Yousefi, and Alhemaid (2022). Two dialects of Saudi Arabic are of interest: Najdi (NA) and Hijazi (HA). The relevant properties of these two dialects (Alghmaiz 2013; al-Mohanna 1998) are shown in Table 3.17.

Table 3.17. SYLLABIC PROPERTIES OF TWO SAUDI ARABIC DIALECTS

L1	sC onsets	Branching onsets	Appendices	% Errors
NA Arabic	No	Yes	Yes	??
HA Arabic	No	No	Yes	??

Neither dialect allows sC onsets, and both dialects allow right-edge appendices (like Persian). Where the two dialects differ is that Najdi allows branching onsets while Hijazi does not. This provides a further opportunity to see whether having an L1 with branching onsets facilitates the L2 acquisition of sC clusters. The production and perception scores of both groups are shown in Figure 3.15.

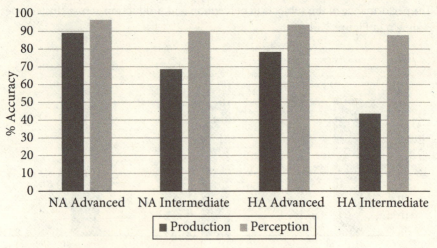

Figure 3.15. Production vs. perception for the Arabic L1 subjects

A comparison of the Persian and Saudi performance is given in Table 3.18.

Table 3.18. Accuracy scores of two Saudi dialects

L1	sC onsets	Branching onsets	Appendices	% Errors
NA Arabic	No	Yes	Yes	7
HA Arabic	No	No	Yes	10

Without doubt, the Saudi listeners are very accurate at perceiving initial sC clusters.

3.7.3.9 Discussion

The Japanese, Thai, and BP subjects do *not* have the building blocks to redeploy to handle sC onsets, and as a result, the perceptual illusion of vowel insertion occurred. This suggests that the 'illusory' vowel is actually part of the stored representation. The Persian and Saudi Arabic subjects, on the contrary, have the L1 building blocks to redeploy and quickly learned that the illusory vowels are not part of the stored representation. Their grammars dictate their reality.

The structure of s-clusters as codas of empty-headed syllables explains the differential prothetic repair of s-clusters versus th epenthetic repair of other clusters. Japanese subjects use only epenthesis as a repair strategy (not prothesis), as shown in (56).

(56) festival → fesutibaru
      strike → sutoraiku

This follows naturally if we assume that these subjects are not setting up s-clusters as codas of empty-headed syllables. However, there is also another possibility we must consider. Japanese does not allow [s] in codas, so could this be what is causing the problem in setting up the representation of s-clusters as codas? I argue that this cannot be the causal factor, as Brazilian Portuguese *does* allow coda [s], and these subjects have difficulty perceiving the English clusters. The feature of licensing right-edge appendices is the causal connection.

3.7.4 'Hearing' sC Sequences

While I believe that this formal account is explanatory in terms of the behavioural groupings of those L1s which can lead to illusory vowels versus those which do not, I would also like to present another aspect to the analysis which focusses on the processing of these s-clusters. To do this, consider the question, *who hears sC sequences?* Viewed in this light, I suggest that speakers of L1s with appendices find the English sC string intelligible (in the sense of Munro and Derwing 1995), while speakers of L1s without appendices find them unintelligible. In its traditional sense, a word which is uttered is intelligible if the listener is able to recover the intended meaning of the speaker. Intelligibility, thus, has a kind of functional definition. However, Archibald (2019) recasts intelligibility in terms of parsing procedures and contextualizes the construct with the word recognition literature. Intelligibility is not only a property of the acoustic signal. It is the result of the listener *parsing* the input. The Persian and Arabic speakers have structures readily available (via redeployment) to which they can map the L2 input segments (e.g. [st]), while the Japanese, Thai, and Brazilian Portuguese speakers lack such structures and cannot map the input onto representational positions.

3.7.5 What about Production?

Yet remember that the Persian subjects (at least the beginning- and intermediate-level subjects) still epenthesize at a high rate in production. Why? In many cases (e.g. Flege 1995) it is assumed that inaccurate (i.e. non-nativelike) production is caused by inaccurate perception. A learner who does not produce an L2 English [ɛ/æ] contrast is probably not accurately discriminating between these vowels. However, in the Persian case we are discussing, the subjects can accurately discriminate between [sC] and [esC] strings, yet they produce target sC words with epenthetic [e] more than 50% of the time. Why?

One possible explanation, following Abrahamsson (2003), is that the subjects are using epenthesis as a communication strategy to make the task of the native listener easier. Abrahamsson looks at Mandarin speakers of Swedish and their production of Swedish codas. Beginning-level L2ers would delete the Swedish coda consonants because they are not licensed by their L1 grammar. An English analogue would be if words like 'wet' and 'when' and 'went' were all pronounced [wɛʔ]. Without sentential or pragmatic context, it might be difficult for the native listener to reconstruct the intended word.

However, over time (as their Swedish proficiency increased) the subjects switched from a deletion strategy to an epenthesis strategy. The English analogue would result in the pronunciations given in (57).

(57) 'wet' → [wɛtə]
'when' → [wɛnə]
'went' → [wɛntə]

This repair strategy (which is not L1 based) seems to make it easier for the native listener to identify the intended meaning.

To my mind, it seems highly unlikely that the Persian speakers (even the advanced speakers) are epenthesizing on sC onset clusters to make it easier for the native listeners. For one thing, given the serial nature of lexical search and activation, epenthesis would make it *harder* for the listener. Hearing a string like [est], the listener would begin by activating lexical cohorts which begin with [e], then [es], and so on. Such a strategy would slow down the processing, certainly compared to the candidate set when hearing a string like [wɛn].

The most obvious answer is that they are still relying on L1 motor routines in producing the L2 clusters even though their perception is accurate. This would be consistent with the two groupings we have seen. Japanese subjects, on the one hand (following Matthews and Brown 2004), have lexicalized vowels in words like s[u]*low* and produce these vowels as a result of accessing their lexicon. Persian subjects, on the other hand, do not perceive the illusory vowels and accurately perceive the word *slow*. However, they are still in the process of acquiring the L2 production routine and still tend to produce epenthetic vowels (e.g. [e]*slow*). An analysis of Persian subjects' production by proficiency level reveals that advanced learners have learned not to epenthesize in production, as shown in Figure 3.16.

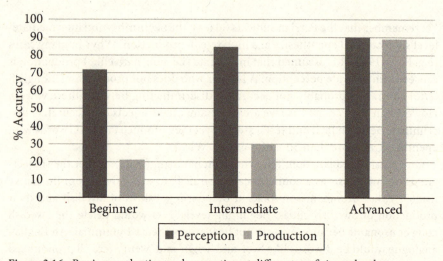

Figure 3.16. Persian production and perception at different proficiency levels

There is also some connection between these issues and recent neurolinguistic work. For example, Blanco-Elorrieta, and Pylkkänen (2015, 2016) focus on the mechanisms of shifting between languages in production and perception. While this is not my focus, this work has implications. Blanco-Elorrieta and Pylkkänen note that there is a close relationship between language control and general cognitive control in production but not in comprehension. Language control in production recruits *domain-general* regions (dorsolateral prefrontal regions bilaterally), while perception recruits *language-specific* regions (anterior cingulate cortex). What this suggests is that the perceptual illusions (or accuracy) are part of *grammar*, while the produced epenthetic vowels are under executive control. This is consistent with the data which show that the Persian subjects get better at production as their proficiency increases. The Advanced subjects were only epenthesizing 10% of the time. We expect practice to have an effect on skills.

3.7.6 Redeployment of Features

Atkey (2001) demonstrates that existing L1 features can be redeployed in new ways in an L2. She looks at the acquisition of palatal stops in Czech by English speakers. She considers both production and perception but, due to space limitations, I will discuss only her perception results. Czech has two palatal stops [c, ɟ] as well as the alveolar stops [t, d], as shown in (58):

(58) [tɛka]   'run' (3 p.s.)   [cɛka]   'wander'
     [dɛkovat] 'to steal'   [ɟɛkovat] 'to thank'

Atkey argues that palatals are phonologically [CORONAL]. She proposes that the feature required to distinguish the alveolar from the palatal sounds is [posterior]. The Czech structures would be those given in Figure 3.17:

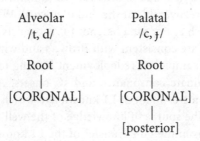

Figure 3.17. Alveolar and palatal stops

As a result of the English contrast of three coronal fricative places of articulation /s, z/ versus /ʃ, ʒ/ versus /θ, ð/, Atkey argues that English has the [posterior] feature. She proposes the representations given in Figure 3.18.

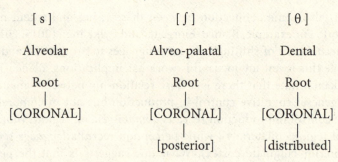

Figure 3.18. [posterior] in English

Therefore, the English speakers should have the building blocks necessary for acquiring the structure of the Czech palatals. Atkey looks at six North American English-speaking adults who were learning Czech in the Czech Republic ranging in exposure to Czech from three months (0;3) to 10 years (10;0). Subjects were given a forced-choice picture selection task which depended on accurate discrimination of alveolar from palatal stops in all syllabic positions. Table 3.19 indicates the percentage of palatal stops perceived correctly by all subjects.

Table 3.19. PERCEPTION OF PALATAL STOPS

Position	ML (0;3)	JD (0;5)	AD (0;11)	SW (0;11)	JA (1;0)	RK (10;0)
Initial	70	90	80	85	80	95
Medial	70	70	80	90	85	90
Final	20	30	50	70	70	80

Clearly the L2 learners can perform this task at greater than chance levels. Native speaker controls scored 100%. The fact that the subjects were much less accurate in final position is due to the reduced saliency of the information on place of articulation recoverable at the end of a word. When a stop is released into a vowel, it is much easier for a listener to recover its place of articulation. Atkey's results, then, are consistent with Brown's and with González-Poot's.

So, we have seen examples of redeployment leading to accurate perception of palatal stops, geminate consonants, and sC onsets. All of these examples involve transfer of some element of L1 knowledge which is used in a new way in the L2 grammar. The source of knowledge of the well formedness of the L2 strings is generated from the Full Transfer of the L1 knowledge.

From these examples, we have seen cases where novel L2 structures can be acquired (i.e. lexicalized/phonologized) as a result of redeployment; accurate perception is a diagnostic of targetlike grammar. There are, however, documented cases where the grammatical representation appears to encode a phonological distinction even though the perceptual ability is lacking.

3.7.7 Direct Mapping of Acoustics onto Phonology (DMAP)

In this section, I want to briefly touch upon a model which arose from a nice study done by Darcy et al. (2012). The basic empirical finding they report is a profile where L2 learners of French (with L1 English which lacks /y/) can distinguish lexical items which rely on a /y/-/u/ distinction while simultaneously being unreliable in discriminating [y] from [u] in an ABX task. This particular profile is taken as noteworthy because of long-standing assumptions that accurate perception was a necessary precursor to accurate production (and representation). They argue that detection of acoustic properties can lead to phonological restructuring (according to general economy principles of phonological inventories) which will result in a lexical contrast, but the phonetic categories may not yet be targetlike. Detection is thought to be preconscious. We know that learners may be attending to different cues than native speakers do (e.g. duration instead of spectral quality in vowels), but this may be enough to determine that a contrast exists. The learners rely on their current interlanguage feature hierarchy to set up contrastive lexical representations even as phonetic category formation proceeds. This is reminiscent of the Goto (1971) study, where Japanese learners were able to produce an /l/-/r/ liquid contrast even while not being able to discriminate between them in a decontextualized task. It could be that the tactile feedback received in the production of these two sounds and the orthographic distinction between 'l' and 'r' were able to cue the learners' production systems. This sort of metalinguistic knowledge can affect production.

A number of researchers have found evidence of subjects who show knowledge of lexical contrasts but demonstrate unreliable performance on discrimination tasks (Escudero, Hayes-Harb, and Mitterer 2008; Hayes-Harb and Masuda 2008). At first blush, such performance would seem surprising. If the L1 does not make an [ɛ/æ] distinction or an [l/r] distinction, then we might expect learners to have a single, homophonous representation for *bet/bat* and for *lock/rock*. There is evidence for this in the phantom activation effects found by Broersma and Cutler (2007). In a left-to-right model of word activation, as listeners process the incoming signal, the number of possible candidates diminishes as more information comes in. Imagine a situation where a listener hears [l]. Many possible words are members of the candidate set. Then the next sound is [i]. There will be fewer choices that begin with [li]. Then the third sound is [n], and the listener would decide that the word was *lean*. Now imagine a listener who does not represent a phonemic /l/ versus /r/ distinction, perhaps a Japanese listener who represents a single non-nasal approximant /ɾ/. When this listener hears an initial [l], then words which begin with both /l/ and /r/ will be included in the set of possible candidates. When the next sound is [i], then words which begin with both [li] and [ri] will be in the candidate set. The members of this expanded set of lexical items waiting to be activated are what Broersma and Cutler call *phantom* competitors. Extra-linguistic factors such as orthographical or metalinguistic knowledge might be implicated in the lexical structure of such subjects who can lexicalize what they cannot discriminate. Darcy and colleagues (2012) maintain a Full Access position, if you will, in that features which are not implicated in the L1 are 'latent' (i.e. available for activation in the L2). They argue that acquiring phonetic distinctions need not precede phonological encoding of contrast. Detection of acoustic properties can lead to phonological restructuring which will result in a lexical contrast, but the phonetic categories may not yet be targetlike.

3.7.8 Universals

Of course, all of our preceding discussion is situated in the long-standing literature which has demonstrated the role of universal properties of language such as markedness and Universal Grammar in L2 phonology.

3.7.8.1 DIFFERING REPAIR STRATEGIES AS EVIDENCE OF KNOWLEDGE OF MARKEDNESS

Broselow (1992) shows that Arabic speakers treat s-clusters that violate the Sonority Sequencing Principle differently than those that do not, as shown in (59):

(59) sweater → [siwɛtar]   study → [istadi]
      slide → [silayd]   ski → [iski]

Singh (1985) demonstrates the same pattern for Hindi speakers shown in (60):

(60) fruit → [fɪrut]   school → [ɪskul]
      please → [pɪlɪz]   spelling → [ɪspɛlɪŋ]

Revisiting these production data within the illusory vowel context illuminates the contribution of grammatical representation. The subjects were hearing vowels that were not in the input in places which can be explained by universal principles. The positioning of these illusory vowels cannot be explained by the input or by transfer. The location can be explained only by the fact that the grammatical representation of the IL grammar is informed by principles of UG. Hearing 'sweater' as [siwɛtar] and 'study' as [istadi] is not explained by the input.

Broselow and Finer (1991) show that the interlanguage systems may be neither L1 nor L2 systems but natural language grammars. Eckman (1991) in his *Structural Conformity Hypothesis* shows that L2 grammars are systems which respect language universals. Major (2001) in his *Ontogeny/Phylogeny* model shows both transfer and universal effects in interlanguage development. Broselow, Chen, and Wang (1998) show that interlanguage grammars could reveal unmarked forms that were not found in either the L1 or the L2. These are only a few examples of this rich literature, and I will not recapitulate it here. In morphosyntax, of course, there is also the vast literature on *access to UG* and particularly the *full access* position of Schwartz and Sprouse (1996).

Finally, when considering the phonetics/phonology interface, Özçelik (2017c) reports on some universal implementation effects. He examined English learners of Turkish (a footless language) and argues that the English L1 participants did not set up a footless grammar for Turkish but rather had either iambic or trochaic feet. Of particular interest to us here is the fact that those subjects with iambic feet manifested stress via duration, while those with trochaic feet signalled stress via intensity and pitch. These implementation strategies adopt the universal tendencies noted by Hayes (1995).

3.8 CONCLUSION

In this chapter, I set out the position that it is productive to maintain a distinction between an abstract, categorical phonological system and a gradient, concrete phonetics. We looked at some of the evidence that L2 phonological behaviour is explained by reference to symbolic systems which are not read easily off the input. As I proposed in the first chapter, the schema of learning, shown in Figure 3.19, situates phonetic data as part of the environment and something that plays a role in the learning theory.

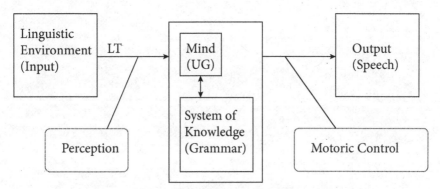

Figure 3.19. Phonetics as input to the phonological grammar

The examples of L2 Japanese moras, illusory vowels and appendices, and feature geometries clearly show that the phonological grammars are not shallow and are governed by the same types of representations and processes as primary languages.

On a broader note, the case study of illusory vowels has implications beyond the redeployment hypothesis and beyond an argument for the presence of appendices in L2 phonological grammars. The construct of Escher's Problem of augmented input, hearing sounds that aren't in the acoustic signal, provides us with some insight into the cognitive architecture of the bilingual grammar. First of all, it is an argument against what Tessier and Jesney (2014) might call the Identity Map lexical-learning strategy, where underlying (input) representations are taken to be faithful to the (environmental) surface forms. These illusory vowels cannot be read off the acoustic signal. Second, it is an argument against exemplar theory (Pierrehumbert 2001). These subjects (a) heard elements *not* found in the input (e.g. illusory vowels), and (b) didn't hear certain elements that were (e.g. lack of ability to discriminate certain environmental contrasts not found in the L1). Finally, it argues that direct realist, sophisticated neo-Behaviourist Bayesian models (Wilson and Davidson 2013), which would require a type of what Dresher and Kaye (1990) would have called *batch processing* of all available input, cannot be the model we seek for bilingual architecture.

In the next chapter, I will show how this model of phonological structure can also provide an explanatory account of the phonology/morphology interface.

4

The Phonology/Morphology Interface

4.1 INTRODUCTION

In this chapter, I begin to explore the central role phonology plays in the broader grammatical architecture as well by focussing on its interaction with morphology. It is clear from basic allomorphic patterns that morpheme choices can be phonologically conditioned as we see in the variation in pronunciation of English plural in forms such as *cat*[s], *dog*[z], and *horse*[əz]. From an acquisition point of view, this is something that has to be acquired by the second language learner.

While other interfaces have been central to the field of SLA—particularly the syntactic interfaces (Montrul 2011; Sorace 2012; White 2011)—the phonology/ morphology interface has not received nearly as much attention. The notable exception is work within the Prosodic Transfer Hypothesis (PTH; e.g. Goad and White 2004, 2006, 2019) which argues that L2 morphemes may be omitted in production due (primarily) to phonological factors rather than any morphological deficit. In other words, missing morphology may be largely a mapping problem not a grammatical feature problem. Goad and White (2019) also suggest that the Prosodic Transfer Hypothesis can apply (following Lieberman 2013) to comprehension as well as production, but I will not pursue that line of inquiry here as the empirical results are still somewhat sparse.

I will not survey here the extensive literature which seeks to account for the oft-observed fact that many L2 learners omit certainly inflectional morphemes in certain tasks (see Lardiere 2007, for a summary). So, for example, an L2 learner might say something like *Yesterday, I walk to school*, with no past-tense suffix on the verb *walk*. Or they might say, *We have three cat at home*, with no plural morpheme added to *cat*. Some attribute the phenomenon to the type of syntactic feature (Tsimpli and Dimitrakopoulou 2007) where it is argued that learners are more likely to omit uninterpretable features (like [3rd person]) but are able to produce interpretable features (like [finite], [plural], and [past]). Others attribute the omission to the pragmatic interface (Sorace and Filiaci 2006). Here it is argued that learners are more likely to show variable production on phenomena which

Phonology in Multilingual Grammars. John Archibald, Oxford University Press. © John Archibald 2024.
DOI: 10.1093/oso/9780190923334.003.0004

are not associated with the core linguistic modules but rather are conditioned by discourse or pragmatic factors. My concern in this chapter is to look at how phonology interacts with the morphological component. First let us examine one mapping account.

4.2 THE PROSODIC TRANSFER HYPOTHESIS

The PTH assumes (Goad and White 2019) that the grammatical representations (in this case, our focus is on the phonological grammar) which transfer to the initial stage of the second language are the full grammar of the L1 (see Schwartz and Sprouse 1996 for more detail on the Full Transfer / Full Access model). A model of prosodic phonology (based on Nespor and Vogel 1986) would assume the levels in the prosodic hierarchy shown in Figure 4.1.

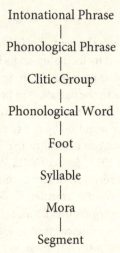

Figure 4.1. The prosodic hierarchy

The details of each level of representation are not critical to our arguments here. Suffice it to say, there are phonological patterns cross-linguistically (e.g. where we find aspiration, or devoicing, etc.) that can be explained with reference to these phonological domains. So, English may aspirate voiceless stops at the beginning of a foot, German may devoice obstruents at the end of a syllable, French may place stress at the end of a phonological phrase, and so on. Crucial to our discussion, though, is the notion that these constituent phrasal structures (e.g. foot, syllable, mora) are what transfers to the L2 grammar and are what will explain the production data (particularly the omission of certain morphemes). Goad and White (2019) propose that if a particular morpheme is not produced, maybe it is because it is composed of sound sequences which are difficult to represent, and not because the morpheme itself (or, rather, its syntactic features) has not

Right-Edge Clusters   131

been acquired. Learners would omit morphemes when the L1 prosodic structure
(which is transferred into the L2) does not license the production of the spell out
of the morpheme. English inflectional morphology is assumed to adjoin to the
Prosodic Word (PWd), as shown in (61) for the word 'helped':

(61) $[_{PWd}[_{PWd}[help]\ t]]$

In other words, we begin with the Prosodic Word *help*, add to it a past-tense
affix [t], and derive a complex Prosodic Word *helped*. Mandarin, by contrast,
adjoins inflectional morphology (like aspect) *within* the Prosodic Word at the
foot level, as we can see in the structure in (62) for the perfective form of the
verb *buy*:

(62) $[[_{PWd}[_{Ft}\ [_{\sigma}mai]\ [_{\sigma}lǝ]]]]$

Once again, the details of the argument of how we can tell that the perfective
affix is attached to a foot and not to a Prosodic Word are not critical. I would ask
the reader to accept the differing structural analyses of the two languages. Note,
then, that the Mandarin speakers have not only to acquire the English tense feature but also to learn to adjoin morphology at the Prosodic Word level. Being
unable to prosodify the structure, the surface inflection will be missing for phonological reasons. This is exactly parallel to a, perhaps, more familiar data set.
An L2 learner may omit consonants if the L1 grammar does not allow coda
consonants. In a word like *help*, the [p] is in the syllable coda. When adding a
past-tense morpheme, we derive a complex coda sequence [pt]. So, if the learner
does not produce the [t] in a past-tense word, it may be for phonological, not
morphological, reasons. The morphology/phonology interface, then, is important for understanding the nature of morphology in developing systems. Let us
explore this in more detail.

4.3 RIGHT-EDGE CLUSTERS

In English, the production of inflectional morphology is confounded with the
presence of right-edge consonant clusters to mark this morphology. The basic
question here is whether what is interpreted as the lack of, say, past-tense morphology is, in fact, the inability to produce consonant clusters. So, if someone
says, 'Yesterday, I [wɑk] to the store', are they producing a non-past verb or a
[+past] marked verb with the final consonant deleted because of L1 transfer?
The answer to this question speaks to the explanation of the phenomenon.

Abrahamsson (2003) looks at a number of aspects of the acquisition of Swedish
consonant clusters by speakers of Chinese. As we will see, the production of these
clusters is influenced by the morphology of the language. Abrahamsson draws

on a fact noted at least since Weinberger (1988), which is that even if clusters are repaired to be produced in a non-nativelike way, they can be repaired in more than one way. Broadly speaking, we see epenthesis strategies and deletion strategies. A deletion strategy would be to produce a word like 'went' as [wɛ] while an epenthesis strategy would be to produce the word 'went' as [wɛntə]. A number of factors influence whether an L2 subject will prefer an epenthesis or deletion strategy. One is the L1. Italian learners of English may epenthesize at the end of a closed syllable in order to produce a CVCV pattern. So, 'bed' might be produced at [bɛdə]. Mandarin, on the contrary, tends to maintain its preference for a CV syllable by deleting coda consonants, so that 'wet' would be pronounced as [wɛ] or [wɛʔ]. But Abrahamsson notes that even the Mandarin L1 subjects produce more epenthetic forms as their L2 proficiency increases. There may well be a communicative reason for this, as the epenthetic forms seem to allow the listener to recover the intended lexical item more easily, as can be seen from the fact that 'wet', 'when', and 'went' might all be produced as [wɛ], which could lead to confusion under a deletion strategy, while epenthesis would more easily allow disambiguation to [wɛtə], [wɛnə] and [wɛntə]. It seems plausible to me that post-coda epenthesis is the result of a communication strategy—but it seems unlikely that pre-sC epenthesis (that we looked at in Chapter 3) has the same source.

I want to digress slightly to explore the notion of communication strategy as something which can consciously influence production. There is a wide literature in SLA on communication strategies (Dörnyei and Scott 2002) which are often operationalized as conscious strategies that learners may employ when their L2 grammar 'fails'. For example, I may draw on the Spanish word for *hammer* when struggling to speak in Italian not because I think that I know the Italian word for *hammer* but because I hope that the Italian listener will be able to figure it out so that the conversation can keep going. Perhaps I would even resort to miming the act of hammering while saying the English word *hammer*. However, this raises an interesting asymmetry in these sorts of epenthesizing repair strategies in different positions in the word.

As we saw in Chapter 3, Section 3.7, learners from many L1s which lack sC onset clusters produce them with a prothetic vowel (e.g. [e]*slow*) even when they can accurately perceive the distinction between [e]*slow* and *slow* (Archibald, Yousefi, and Alhemaid 2022). But it certainly seems that this is *not* the result of a communication strategy.

How do we reconcile the difference between the left-edge and right-edge behaviours? Given that communication strategies are designed to meet the needs of the listener, there is an obvious difference when it comes to the effects of the strategies if we view the listening process as one of word recognition. Of course, listeners can accommodate variety in a speech signal and ambiguity in the input. Yet initial ambiguities will garden-path the word recognition algorithm; wrong competitors will be activated. For example, if the intended word is *slow* and a second language speaker produces [e]*slow*, then the listener may activate lexical candidates such as *escape* or *especially*. It may take the listener more time

Morphological Theories 133

to recover from the wrong choices to find the word which is intended and best matches the acoustic signal.

By the time the listener gets to the epenthetic vowel at the right edge, the final choices are being made. Lexical candidates are eliminated with every additional phoneme that is processed. If the listener parses a word from left to right by the time they get to *prospec-*, for example, there are very few lexical candidates left (i.e. *prospect*). When you hear the string *hippop-* there is really only one word that could be intended. Thus, the farther from the beginning of the word the site of epenthesis, the fewer lexical candidates for the listener to consider.

All of this reveals that inflectional morphemes are not simplistically 'left out' or 'put in' but, as with other aspects of L2 performance, variable and conditioned by a variety of factors. We should note, as well, that from early 'morpheme order' studies (Dulay and Burt 1974) to the recent summary of the PTH (Goad and White 2019), much of the data collection involved production tasks. These production tasks often are designed to reveal properties of the performance system. But let us not lose sight of our central mandate here: the nature of the representational system of the second language learner. To address that issue, we need to adopt a theory of morphology.

4.4 MORPHOLOGICAL THEORIES

There are, of course, many approaches to morphology to choose from (e.g. Construction Morphology (Booij 2010), Amorphous Morphology (Anderson 1992), Word Grammar (Hudson 2010), Prosodic Morphology (McCarthy and Prince 1996)). The model I will adopt and delve into here is Distributed Morphology (Halle and Marantz 1993). This is a model which says much about the architecture of the grammar. We will focus on the nature of the phonology/morphology interface (following Embick 2010), the architecture of the bilingual lexicon (López 2020), and the phenomenon of what has been called *intraword codeswitching* (see Stefanich et al. 2019; Stefanich and Cabrelli 2018) and how Distributed Morphology can explain it.

4.4.1 Distributed Morphology

Distributed Morphology (DM) has interesting implications for the study of what is traditionally referred to as the bilingual lexicon. DM is a theory in which morphological roots are inserted into syntactic trees but only assigned phonological form at a late spell out. This is why it is referred to as a 'late-insertion' model. Such a model is contrasted with a 'lexicalist' model which assumes that a lexicon is pre-syntactic. As Embick (2010) demonstrates, there is competition for allomorphs but not for complex output forms. The bulk of evidence from DM is incompatible with an output-focussed model such as Optimality Theory. It thus behooves us to explore the implications for L2 phonology.

I will begin by providing an (admittedly simplistic) overview of some of the crucial properties of DM:

- Functional morphemes are bundles of features (e.g. [past]) in the syntax which, via a process known as Vocabulary Insertion, are spelled out phonologically.
- There is competition for allomorph selection (e.g. which plural allomorph attaches to *cat*, which attaches to *ox*?) but, crucially, no competition between complex multimorphemic objects
- A syntactic derivation is sent to spell out (probably in phases) which is then sent to both phonetic form (PF) and logical form (LF). PF and LF are the interfaces with the sensory-motoric and logical-conceptual systems, respectively.
- There is a matrix of features on the syntactic terminal node and various vocabulary items would compete for insertion by seeing which affix matched the most features.

DM is a single-engine account for both word and sentence construction (Halle and Marantz 1993). Embick (2010) was seminal for me in triggering the idea that the phonology/morphology interface was critical to SLA. He argues for a local, serial model of the interface, which has implications for both the phonetic and syntactic interfaces as we build a unified architecture to account for the varied aspects of second language phonology.

The store of category-neutral roots contains no phonological information (which is reminiscent of the more traditional psycholinguistic notion of *lemmas*—which have conceptual structure but no phonological content (Levelt 1989)). In DM terms, these would be represented as √*dog* and √*chien*. Grammatical categories are established in the syntax via functional heads (such as *v* or *n*) which will be combined with the roots via the Merge operation.

I would now like to turn to four case studies which demonstrate the utility of Distributed Morphology for the understanding of L2 phonological phenomena.

4.5 CASE I: WORD RECOGNITION AND THE BILINGUAL LEXICON

For many years, investigation into the processes of bilingual lexical access has been ongoing. A consensus (Gollan, Forster, and Frost 1997; van Leerdam, Bosman, and de Groot 2009; Dijkstra, Grainger, and Van Heuven (1999) emerged that bilinguals always activate words in *both* languages (regardless of linguistic context). I will briefly summarize some of the work which demonstrates the behaviour of what are called interlingual homographs and interlingual homophones in lexical processing. Dijkstra, Grainger, and Van Heuven (1999) crafted some elegant experiments using lexical decision tasks which reveal the complexity of what had been known simply as 'cognates' before. This sort of

Case I: Word Recognition and the Bilingual Lexicon   135

research shows that if we were interested in a question like, *are words in both languages activated in a monolingual environment?*, then we needed to ask a subtler question than that. Not all 'words' were created the same. Table 4.1 sets up different categories of cross-linguistic relation between English and Dutch where the acronyms reveal what is shared across lexical items (S = semantics; O = orthography; P = phonology). Of most interest at this point is the difference between the items which share only orthography (what are called interlingual *homographs*) and the items which share only phonology (what are called interlingual *homophones*).

Table 4.1. INTERLINGUAL HOMOGRAPHS AND HOMOPHONES

SOP cognates	**SO cognates**	**SP cognates**
hotel	fruit [frøyt]	news/nieuws
film	chaos [xaɔs]	boat/boot
lip	jury [ʒyri]	wheel/wiel
OP false friends	**IL homographs (O)**	**IL homophones (P)**
step (scooter)	glad	[lif]
arts (doctor)	[xlɑt] (slippery)	'leaf' 'lief'
kin (chin)		(dear)

In lexical decision tasks, Dijkstra, Grainger, and Van Heuven (1999) found that interlingual homographs had faster decision times than control items, while interlingual homophones had slower decision times than control items.

Nakayama and Archibald (2005) replicated this finding via a task with more ecological validity than a lexical decision task: eye-tracking. In an eye-tracking task, subjects are simply reading sentences on a computer screen. During this task, we can track where and how long the eyes are fixating in a sentence. The question we probe is, *do interlingual homographs and interlingual homophones behave differently in a monolingual, silent reading task?* We had fourteen Dutch/ English bilinguals in Calgary read sentences which had either IL homographs or homophones embedded in English sentences. The fixation times on each were compared to control words which were matched by word length, frequency, and predictability. Examples of the two experimental categories (before the solidus with the control item after) are shown in (63).

(63)   IL Homographs: An **angel/elbow** can be damaged easily.
       IL Homophones: I had never seen a single **oar/oat** before.

The results on analysis of fixation time for the interlingual *homophones* are given in (64).

(64)   Mean Control fixation: 239 ms
       Mean Experimental fixation: 280 ms

136   THE PHONOLOGY/MORPHOLOGY INTERFACE

This difference of +41 ms *inhibition* on the experimental items was significant (p < .05). The results on analysis of fixation time for the interlingual *homographs* are given in (65).

(65)   Mean Control fixation: 284 ms
        Mean Experimental fixation: 255 ms

This difference of −29 ms *facilitation* on the experimental items was significant (p < .05). Thus, the interlingual homographs *facilitate* lexical access, while the interlingual homophones *inhibit* lexical access. In a monolingual English context, bilinguals cannot suppress access to the other language. Properties of these *Dutch* words explain the *English* reading behaviour. So, lexical activation (including by silent reading) taps into phonology.

Recall that Embick (2010) argues that there is only competition for allomorphs (i.e. between items with the same meaning but different phonological form); there is no global parallel competition between forms other than this. There cannot be competition for other forms because the grammar outputs a single node to be filled. Here, there are implications for the bilingual mind. If interlingual homophones are significantly slower to access than other forms, it may be because of the mismatch of the mapping of phonology to morphology in the two languages (in addition to the cross-linguistic differences in phonetics even in what have been called homophones). Similarly, we could argue that, say, 'dog' and 'chien' are allomorphs competing for insertion into a syntactic tree. But here, we must note that a traditional lexical decision task doesn't tap into syntactic structure or grammatical features. However, Nakayama and Archibald (2005) show that the behaviour of these interlingual homographs and homophones is also revealed in a *sentence* reading task as measured by eye-tracking. Interlingual homographs had shorter fixation times, while interlingual homophones had longer fixation times. Thus, in reading an English sentence like 'The leaf/fair was a sign that autumn had come,' the Dutch word [lif] and the English word [lif] were competing for insertion into the sentence. The reading times (and patterns) in the *English* sentence were explained by properties of the *Dutch* words. These data are evidence of competition for homographs and homophones as well as allomorphs post-syntactically for the bilingual. This is consistent with Embick's argument and with the tenets of Distributed Morphology.

This type of model also receives support from the cognitive neuroscience literature. Pylkkänen, Llinás, and Murphy (2006) argue in an MEG study that different senses of a polysemic word (such as *paper* in English) do not have distinct lexical entries but rather share a morphological root. In the DM literature, these roots are where the sound-meaning pairings in language are established.

4.5.1 Phonology Meets the Lexicon

In this section, we are going to explore the lexicon in the mind and the brain. We will explore elements of phonology and morphology in the bilingual lexicon.

4.5.2 Psycholinguistic Methods

But we don't need to do actual brain scans to probe how people actually use language in real time. There is a range of psycholinguistic techniques which can provide data to inform our theories of mental representation. A lexical decision task (LDT) is designed to give a picture of language processing in real time by probing the effects of activating particular lexical items. These tasks draw on properties of lexical networks (or spreading activation) whereby the access of one word might spread to another word which is somehow similar (e.g. in meaning or sound). The activation effect shown in Figure 4.2 is referred to as *priming*.

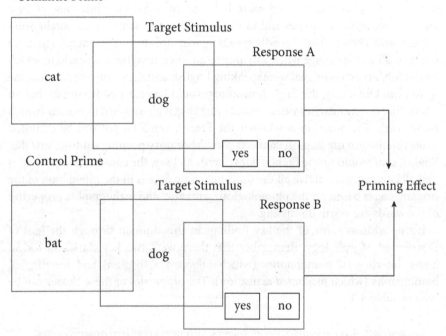

Figure 4.2. Priming studies
SOURCE: Adapted from Libben (2021)

In this figure, when we measure the response time on the button pressing on *dog* under the two conditions, we would expect that the response on *dog* when it follows *cat* will be faster than the response on *dog* when it follows *bat*. *Cat* is said to prime *dog*. Another way of describing this is that the activation of *cat* facilitates the activation of *dog*. Priming is a technique, then, which can help us to understand the processes and networks of lexical activation. Of course, this is most relevant to us in the investigation of bilingual lexical activation. Before getting into some of the details of those issues, though, I want to step back briefly to introduce Libben's *Homogeneity Hypothesis*. In the year 2000, Libben, one of the pioneers in the study of the bilingual lexicon, first proposed his idea that the types of representations and processes invoked by bilinguals were exactly the same as the types of representations and processes invoked by monolinguals (Libben 2000: 229): 'The essence of the Homogeneity Hypothesis is that monolinguals, bilinguals, and second language learners possess the same kinds of lexical representations and employ the same kinds of processes in the activation of words in the mental lexicon.' With that background, let us now turn to empirical studies of the bilingual lexicon.

4.5.3 The Bilingual Lexicon

Studies such as Dijkstra, Grainger, and Van Heuven (1999) argue for a non-selective bilingual lexicon, and there is broad consensus for this view at least for word recognition studies and in the early stages of sentence comprehension (Libben and Titone 2009). Broadly speaking, what this means is that bilinguals do not turn off one language when listening to another. Imagine a scenario in which an English/French bilingual were speaking English and they happened to hear the word *chat*. Obviously, the English meaning would be activated (*to speak*), but an interesting question arises when we note that *chat* is also a word in French (which means *cat*). The question is whether the French word for *cat* will be activated while listening to the English conversation. Laboratory priming studies show that English *chat* would prime French *dog* (*chien*). As I say, the consensus view then is that all languages are active all the time, but some details in the interaction of the two languages based on the phonological, semantic, and orthographic properties of the words are worth discussing.

Let us address some of the key findings in this domain through the lens of Distributed Morphology. Remember that there were two key classes of lexical items: interlingual homophones (which *inhibited* activation) and interlingual homographs (which *facilitated* activation). The properties of these classes can be seen in Table 4.2.

Table 4.2. INTERLINGUAL HOMOPHONES AND INTERLINGUAL HOMOGRAPHS

Interlingual homophones	**Interlingual homographs**
e.g. English/Dutch	e.g. English/Dutch
[lif] 'leaf'/'dear'	'glad' [glæd]/[xlat] (Dutch: 'slippery')
-Slower (inhibited) activation	-Faster activation
-Don't share a root (*leaf/dear*)	-Don't share a root (*glad/slippery*)
-Same spell out	-Different spell out (matched by letters, predictability, etc.)

So, priming studies can provide evidence of cross-linguistic activation, activation below the threshold of consciousness. Neither of the above examples

Case I: Word Recognition and the Bilingual Lexicon   139

shares a root. It is the phonology which determines the priming effect. Let us consider these results in light of the Homogeneity Hypothesis by referring to studies of monolinguals. MEG studies on polysemy (e.g. Pylkkänen, Llinás, and Murphy 2006) show that the different senses of a polyseme (a word which sounds the same and has related meanings, vs. homophones, which are words which sound the same but have unrelated meanings) have facilitating latencies, while Beretta, Fiorentino, and Poeppel (2005) show that polysemy is facilitative but homonymy inhibitive in a lexical decision task. These results are summarized in Table 4.3.

Table 4.3. Polysemes and homophones

Polysemes	Homophones
The *paper* is A4.	He fell off the *bank* of the river.
The *paper* is owned by Rupert Murdoch.	She opened a savings account at the *bank*.
The *paper* was written by Walcir.	Townshend stared at the *bank* of amplifiers.
-Faster activation	-Slower activation
-Share root	-Don't share root
-Same spell out	-Same spell out

So, polysemes have faster activation and related meanings. This is clearly analogous to translation equivalents in two languages. Let us explore how that comes to pass.

4.5.4 The Role of Phonology

There is a rich psycholinguistic literature on translation equivalents. The role of phonology in bilingual access has been clearly demonstrated, as shown in Table 4.4. The table adopts the standard terminology of psychological approaches (to aid the reader in accessing the primary literature), but I will include interdisciplinary translation equivalents, if you will. *Cognate* translation equivalents have similar phonology (so note this is not the historical linguistics notion of a cognate sharing a common linguistic ancestry), while *non-cognate* translation equivalents do not have similar phonology (Nakayama et al. 2014).

Table 4.4. Translation equivalents

- Cognate words are easier to recognize than non-cognates in LDT (Lemhöfer, Dijkstra, and Michel 2004)
- Cognate words are translated more quickly than non-cognates (de Groot 1992)
- Voga and Grainger (2007) demonstrate that cognate translation equivalents show facilitative priming relative to matched phonologically related primes. The primes were Greek (L1), and the targets were French (L2).

Here I observe that the semantic relatedness combined with phonological similarity leads to *facilitated* access. Note this is different from the previously discussed interlingual homophones (Dutch/English [lif]) which inhibited access. This leads us directly to look further at what are traditionally called *translation equivalents*. For example, English *dog* and French *chien* are translation equivalents. I would propose that we refer to them as *interlingual allomorphs* in that they share a root but have different spell out at PF. In a bilingual speech context, this is equivalent to polysemy.

4.5.5 Competition for Root Insertion

Traditional approaches to DM assume that there is competition for allomorphs (such as *cat[s]* vs. *dog[z]*) but not for roots (e.g. √dog vs. √cat). However, Haugen (2008) and Haugen and Siddiqi (2013) argue that there is competition for roots and therefore the root is part of the vocabulary list.

We can frame this psycholinguistic discussion in a linguistic model by incorporating insights from Distributed Morphology. Translation equivalent primes—both cognate (i.e. those with phonological overlap) and non-cognate—produce facilitation effects via their shared meaning representation. Like polysemy, these translation equivalents (*interlingual allomorphs*) share a root. Cognate translation equivalents produce stronger priming effects than do non-cognate translation equivalents (Voga and Grainger 2007; Nakayama et al. 2013). Consider the cognate versus non-cognate translation equivalents in Japanese/English shown in (66).

(66)   • Cognate: /remoN/ 'lemon'
       • Non-cognate: /josei/ 'woman'

When activating the same root, the phonological overlap facilitates recognition. Thus, we see competition for root insertion across languages which is consistent with Libben's (2000) Homogeneity Hypothesis (Libben and Goral 2015). It is consistent because we see exactly the same thing happening in monolingual activation. The English word *bug* can have (at least) two meanings: 'insect' and 'covert listening device'. Even in a context which promotes one rather than the other (e.g. *I was in the garden weeding when I saw a bug on the leaf*), it has been shown (Marcel 1983) that both meanings are initially activated and then the less likely meaning (*covert listening device*) is suppressed.

We see competition for root insertion across languages. Consistent with Libben's (2000) Homogeneity Hypothesis, the DM vocabulary must be non-selective. There is some debate on this in the literature, with Burkholder (2018) arguing for separate lexicons, while López (2020) argues for a single store of vocabulary items. Burkholder (2018) suggests that bilinguals have functionally separate distributed lexicons but mitigates this claim by also noting that during language mixing, neither language is inhibited. My preference is to achieve this representationally via language tags (see Archibald and Libben 2019) and to handle it in production as outlined in Stefanich and colleagues (2019). So, a verb's stored information might include such properties as transitive, takes animate subject, English. Given that multilingualism is more common than monolingualism and given that unpredictable information about lexical items needs to be stored somewhere in any theory, the default assumption should be that vocabulary items include information on which language they belong to. We know that monolinguals have sub-lexicons which encode things like Latinate versus non-Latinate vocabulary (in English) to explain such things as the dative alternation (compare *I gave the library a book* to **I donated the library a book*) or phonological strata in Japanese (Itô and Mester 2017). Consistent with the Homogeneity Hypothesis, multilinguals are no different. What this suggests is that all lexical roots and affixes in a given language would, in fact, be tagged (as English, or German, or Danish) even in monolingual speakers. Green and Abutalebi (2013) and Green (2018) note how we can suppress the language items which, while activated, do not belong to the language of the conversation or context. Which items get suppressed? The items of a particular language tag.

In this section, we have seen that adopting a model of the phonology/morphology interface consistent with Distributed Morphology can help to understand findings from the traditional literature on the bilingual lexicon.

4.6 CASE II: ABRAHAMSSON REVISITED: A DISTRIBUTED MORPHOLOGY ANALYSIS OF SWEDISH CODAS

Distributed Morphology also allows us to gain greater insight into some previously reported data on L2 coda clusters. For years, Abrahamsson has been producing fascinating work on both the structural properties of L2 phonology and on the extralinguistic factors that influence production and proficiency. Abrahamsson (2003) reports on the acquisition of coda consonants in L2 Swedish by native speakers of Mandarin. In this study, he invokes a principle of *recoverability* to account for the repair strategies and the accuracy of L2 codas. What I will argue here is that a DM feature-bundle-style analysis is preferable for the inflectional data.

Abrahamsson reports on the fact that if [r] was the coda of a monomorphemic stem, then it was pronounced more accurately than if it was either a present-tense or a plural affix. He argues that the retention of the [r] in a monomorphemic form helped the recoverability more than the retention of [r] in affixes, as there were *redundant* cues to elements like tense and plural. For example, in the discourse there will be other cues to temporality or quantity. He presents the examples shown in Table 4.5.

Table 4.5. Final -r words in Swedish

Present tense		Plural		Monomorphemic	
kasta-r	'throw[s]'	sko-r	'shoes'	dyr	'expensive'
gå-r	'walk[s]'	bil-ar	'cars'	klar	'ready'
sitt-er	'sit[s]'	röst-er	'voices'	hår	'hair'
		blomm-or	'flowers'	doctor	'doctor'
				mer	'more'
				när	'when'
				ner	'down'
				ungefär	'approximately'

All subjects had significantly more errors for multimorphemic words than for monomorphemic words. The errors cannot be explained by phonology alone, as all words contain singleton [r]. This difference in error patterns between inflected and uninflected forms implicates syntactic features in the explanation. There is, of course, a rich literature on missing surface inflection (e.g. Jensen, Slabakova, and Westergaard 2019; Prévost and White 2000), but the question of interest here is the difference between the subjects' performance on the [past] affix versus the [plural] affix. Remember that Abrahamsson invokes a functional explanation: unique markers would be retained more than redundant markers. However, as he acknowledges, it is not straightforward to tell whether tense or number is more redundant in Swedish. Let us consider two hypotheses, where >> is meant to be read as *is produced more accurately than*.

Hypothesis A: Present >> Plural

Hypothesis A predicts that *present* should be more accurate than *plural* to avoid ambiguity between the infinitive and the present tense, as shown in Table 4.6. We see that if the final -r is deleted in a target present form, then the resulting form would be identical to an infinitive. This is unlike the plural suffix because if the final -r is deleted, then the resulting form is not homophonous to the stem.

Table 4.6. Present and Plural Morphemes in Swedish

Present marker		Plural marker	
tala/tala-r	talk/talks	häst/häst-ar	horse/horses
gå/gå-r	walk/walks	röst/röst-er	voice/voices
se/se-r	see/sees	flicka/flick-or	girl/girls

If the [r] were omitted from the first column, then the two forms (infinitival and inflected) would be identical (e.g. 'tala' (infinitive) / 'tala' (present)), whereas if the [r] were omitted from the second column, then the two forms would remain distinct (e.g. 'häst' (horse) / 'hästa' (horses)). A principle of recoverability would predict that the present morpheme should be produced more accurately than the plural morpheme.

Hypothesis B: Plural >> Present

Hypothesis B, according to Abrahamsson, predicts that present-tense forms should be more accurate, as they are more predictable (and hence redundant) than plurals, because the tense of a sentence can often be inferred from the conversation. Number, conversely, cannot be predicted from the conversational turn and must, therefore, be specified on each noun. Plural is viewed as being more marked (when contrasted with singular), making it more important to preserve a surface plural [r] than a surface present [r].

4.6.1 The Data

Abrahamsson's data show that Hypothesis B is confirmed as the plural forms are produced more accurately than the present forms.

4.6.2 A Distributed Morphology Reanalysis

But let us consider what a representational (as opposed to functional) account of these facts would look like. Zhang (2014) proposes the structure of (67) for Mandarin plural marking.

(67)
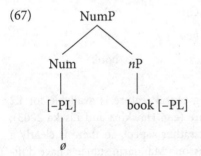

Singular Num head is null, but [PL] (and numerals) must be marked morphologically (Hsieh 2008; H. Yang 2005), as we see in (68).

(68)
Plural

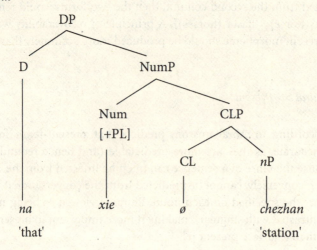

Numerals

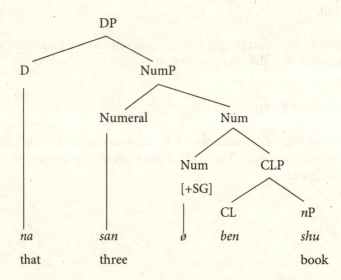

Thus, under this analysis, the L1 underlying plural feature is available for L2 spell out. As is well discussed in the literature (e.g. Hawkins and Liszka 2003), Mandarin does not have a tense feature but rather aspect, so there is clearly a learning task here for the L2er, and Abrahamsson's Mandarin subjects have difficulty with English tense marking. We do not need recourse to a functional principle such as *recoverability*.

Mandarin, however, does have a [finite] feature. Let us put this in the context of the data from Lardiere's (2007) subject Patty. Lardiere presented both spoken and written data which are illuminating, noted in Table 4.7.

Table 4.7. PATTY'S PAST AND PLURAL MARKINGS

Past tense production in obligatory contexts	Spoken: 35%
	Written: 78%
Plural marking in quantified expressions	Spoken: 58%
	Written: 85%
Plural marking in unquantified expressions	Spoken: 55%
	Written: 70%

Lardiere adopts the Prosodic Transfer Hypothesis (Goad and White 2006, 2019) to account for the lack of spoken affixes in English (where affixes adjoin to a Prosodic Word), unlike Mandarin (where they adjoin to the lexical root inside the Prosodic Word). However, the Prosodic Transfer Hypothesis would *not* explain the Swedish production data, which all have a singleton coda [r]. Thus, once again, morphosyntactic features are implicated in explaining the L2 Swedish data. The explanatory adequacy of such a Distributed Morphology–type analysis again reveals that we do not need to appeal to functional accounts of phonological phenomena. The representational linguistic models provide a satisfying account of morphological phenomena at the phonological interface.

4.7 CASE III: L2 ALLOMORPHY

In this section, I present the results of a project which investigated the acquisition of German plural affixes in second language learners. The literature on German phonology (e.g. Wiese 1996) has documented the various patterns extensively and noted the challenges of determining an adequate explanation for the observed alternations. Wiese (1996) observes that the German plural forms are prosodically homogenous in that they all consist of a $(\sigma_{strong} \cdot \sigma_{weak})$ pattern, but they are segmentally heterogeneous as illustrated in Table 4.8.

Table 4.8. GERMAN PLURAL VARIANTS

Singular form	Plural form	Affixation
Pelz (fur)	Pelz[ə]	Affixation of -ə
Kind (child)	Kind[ɐ]	Affixation of -ɐ
Held (hero)	Helden	Affixation of -n
Stecken (stick)	Stecken	Ø-Affixation

In addition to affixation (e.g. -ə, -ɐ, -n), plural can also be marked by umlauting, as shown in (69).[1]

(69) (a) Thron → Thron[ə] (throne)
      (b) Sohn → Söhn[ə] (son)
      (c) Mund → Münd[ɐ] (mouth)
      (d) Bund → Bünd[ə] (federation)

In 69(b) and 69(d) we see that the umlauted form can co-occur with the schwa suffix. In 69(c) we note that the umlauted form can co-occur with the dark-schwa suffix [-ɐ]. We can also note a learnability challenge in this tiny data set by comparing the segmentally similar forms in (a) and (b) and noting that one umlauts and the other does not. Compare this with (c) and (d), where the forms are again segmentally similar, but both umlaut while one takes the schwa and the other takes the dark schwa. For the phonologist, it is a challenge to state the generalization. For the L2 learner, it is a challenge to learn how the plurals are formed.

In addition to this productive variation, there is an interesting constraint on plural formation, which is that plural -n cannot co-occur with an umlauted vowel. So, the plural form for *godparent* is generated as shown in (70).

(70) Pat[ə] → Pate-n/*Päte-n

Note that the sequence of non-umlauted vowel ([a]) followed by the plural suffix -n is well formed, while the umlauted vowel ([ä]) followed by plural -n is ill formed. By contrast, -n which is non-plural *can* co-occur with an umlauted vowel with the plural form of *store* being generated as shown in (71).

(71) Laden → Läden

From an acquisition perspective, these patterns are interesting because they involve the acquisition of *multiple exponence*, which according to Matthews (1974: 149) is a phenomenon 'in which a category if positively identified at all, would have exponents in each of two or more distinct positions'. This can be shown in Table 4.9.

Table 4.9. MULTIPLE EXPONENCE
IN GERMAN PLURAL

Singular	Plural	
Arm	Arme	'arm'
Vater	Väter	'father'
Hals	Hälse	'neck'

---

1. From Wunderlich (1999).

Case III: L2 Allomorphy   147

The plural form of *neck* is different from the singular in that it has both an affix *and* the umlauted vowel, an example of multiple exponence.

The focus of this case study, though, is on the acquisition implications of the interaction between the *-n* suffix and the umlauting process. We see from the form *Hälse* in Table 4.9 that multiple exponence occurs in German. As defined by Harris (2017: 9), 'Multiple exponence is the occurrence of multiple realizations of a single morphosemantic feature, bundle of features, or derivational category within a word.' However, 'an alternation introduced by a phonological rule is not considered an exponent, and hence the alternation cannot involve this as one of the two morphemes in a relation of multiple exponence'. Thus, phonologically conditioned morphological phenomena are not instances of multiple exponence. As acquisitionists, the question that interests us is, *what are the learners acquiring when they are acquiring the knowledge that umlaut and plural -n cannot co-occur?*

This study is guided by the work of Trommer (2015, 2018). The theoretical machinery is designed to handle the spell out of a grammatical feature. Such a relationship of exponence is shown in (72).

(72) $[F] \Leftrightarrow \phi$

The schema in (72) is read as, 'the feature [F] has exponent phi.' For example, if the grammatical feature in English is the present participle, then this feature is realized as [ɪŋ]. We also need to be able to handle cases of contextual allomorphy (Bonet and Harbour 2012), as shown in (73).

(73)

$$[F] \begin{cases} \phi_1 \text{ Context}_1 \\ \\ \phi_2 \text{ Context}_2 \end{cases}$$

In such instances, the spell out of a single grammatical feature can vary predictably. This is not multiple exponence.

So, how does this connect to the German data in question? According to Trommer (2015, 2018), there is only a single plural affix. The relationship is as shown in (74).

(74) $[+pl]$ affix $\Leftrightarrow$ •
$$\mid$$
$$[\textsc{cor}]$$

The plural is spelled out as an underspecified CORONAL node. Feminine plural is spelled as shown in (75).

(75)   [+pl +fem] ⟷ [NASAL]

This then leads us directly to the question of why an umlauted vowel and the plural -n suffix cannot co-occur. The answer has to do with basic, universal properties of phonological architecture such as the architecture of feature dependency and the behaviour of association lines in (76).

(76)   *Feature Geometry*

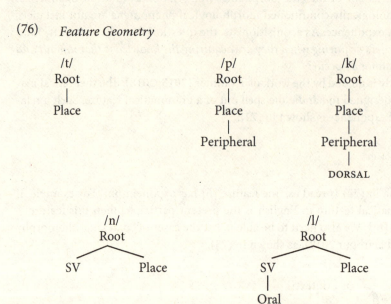

In terms of dependency relationships, we see that [peripheral] is a dependent of [place], while [DORSAL] is a dependent of [peripheral]. It is possible to have a bare Place node ([t]) or a bare Sonorant Voice (SV) node ([n]), but note that a structure where [peripheral] is a dependent of [DORSAL] is not sanctioned by general phonological principles (or UG).

Remember that Trommer (2015) notes the two spell outs of features (in German) given in (77).

(77)   [+pl] ↔ COR
       [+pl +fem] ↔ NAS

Case III: L2 Allomorphy

In terms of feature geometric representations, then, this would lead to the representations shown in (78).

(78)
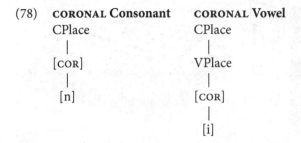

Crucially, the [CORONAL] feature can be expressed either as a vowel *or* as a consonant, but not both. I will return to the explanation of the ill formedness of jointly linked forms in Section 4.7.1.8 when I discuss the results of an experimental study.

4.7.1 L2 Learners

Archibald (2022c) looked at 154 learners of L2 German in an introductory university class in North America. The data were collected as part of the regular instruction of the university class. No other information on the subjects was collected. The tests were taken in class and marked by the regular instructional team. The anonymous test papers were passed on to me to analyse the plural data provided by the subjects. The main research question was, *will they produce [umlaut]$_{Root}$ + -n forms?* If so, they might be violating certain phonological universals.

4.7.1.1 METHODOLOGY
The data were gathered via two fill-in-the-blanks tests (approximately one month apart) which included sections on German plurals. The tests were administered in class and later marked by the professors and teaching assistants. At Time 1, the question would give the article + noun and ask the student to write in the plural form, as shown in (79).

(79) Der Apfel _____

At Time 2, the question would show a picture of the target noun, as shown in Figure 4.3, and ask the student to write in the plural (including the article).

Die Geschenk   Die Zeitungen

Figure 4.3. Picture task

Test Items T1

> Der Apfel (apple)   Die Äpfel
> Die Wurst (sausage)   Die Würste
> Die Tomate (tomato)   Die Tomaten
> Die Suppe (soup)   Die Suppen
> Der Salat (salad)   Die Salate
> Das Ei (egg)   Die Eier

Test Items T2

> Die Haltestelle ((bus) stop)   Die Haltestellen
> Der Zug (train)   Die Züge
> Das Geschenk ((birthday) present) Die Geschenke
> Das Taxi (taxi)   Die Taxis
> Der Koffer (suitcase)   Die Koffer
> Die Zeitung (newspaper)   Die Zeitungen
> Das Flugzeug (airplane)   Die Flugzeuge

Having received the anonymized student tests, I tabulated the results, and then looked at the wrong answers to assess what *type* of wrong answer it was. I classified the errors in one of two ways. A Type A error on the one hand consisted of choosing the wrong (but a *possible*) allomorph as shown in (80).

(80)   Wursten; Wurste   ←   <u>Würste</u>

In this case, for the singular *Wurste*, the student would not choose the actual plural *Würste* but would write either the *-n* suffix without umlauting (*Wursten*), or neither umlauting nor writing the *-n* suffix (*Wurste*); both forms are phonologically

Case III: L2 Allomorphy

well formed (i.e. possible German words). A Type B error on the other hand consisted of choosing the wrong (and an *impossible*) allomorph as shown in (81).

(81) **Würsten** ← Würste

In this case, the student produces a form which has *both* the umlauted vowel *and* the *-n* suffix; this is not phonologically well formed and is an impossible German word.

Let us explore, then, why some non-targetlike answers are possible (Type A) but other answers are impossible (Type B). Both of the forms in (80) are well formed, as they follow the conventions of feature dependency and none of the association lines crosses, as shown in (82).

(82)

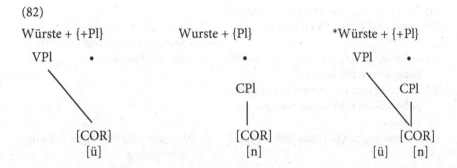

However, the form in (81) would be ill formed because the doubly linked [CORONAL] feature would entail the crossing of association lines as shown in (83).

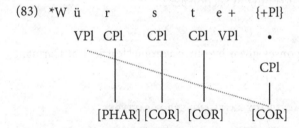

At this point, we are able to articulate the first pass at a hypothesis: *if* the L2 learners' interlanguage phonological grammars respect the universal principles of CORONAL licensing and association lines, *then* forms with doubly associated coronals should not occur systematically.

4.7.1.2 THE TASK
However, for that hypothesis to be coherent, we want to be confident that the task taps into phonological knowledge. My short answer is *yes, it does*.

4.7.1.3 Phonology, Silent Reading, and Lexical Activation

There is much literature which demonstrates that silent reading activates phonology. Table 4.10 summarizes very briefly some of the evidence.

Table 4.10. Phonology in silent reading

Task	Phonological effect
• Acoustic influence in letter cancellation. Cross-out the letter *e*. (Corcoran 1966, 1967)	• More errors result when the *e* is not pronounced
• Visual tongue twister effects (McCutchen and Perfetti 1982)	• Tongue twisters take longer to read silently
• Prosodic constraints on reanalysis (Bader 1998) 　(a) *In order to help the little boy put down the package he was carrying.* 　(b) *Peter knew the answer would be false.*	• More effortful to reanalyse longer embedded clauses
• Relative clause ambiguity attachment (Fodor 2002) 　(a) Someone shot the servant of the **actress** [**who** was on the balcony] 　(b) Someone shot the **servant** of the actress [**who** was on the balcony with her husband]	• Short RCs tend to have low attachment while long RCs have high attachment
• Electromyography (McGuian and Dollins 1989)	• Muscular activity triggered during silent reading

4.7.1.4 Bilingual Lexicon and Non-selective Access

There is also a large body of psycholinguistic literature on the architecture of the bilingual lexicon which shows the role of phonology in silent reading lexical access tasks. We reviewed this literature in Section 4.5.3.

4.7.1.5 Results

Let us now look at the responses given by our classroom learners of German, shown in Table 4.11.

Table 4.11. Accuracy rates and error patterns

	Time 1	Time 2		Totals	
Subjects	87	67		154	
Test Items	522	469		991	
Correct	292	239		531	
Type A Error	225 (43%)	71 (15%)	159 (33%)	296 (30%)	159 (16%)
Type B Error	5 (.9%)	2 (.4%)		7 (0.7%)	

NOTE: The second cell for Type A errors under T2 and Total (enclosed in a box) indicates that the test item was left blank.

Case III: L2 Allomorphy   153

As would be expected from introductory-level students, they made plenty of errors. Remember that the T2 test had only a picture as the stimulus (not the singular word). This different task accounts for the high number of blank responses at T2. I have scored them as errors but have separated them out in the accounting. Note that the Type B (i.e. impossible) errors are very infrequent, at seven out of 991 items (0.7%). The actual Type B errors are given in (84), where the doubly assigned [CORONAL] is bolded.

(84)   Die Zügen (*trains*)
        Die Zeitüngen (*newspapers*)
        Die Tömaten (*tomatoes*)
        Die Würsten (*sausages*)
        Die Süppen (*soups*)

The question we must ask is, *are these* errors *or* mistakes? I am drawing here on the traditional applied linguistics terminology (Corder 1967) in which systematic deviations are referred to as errors (and are assumed to reflect the learner's actual linguistic competence) while non-systematic deviations are referred to as mistakes (and are assumed to be performance phenomena). Before looking at the statistical analysis, it is worth noting that none of these forms involved umlauting a front vowel; they seem to know what umlauting is/does.

To see whether there was a significant difference in the frequency of Type A versus Type B errors, I ran a chi-squared test, and the results are given in Table 4.12.

Table 4.12. CHI-SQUARED RESULTS OF TYPE A VS. TYPE B ERRORS

	Observed N	Expected N	Residual
Type A	296	151.5	144.5
Type B	7	151.5	−144.5
Total	303		

chi-squared	275.64
df	1
asymptotic significance	.000

The chi-squared results show clearly that the Type B errors occurred significantly less often than the Type A errors. For this reason, it would be more accurate to refer to these deviations from the native target as *mistakes*.

The pattern that we see here, I would argue, is *not* that they don't produce things they don't hear, and they never hear umlaut+n. Rather, it would be more accurate to note that they don't produce *illegal* structures that they don't hear but they produce *legal* structures that they don't hear. The legal structures are structures licensed by universal properties of phonological representations. In Table 4.13, the target form is in the right-hand column, and the erroneous forms produced by the subjects (which are never heard in the input) are in the left-hand column. These erroneous forms are, however, well-formed possible plurals.

Table 4.13. WELL-FORMED (TYPE A)
ERRORS WHICH ARE NOT IN THE INPUT

Wursten; Wurste	←	Würste
Apfels; Apfelen	←	Äpfel
Süppe	←	Suppen
Tomate; Tomates	←	Tomaten

But what of the ill-formed items (which occur 0.7% of the time)? To delve into why they are not possible hypotheses in the interlanguage grammars of our subjects, let us turn to the question of what makes an impossible grammar impossible. Ultimately, this is what will allow me to argue that the 0.7% of the forms are, in essence, noise in the data, performance errors which do not reflect grammatical competence.

4.7.1.6 NO IMPOSSIBLE (L2 TURKISH) GRAMMARS

Özçelik and Sprouse (2016) investigated the acquisition of a type of vowel harmony they refer to as 'non-canonical' in L2 Turkish learners. Vowel harmony is an example of what looks like a non-local spreading operation, but when viewed with a particular phonological model, the harmony process is governed by tier-based locality. As we saw earlier, feature geometry encodes markedness and dependency relations. Place features (such as [CORONAL] or [DORSAL]) can be found on either consonants or vowels. A [CORONAL] consonant might be a consonant made at the alveolar ridge like [t] or [d], while a [CORONAL] vowel would be a front vowel like [i] or [e].

The example in (85) shows how the [CORONAL] feature under the Vowel Place (VPlace) node spreads to the right so that the two vowels in the word agree in place (i.e. are both front ([CORONAL]) vowels). This would be 'canonical' vowel harmony.

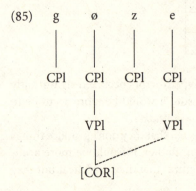

4.7.1.7 Secondary Feature Spreading

The example in (86) shows that the [CORONAL] feature can also be found on a Consonant Place (CPlace) node to indicate secondary articulation. A secondary [CORONAL] feature represents palatalized consonants.

(86)
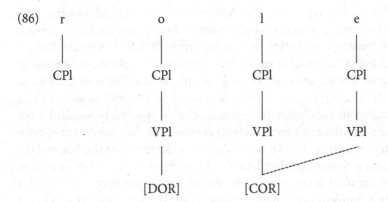

In this form, the word contains both a back vowel and a front vowel. The place feature of the front vowel [e] is the result of the spreading of the [CORONAL] feature from the adjacent palatalized [l].

4.7.1.8 No Crossing Constraint

There is a general phonological principle that blocks the crossing of association lines. Thus, the form given in (87) with two back ([DORSAL]) vowels is ill formed, as it would require the crossing of association lines. The vowel feature from the /o/ cannot spread to the /a/.

(87)
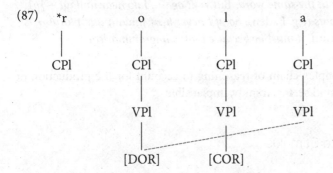

Özçelik and Sprouse (2016) explore the implications of these phonological principles with respect to learner grammars. Strikingly, they observe that the learners do not entertain hypotheses which include such ill-formed structures.

They note that learners receive no classroom instruction on these (relatively infrequent) forms. In spite of the lack of input, the grammars manage to be consistent with universal representational principles.

4.7.1.9 NO IMPOSSIBLE (L2 GERMAN) GRAMMARS

I argue that the classroom learners in Archibald (2022c) are not hypothesizing 'impossible' German grammars which contain doubly associated [CORONAL] features with crossing association lines as we saw in (83). Furthermore, I argue that the blocking of the multiple association of [CORONAL] (which would result in the co-occurrence of an umlauted vowel with a plural -*n* suffix) is an instance of the poverty of the stimulus. Let us consider other possible explanations. To rule out the most obvious possibility, the ungrammaticality of umlaut+plural[n] is not taught in class. For the most part, students are told that they need to memorize the plural form of a given singular noun. But the students make mistakes, and the mistakes generate forms that they have not heard from their teacher or read in the textbook. So, what licenses a certain class of mistake but bans another? This is potentially a problem of indirect negative evidence (see Schwartz and Goad 2017). If it is not a delimiting of the hypothesis space which blocks the Type B errors, then we would have to ascribe a reasoning process to the learner along the following lines:

Sometimes I hear umlaut in plural words (e.g. Würste*). And the plural word can include and umlaut and a suffix.*

> 'Sohn' → 'Söhne' {umlaut + [ə]}
> 'Mund' → 'Münder' {umlaut + [ɐ]}

Sometimes I hear -n in plural words (e.g. Suppen*). But wait, I never hear umlaut and plural -n together in the same word. But wait again, I do hear umlaut + [n] in monomorphemic roots (e.g.* Läden*). So, if I never hear umlaut and plural -n together in the same word, it must be because that is ungrammatical.*

To rely on such a complex chain of reasoning to account for the production of virtually *all* of the stimuli seems, frankly, implausible.

4.7.2 Poverty of the Stimulus

The argument for the poverty of the stimulus succeeds when we note that the environmental evidence for the learner to hypothesize a ban on the [CORONAL] node to the CPlace suffix and the VPlace root vowel is without a doubt impoverished. And yet, this is the ban that seems to describe the grammar.

Trommer's (2018) version of the No Crossing constraint adopted by Özçelik and Sprouse (2016) includes the two constraints given in (88).

Case IV: Intraword Codeswitching   157

(88)   • No Crossing Lines
          • A Place node dominated by a CPlace node may not associate across
            another CPlace node
       • No multiple linking
          • [COR] links to *either* CPlace OR VPlace

The behaviour of the subjects in this project is consistent with these principles. In acquiring this instance of phonologically conditioned allomorphy (not multiple exponence), their IL grammars respect the universal principles evident at the morphology/phonology interface.

4.7.3 Summary

The data collected from the 154 introductory German students confirm that their interlanguage grammars do not allow the crossing of phonological association lines, thus suggesting that they are grammars constrained by universal phonological principles. It has oft been suggested that linguistics is a bit of an outlier in the social sciences or humanities in that data on what is *not* allowed or *not* observed is paramount, but that is the critical pattern in the data here. As would be expected, students in an introductory foreign language class make numerous errors. However, the correct forms (531) and Type A errors (296) don't tell the whole story. The 7/991 (0.7%) are notable in their absence, and that is part of the tale as well.

This case study has shown us how phonological theory can help us to understand L2 morphological behaviour and also can add to our understanding of the nature of bilingual representation. The next phenomenon we will turn to is also illuminating when it comes to documenting and explaining the complexity of bilingual knowledge and ability.

4.8 CASE IV: INTRAWORD CODESWITCHING

There is a growing literature on language mixing and Distributed Morphology (see Alexiadou et al. 2015; Stefanich et al. 2019; López 2020). These works probe the fascinating phenomenon of intraword code switching (ICS) such as the forms in (89) taken from bilingual Norwegian/English speakers:

(89)   Så   play-de   dom   game-r
       then   play-PAST they   game-INDEF.PL
       'Then, they played games.'

       Så   close-a   di   åpp   kjist-å
       so   close-PAST they   up   casket-DEF.SG.
       'Then they closed up the casket.'

The affixes come from the terminal nodes on a Norwegian syntactic structure. However, note that an L2 (English) lexical item can get inserted into an L1 syntactic skeleton, as is evidenced from the Norwegian sentence structure (with the verb in second position (V2)); English does not evidence V2 syntax. Such intraword codeswitching is found in many language pairs. An example of Spanish/English intraword codeswitching would be as in (90).

(90) Voy a *hang*ear con mis amigos
      'I'm going to hang with my friends.'

Stefanich (2019) surveyed 57 case studies and noted the following facts:

- Switches between derivational and inflectional suffixes are not attested in the corpora. That is to say, the derivational and inflectional suffixes are always in the same language. One example is kalp-ify-ed (with a Telugu root and English affixes; from Bandi-Rao and den Dikken (2014)).
- As far as can be determined from the corpora, the phonology of a morphologically mixed word will come from the language of the *affixes*.

4.8.1 ICS and Phonology

Stefanich (2019) also conducted some insightful experiments to probe the question of whether the mixed words in question showed evidence of one single phonology or two phonologies mixed.

The first phase of the project tested which phonological system(s) a Spanish/English bilingual utilizes in the production of verbs with English roots and Spanish affixes. The hypothesis to be tested was that Spanish phonology would be exclusively applied across the word since Spanish is the language of the affixes. To test this claim, elicited production tasks were completed by 19 English-dominant US English / Mexican Spanish bilinguals who identified as naturalistic code-switchers and had positive attitudes towards codeswitching (CS). The attitudinal factor was important to control for (see Badiola et al. 2017, for a discussion of effects of attitude on CS behaviour), given that in some environments codeswitching is judged negatively; think of the negative connotations of words such as *franglais* or *Spanglish*. Nonce verbs were used to address the challenges of teasing apart codeswitches (a change from one language to another) from borrowings (in which a word from one language has been incorporated into the lexicon of the other). To identify any instances of phonological switching, each English verb in the codeswitching task contained one of three phonemes that are not part of Mexican Spanish: /z/, /θ/, /ɪ/. Thus, if these sounds are used, it is diagnostic of a switch to English phonology. The task is outlined in (91).

Case IV: Intraword Codeswitching 159

(91) Slide 1: *Repite por favor* [please repeat]. To mip.

Slide 2: To mip *es cuando bailas* [is when you dance] to your favorite song in an empty room. *Angela* lives in a studio apartment and she mips every night. *¿Qué está haciendo en la foto?* [What is she doing in the picture]

Slide 3: *Está* _____.   Expected answer: *Está mipeando.*

Stefanich (2019) finds evidence of application of Spanish phonology across the three English phonemes. English /z/ was produced as a Spanish-like [s] in the English root of the mixed word by 50% of the bilinguals. The remaining participants produced [z], which might have been construed as the application of English phonology. However, analysis of these participants' monolingual Spanish production of /s/ in a voicing assimilation context revealed production of [z] in this context. This could be a case of phonetic drift (see Chang 2019). The bilinguals produced /ɪ/ as [i] in the codeswitching task, which she takes as an indication that the participants applied only Spanish, and not English, phonology in morphologically switched words. In the case of mixed words with /θ/ in the English root, she finds evidence of substitution of /θ/ via a handful of Spanish-like sounds, namely [t̪], [s], [z], [v], and [f].

To complement the production study, Stefanich conducted an aural judgement task (with 30 early Spanish/English bilinguals as judges) to tap the participants' I-language by testing the acceptability of phonologically codeswitched words (see e.g. González-Vilbazo et al. 2013; Schütze and Sprouse 2014, for motivation for this type of method). The task consisted of morphologically switched verbs with English roots and Spanish progressive morphology; the stimuli were the same as those used in the production task in the codeswitching session. Each trial belonged to one of three conditions: items produced with English phonology only, Spanish phonology only, or phonology matching the morphology of the item (i.e. English phonology in the root and Spanish phonology in the affixes). The results confirmed the findings from the production task. The judges rated the words using a scale of 1 (completely unacceptable / not a possible answer in Spanglish) to 7 (completely acceptable / a possible answer in Spanglish). The rating scores were z-score transformed to account for individual variation in scale use. The bilingual judges assigned the highest ratings to items produced with Spanish phonology (the language of the affixes), lower ratings to the phonologically switched items (i.e. two phonologies), and the lowest ratings to items produced with English phonology. This is in line with the hypothesis that the phonology of a morphologically switched word must be the language of the affixes.

The acceptability judgement task is also revealing in that it taps into the I-language of bilinguals. It demonstrates that the lack of phonological switching within a word is not merely the result of physical constraints on the switching system. The results suggest this is not a production issue.

4.8.2 Why No Phonological Switching?

This raises the interesting question of why our grammars allow morphological switching but not phonological switching. As Stefanich (2019) notes, lexicalist approaches such as MacSwan and Colina's (2014) PF Interface Condition assume that morphology and phonology should pattern together. However, building on work within a non-lexicalist framework (González-Vilbazo and Lopez 2011; López, Alexiadou, and Veentra 2017), we can see that the empirical data are consistent with Distributed Morphology (Halle and Marantz 1993) insofar as the vocabulary items are delinked from their phonological spell out and there is a single-engine underlying word and phrasal behaviour.

It strikes me that there are two possible classes of answers to the question of intraword phonological integrity. The first is that it has something to do with the production system or perhaps neurolinguistics processing (Gwilliams et al. 2018). Perhaps humans are unable to switch within a complex unit that could be spoken in 500 ms. There is a cost to switching. Blanco-Elorrieta, Emmorey, and Pylkkänen (2018: 9708) in an investigation of language switching in bimodal (ASL/English) bilinguals show that 'the burden of language switching lies in disengagement from the previous language as opposed to engaging a new language and that, in the absence of motor constraints, producing two languages simultaneously is not necessarily more cognitively costly than producing one'. If we extrapolate from these findings and we take the language of the syntactic frame to be the one which generates the language of the affixes and Selkirk's (2011) Match Theory (to be discussed again in Chapter 5) dictates that the phonological word match the language of the X^0, then it follows that it would be costly to disengage this language and switch to the phonology of the root. We can certainly argue that the tendency to phonological uniformity does not arise from seeking to meet the needs of the listener. We know that listeners can comprehend language that consists of the properties of more than one language. This is what happens in the everyday phenomenon of listening to accented speech. Blanco-Elorrieta and colleagues (2021) describe the neurological mechanisms by which 'humans adapt to systematic variations in pronunciation rapidly'. In more traditional second language acquisition research, this has been demonstrated by Clarke and Garrett (2004) and Reinisch and Weber (2012). It is also well supported by the work of Munro and Derwing (1995), which demonstrates that highly accented speech can be perfectly intelligible. Archibald (2019) places this notion of intelligibility within the context of models of word recognition.

Another possibility is that the block of phonological switching results from the process of derivation, particularly derivation by phase. Collins and Stabler (2016: 44) label this spell-out process *transfer*: 'Transfer is an operation that maps the syntactic objects built by Merge to pairs <PHON, SEM> that are interpretable at the interfaces.' Perhaps transfer is not fine grained enough to send units smaller than the phonological word (see Newell and Piggott (2014), for interesting discussions of phonology and derivation by phase).

Marantz (2001: 6/,7) notes that little x's determine the edge of a phase. So the 'combination of a root and little x is shipped off to LF and PF for phonological and semantic interpretation', as shown in (92).

(92)

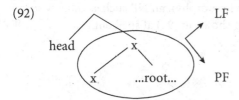

This idea is explored further in López, Alexiadou, and Veenstra (2017: 4), who argue for what they call the Phase Head Hypothesis, in which 'the phase head determines grammatical properties of its complement'. Furthermore (ibid.), they adopt the *Block Transfer Hypothesis*, which maintains that 'the material that is transferred to the interfaces is sent in one fell swoop'. The fact that the derivational morpheme decides the relevant phonology falls out from their Phase Head Hypothesis, given that the derivational morpheme is the spell out of the functional head which is the head of a phase. Such a model suggests that the contents of a phase would remain phonologically intact. This is supported by Dobler and colleagues (n.d.), who propose the notion of *phonological persistenc*e given in (93).

(93)　In the computation of phonology, there is a tendency to retain the phonological form that has been previously mapped to each individual phase constituent during later computation; that is, the phonology assigned to a phase will be maintained as much as possible during subsequent computation.

This means that phonological processes which target elements within a phase will be more 'destructive' than operations which occur across a phase boundary. Following this, a switch from language x to language y between tautophasal morphemes would be costly.

There is an additional reason why we would not expect intraword phonological switches, and that has to do with the nature of the phonology syntax interface. So, how are syntactic and phonological structures related? A consensus view has emerged recently (Yu 2019) that there is, by default, a correspondence between the two. This correspondence can be violated under certain circumstances. Such correspondences are articulated in Match Theory (e.g. Selkirk 2011; Tyler 2019).

Match Theory, broadly speaking, begins with the assumption of syntax-prosody isomorphism. Phonological structure is modelled via the Prosodic Hierarchy (Nespor and Vogel 1986) with modifications to earlier proposals which recognize that (a) not all languages may encode all levels (see Özçelik 2017b), and (b) recursive structures are permissible. The preferential mapping is between (a) syntactic phrases (XPs) and phonological phrases (φ), and (b) syntactic heads (X⁰s) and prosodic words (ω)[2]. Furthermore, it is assumed that CPs are mapped onto intonational phrases (ι). Within such a model (e.g. Tyler (2019) using a Bare Phrase Structure tree to emphasize the isomorphy), an NP such as *shallow structure* would have the structural mapping shown in (94) at spell out.

(94)

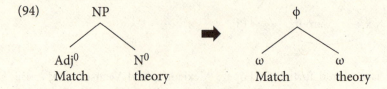

What this suggests is that the principles of Match Theory would dictate that the X⁰ (from a particular language) would map onto a phonological word (from the same language). Match Theory is easily adaptable to a multilingual context by introducing language tags (Archibald and Libben 2019), as previously discussed in Chapter 1, Section 1.4. The phonological spell out must match the language which triggers the generation of the syntactic structure. And the language of the X⁰ must match the language of the ω. Again, no special architecture is required to account for either the morphology or phonology of intraword codeswitching.

4.8.3 Summary

I think that we can draw some fairly broad conclusions from the intraword codeswitching literature. First of all there are descriptive patterns:

1. The affixes come from the language of the syntactic tree.
2. The root might be from either language.
3. The phonology is from the affix language and does not switch across morphemes.

There are also theoretical consequences that flow from these empirical facts:

1. The insertion of a root from the non-dominant language suggests root competition in the spirit of Distributed Morphology. Just as affixes compete for insertion, so do roots across languages.

---

[2]. These preferences are, in fact, modelled as violable constraints, the details of which are not crucial to my argument.

Conclusion 163

2. The fact that the phonology does not switch across morphemes is consistent with what we would expect if interlanguage grammars are subject to the principles of derivation by phase (i.e. phonological persistence) and the constraints of Match Theory (where $X^0 = \omega$).

4.9 CONCLUSION

In Chapter 3, I set the foundation of a model of SLA at the phonetics/phonology interface which is built upon complex abstract representational models of phonological knowledge. What I have argued via the case studies in this chapter is that such a model is consistent with the empirical facts that we see at the phonology/morphology interface and consistent with the architecture outline by Embick (2010).

I have illustrated the role of phonology in the acquisition of morphemes and in multilingual lexical representation and access. I have supported the Homogeneity Hypothesis and argued for the explanatory adequacy of Distributed Morphology when it comes to root competition (interlingual allomorphs) in the bilingual lexicon. Distributed Morphology was also shown to be relevant in that it predicted the fact that codeswitching should be found at both the word and sentence level given the single engine of complex structure which drives the model. We also saw how the construct of Match Theory (which connects phonological and morphological words) could also explain elements of interlanguage grammars. The IL grammars are constrained by such universal properties. The case study of phonologically conditioned allomorphy also showed how interlanguage grammars were constrained by universal principles and processes of phonology.

What we turn to in the next chapter is a discussion of the phonology/syntax interface. We will see the central role that abstract, complex phonological representations play at this interface too.

5

The Phonology/Syntax Interface

5.1 INTRODUCTION

In the field of generative approaches to second language acquisition (GenSLA), I think it is fair to say that little attention has been given to the phonology/syntax interface (cf. Fodor 2002) in SLA, though, of course, it has been addressed in the theoretical literature (Elfner 2015). In this chapter I present two distinct research projects. The first has to do with sentence processing in Deaf learners of English, the second with L2 learners of Japanese WH-questions. What these case studies show is that complex, abstract models of phonology are central to accounting for linguistic phenomena at this interface. The first demonstrates this with respect to syntactic comprehension, the second with respect to syntactic production.

5.2 L2 SENTENCE PROCESSING

Sagae (2007) shows how phonology affects L2 syntactic interpretation. Her work also provides an interesting case which expands our understanding of *redeployment* and which further demonstrates the need for viewing phonology as cognition.

Sagae looks at the sentence processing strategies and preferences of Deaf learners of English. Her data reveal that representations from a gestural language can be redeployed into a spoken L2. By discussing her work, I hope to show (a) how phonology can affect syntax, and (b) how redeployment can take place cross-modally (from gestural phonology to spoken phonology). Such facts support the view of phonology as cognition, given that the processes are not articulatorily driven.

As we will see, there is a relationship between prosody and sentence processing in silent reading. Even though silent reading does not involve articulation, it does involve phonological processing. Many questions arise in the field, but the one I focus on here is the question of whether people with hearing

---

Phonology in Multilingual Grammars. John Archibald, Oxford University Press. © John Archibald 2024.
DOI: 10.1093/oso/9780190923334.003.0005

deficits can acquire the necessary phonology in a spoken language to engage in the phonological processing necessary for the silent reading of sentences.

5.2.1 The Reading Process

Rayner and Pollatsek (1989) outline a model of reading which addresses word recognition and lexical access from long-term memory. In sentence reading, we certainly activate working memory as well, and working memory includes such elements as (a) a syntactic parser, and (b) a module for *inner speech*. Inner speech saves phonologically coded information which has been converted from the written input.

5.2.2 The Sentence Parser

Without getting into much detail at this point, the function of the parser is to assign a well-formed structure to an input string (see Berwick and Stabler 2019). There are points in a parse where more than one option is available, and, in a deterministic parser, a choice must be made. So, in a garden-path sentence such as *The horse raced past the barn fell*, the initial assignment of *raced* as the past-tense verb of the main clause has to be undone and reassigned as the participle of a reduced relative clause. Note how this ambiguity is resolved with different morphology as in *The horse taken past the barn fell*. Several principles have been invoked to guide the actions of the parser: late closure (Frazier 1978), early closure (Kimball 1973), dependency locality (Gibson 2000), relative clause attachment ambiguity (Cuetos and Mitchell 1988).

The details are not important, but these strategies are all designed to account for ambiguities which arise in sentences like those in (95).

(95) (i) Hans claimed he went to London last week.
(What happened last week, the *claiming* or the *going*?)
(ii) The boat floated on the water sank.
(Is *float* in the main clause?)
(iii) They knew the girl was in the closet.
(Is *the girl* in subject or object position?)
(iva) The reporter who attacked the senator admitted the error.
(ivb) The reporter who the senator attacked admitted the error.
(Why is the second sentence harder to process?)
(v) Someone shot the servant of the actress who was on the balcony.
(Who was on the balcony?)

It is sentences of types (iv) and (v) which we will focus on here. We need to go into a bit of detail to establish terminology, and I will do so in order of sentences given. First, the issues which arise from sentence of type (iv): the two areas of interest are (i) prosodic constraints on reanalysis, and (ii) relative clause attachment.

5.2.3 Prosodic Constraints on Reanalysis

As we saw from the garden-path sentences earlier, different grammatical sentences can have different degrees of processing complexity. At times the parser has to reanalyse the initial structure that is constructed and repair it. In both of the (b) sentences in (96), the second noun phrase (NP) is initially thought to be a direct object but then has to be reanalysed as the subject of an embedded clause:

(96) (a) In order to help the little boy Jill put down the package she was carrying.
    (b) In order to help the little boy put down the package he was carrying.

    (a) Peter knew the answer immediately.
    (b) Peter knew the answer would be false.

The (b) sentences are more difficult to process than the (a) sentences (Ferreira and Henderson 1991; Frazier and Rayner 1982). But note also that even though both (b) sentences require the same type of syntactic reanalysis, the second one (*Peter*) is much easier to process than the first one (*little boy*) (Gibson 1991; Gorrell 1995). What causes this differential difficulty?

Bader (1998) proposes the Prosodic Constraint on Reanalysis (PCR). He suggests that phonological encoding is implicated in silent reading, and that it is prosodic reanalysis which differentiates between the sentence types. His hypothesis is stated in (97):

(97) Revising a syntactic structure is difficult if it necessitates a concomitant reanalysis of the associated prosodic structure.

We will return to these structures, but we will also look at another set of structures which implicate the role of phonology in sentence processing.

5.2.4 Relative Clause Attachment Preferences and Prosody

Consider the sentence in (98):

(98) Someone shot the servant of the actress who was on the balcony.

If it is the *servant* who was on the balcony, we say that this is *high attachment* (HA). The structure for this interpretation is shown in (99).

(99)
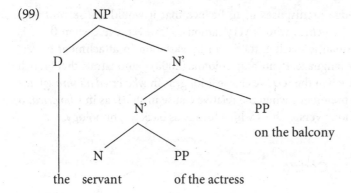

However, if the *actress* is on the balcony, we say the relative clause evidences *low attachment* (LA) in the syntactic structure. The structure for this interpretation is shown in (100).

(100)
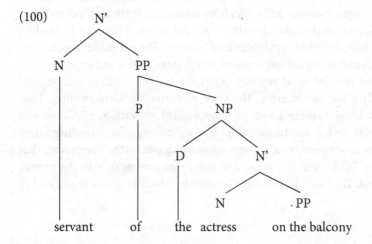

These attachment preferences vary cross-linguistically. English speakers prefer LA (Cuetos and Mitchell 1988). Spanish speakers prefer HA (Fernández 1998, 2003). Japanese speakers prefer HA (Kamide and Mitchell 1997). For the most part, the studies are reading studies, but Goad, Guzzo, and White (2020) demonstrate the influence that aural stimuli can have on the interpretation of ambiguous sentences in L2 learners. Of course, preference can be forced or biased pragmatically, as shown in (101).

(101) Someone photographed the servant of the actress who was serving tea.
       Someone photographed the servant of the actress who was very famous.

Our world knowledge predisposes us to believe that it would the *servant* who is serving tea and the *actress* who is very famous. However, even when there is no pragmatic or semantic biasing, there can be variation in attachment preference within a single language. Pynte and Colonna (2000) demonstrate that French speakers prefer HA when the relative clause is long, as in *who cried all through the night*, but show no preference when the relative clause in short, as in *who cried*. It is this construct of long versus short which brings us back to phonology.

5.2.5 Phonological Coding

There is much evidence to show that there is phonological activation (or *inner speech*) in silent reading. Corcoran (1966) showed that in a proofreading task where the instructions were to cross out the letter *e*, subjects were more accurate in crossing out *Es* that were pronounced compared with silent *Es*. Haber and Haber (1982) investigated the same question by looking at tongue twisters. By definition, tongue twisters are difficult to articulate. If there is no articulatory or phonological activation, then there should be no difference in reading speed between tongue-twister sentences and controls. The paired sentences were controlled for syntactic structure, number of syllables, and number of stresses. They found that the out-loud reading times for tongue twisters was significantly longer than for the controls. The same was true for silent reading. They concluded that silent reading involved phonological activation. McGuian and Dollins (1989) recorded electromyographic data during silent reading. They found that when silent-reading a 'p', there was contraction in the lip muscles (but not the tongue). When silent-reading a 't', there was contraction in the tongue (but not the lips). They concluded that phonological encoding was implicated in silent reading.

5.2.6 The Implicit Prosody Hypothesis

Fodor (2002: 113) proposed the Implicit Prosody Hypothesis (IPH) given in (102).

(102) In silent reading, a default prosodic contour is projected onto the
       stimulus, and it may influence syntactic ambiguity resolution. Other
       things being equal, the parser favors the syntactic analysis associated
       with the most natural (default) prosodic contour for the construction.

It is the IPH which is used to explain the variable attachment preferences we have seen. For short relative clauses (RCs) (e.g. *who cried*), there is a preference for LA. For long RCs (e.g. *who cried all through the night*), the preference is HA. Selkirk (2000) and Nespor and Vogel (1986) refer to a phonological domain between the Prosodic Word and the intonational phrase. We will call that (following Selkirk) a Major Phonological Phrase. A Minor Phonological Phrase combines Prosodic Words and Clitics into a single domain. Selkirk (2000) argues that the optimal length of a Major Phrase is *two* Minor Phrases (not one or three). Fodor (1998b) argues that there should be congruency between the syntactic structure and the prosodic structure (similar to the assumptions of Match Theory, which I introduced in the previous chapter and which we will return to in Section 5.3.2). She demonstrates this by considering the interpretation of a Japanese phrase like *the extremely kind student's sister*. This is a potentially ambiguous sentence which could mean (a) the sister of an extremely kind student, or (b) the extremely kind sister of a student. The preferred reading is (b), and the explanation is as follows. We assume something like the structure shown in (103) as the syntactic structure of the phrase:

(103)

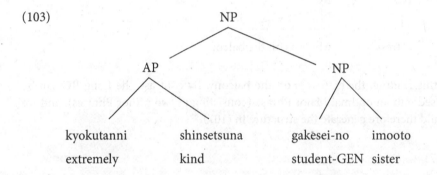

Note that the number of nodes on the left branch is the same as the number of nodes on the right branch (what Fodor calls a *balanced* structure). Let us look at the prosodic phrasing of the two examples in (104).

(104)   [[extremely kind student]'s // [sister]]   (3 Minor Phrases // 1 Minor Phrase)
       [[extremely kind] // [student's sister]]   (2 Minor Phrases // 2 Minor Phrases)

Given that the optimal length of a Major Phrase is 2 Minor Phrases and that we prefer congruent structure, the preferred parse is to have the two-Minor-Phrase structure map onto the binary-branching syntactic structure, and, as a result, the preferred interpretation is *the extremely kind sister of a student*.

Let us bring this discussion back to RC attachment preferences (short RC implies LA; long RC implies HA) in the kinds of sentences shown in (105) (where the bolding indicates the accented elements):

(105) (i) Someone photographed [$_{NP1}$ the **servant**] [$_{NP2}$ of the **actress**] [$_{SHORT RC}$ who was on the **balcony**]
(ii) Someone photographed [$_{NP1}$ the **servant**] [$_{NP2}$ of the **actress**] [$_{LONG RC}$ who was on the **balcony** with her **husband**]

Each instance of NP1 and NP2 is a Minor Phrase. The Short RC consists of a single Minor Phrase, while the Long RC consists of two Minor Phrases. Therefore, the Short RC in (105) above cannot stand alone as a Major Phrase and is, therefore, adjoined to the preceding phrase, as shown in (106).

(106)

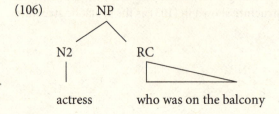

In this reading, the actress is on the balcony. By contrast, the Long RC can be parsed into an optimal Major Phrase (consisting of two Minor Phrases), and we would therefore generate the structure in (107).

(107)

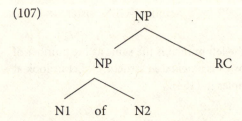

In this reading, the *servant* is on the balcony.

In summary, the RC length (as measured in phonological phrases) affects the RC attachment preference. To repeat the IPH, 'the parser favours the syntactic analysis associated with the most natural (default) prosodic contour for the construction.'

All of this clearly shows that the second language learner has to acquire not only the grammar of the new language but also the parsing procedures and preferences. The details of this cross-linguistic parsing literature are not, however, our focus here.

5.2.7 Phonological Coding and Hearing Loss

The question that interests us here is whether Deaf and Hard-of-Hearing subjects employ implicit prosody or inner speech in their silent reading of English. This is a question of some empirical import as it may affect their comprehension abilities in the L2. The two examples we have seen here have to do with processing difficulty and relative clause attachment interpretation. There are many complexities surrounding the study of the language and culture of Deaf communities, as well as complexities in probing the behaviour and educational needs of the Hard of Hearing. I do not claim to do the complexity justice here, as my focus will be narrow. Students with hearing loss have difficulty acquiring reading skills (as measured by comprehension tests) in the spoken language of the majority environment (Monreal and Hernandez, 2005). But how does this affect parsing routines or comprehension preferences which are implicated by phonological coding of the target language? Do hearing-loss subjects have inner speech? If they cannot hear and cannot speak, do they have phonological representations? Again, I am not delving into many of the complexities of ASL (or other gestural languages') phonology. We know that these gestural languages are natural languages which have phonological structure (though a different type of phonological structure than a spoken language has—see Sandler 2012). Treiman and Hirsh-Pasek (1983) look at second-generation Deaf subjects who had learned ASL from their parents. They asked them to judge the acceptability of the kinds of ill-formed English sentences given in (108).

(108) (i)   He doesn't like to eat meet.
       (ii) His favorite color is blew.
      (iii) He doesn't like to eat melt.
      (iv) His favorite color is bled.

If phonological encoding is implicated then sentences like (i) and (ii) would be more difficult than sentence (iii) and (iv). The hearing subjects made significantly more errors when judging the homophone sentence (i.e. *meet/meat*; *blew/blue*) than on control sentences (*melt*; *bled*). However, the Deaf subjects did not treat the categories differently, which indicates that they did not access phonological representations. However, a study by Hanson, Goodell, and Perfetti (1991) argued that native signers did show evidence of consulting English phonological representations when judging the acceptability of English tongue-twister sentences. Response times were longer, and error rates were higher for the tongue-twister sentences, which is consistent with the activation of added phonology; if it were just a visual task, then tongue-twister status should not have influenced reading time.

172 THE PHONOLOGY/SYNTAX INTERFACE

5.2.7.1 THE SUBJECTS AND METHODS

Sagae (2007) looked at subjects who had started their hearing loss before entering school. Some of the subjects had English as an L1, some had ASL. Their first written language was English. She administered an offline questionnaire study and an on-line eye-tracking task to the subjects. The questionnaire allowed them to indicate which sentence they found more difficult to comprehend, including sentences which required various combinations[1] of syntactic and prosodic reanalysis such as those in (109):

(109) According to her studies predict the volcano would erupt in less than
         one year.
         According to her studies the volcano would erupt in less than one year.
         Every time Harry calls his mother she is out.
         Every time Harry calls his mother is out.

5.2.7.2 PROSODIC CONSTRAINT ON REANALYSIS IN HARD OF HEARING

Frazier and Clifton (1996) find that there is a tendency to insert a prosodic break before a long adverbial phrase, which removes the need for prosodic reanalysis. This is revealed in the sentences given in (110).

(110) (a) John will explain to the kids that their grandfather died [$_{AP}$ after
              they come home from school].
        (b) ($_{CP}$ John will explain to the kids) ($_{CP}$ that their grandfather died
              [$_{AP}$ tomorrow]).

In (110b) the readers initially assign *tomorrow* to the adjacent verb phrase (VP) *died* because the short adjective phrase (AP) is included in the same embedded complementizer phrase (CP), but when this parse fails, the AP must be reassigned to the VP *explain* higher up. This requires both syntactic and prosodic reanalysis as shown in (111).

(111) ($_{CP}$ John will explain to the kids that their grandfather died) // ($_{CP}$ tomorrow)

I introduce the // notation to indicate a prosodic break. In the (110a) sentence, though, the prosodic break is inserted initially, which blocks the adjunction of the long AP to the lower verb *died*, as shown in (112).

---

1. There were several different kinds of sentences, and I won't get into the details. They involved such structures as subject-extracted versus object-extracted relative clauses, and long versus short relative clauses, etc.

(112) ($_{CP}$ John will explain to the kids that their grandfather died) // ($_{CP}$ after
they come home from school).

What I have shown here is that prosody plays a role in sentence processing. The
question we turn to now is how Deaf and Hard-of-Hearing (DH) subjects fare in
processing these types of sentences in English.

5.2.7.3 OFFLINE RESULTS
In the questionnaire, both hearing and DH subjects were similar in their
results: there was overwhelming consensus for the judgment that sentences
which required both syntactic and prosodic reanalysis were more difficult than
sentences which required no reanalysis. For the hearing subjects the ratio was
12:80 (i.e. there were 12 out of 80 instances where the subjects found the *no
reanalysis* sentence easier), and for the DH subjects the ratio was 26:74 (i.e.
there were 26 out of 74 instances where the subjects found the *no reanalysis*
sentence easier). In this case, we see that there is no difference between the
populations. The DH subjects are behaving like the NS of English, and we
might infer that they are doing so because they are invoking phonological
encoding.

5.2.7.4 EYE-TRACKING AND REANALYSIS
In the eye-tracking study, subjects were given 20 sentences which required no
reanalysis and 20 sentences which required both syntactic and prosodic reanalysis.
One of the key measurements was the fixation time on the items which were
candidates for reassignment, as in *the little boy* in the examples in (113).

(113) (a) In order to help *the little boy* // put down the package he was carrying.
       (b) In order to help *the little boy* put down the package he was carrying.

In the (113a) sentence we would expect longer fixation times on *the little boy* both
because it occurs before a prosodic break and because there will be regressions
back to this phrase as the parsing failure is discovered later in the sentence. In
the (113b) sentence, we would expect shorter fixation times on *the little boy* because no reanalysis is necessary. Therefore, the fixation times can be used as independent measures to processing cost.

We will see that the DH subjects were behaving very much like the hearing
subjects in that there was much more regression in the sentences which require
reanalysis than in the sentences which do not. The hearing subjects regressed significantly on 17 out of the 20 sentences, while the DH subjects did so on 15 out of
20. The gaze durations were significantly longer for the hearing subjects on 15 out
of 20 sentences and for the DH subjects on 16 out of 20.

The reanalysis result in both offline and online tasks indicate that the DH subjects are sensitive to the prosodic encoding of English sentences in silent reading and that this is influencing their parsing strategies.

5.2.7.5 IMPLICIT PROSODY AND RC ATTACHMENT IN HARD OF HEARING

Sagae (2007) looks at subjects who had started their hearing loss before entering school. Some of the subjects had English as an L1, some had ASL. Their first written language was English. She administered an offline questionnaire study and an online eye-tracking task to the subjects. The questionnaire allowed them to state their preferred interpretation of sentences such as those in (114).

(114) (i) Julia saw the secretary of the lawyer that was on vacation (short RC).
       (ii) Julia saw the secretary of the lawyer that was speaking on the phone all morning (long RC).

5.2.7.6 RESULTS: OFFLINE TASKS

On the task of determining which sentence was the most difficult to understand, there were no differences between the DH and the hearing subjects. Any difficulty in understanding the sentences could not be attributed to the length of the RC. What about attachment preference? All of her DH (Sign) subjects preferred HA in long RCs, and all but one preferred HA in short RCs. Thus, they were performing differently than the hearing subjects (who preferred LA) on these offline tasks, as shown in Table 5.1.

Table 5.1. ATTACHMENT PREFERENCES OF THREE GROUPS

	DH (Sign)		DH (English)		Hearing (English)	
	Short RC	Long RC	Short RC	Long RC	Short RC	Long RC
Preference	HA	HA	No preference	No preference	LA	LA

5.2.7.7 RESULTS: ONLINE TASKS

The same subjects were also participants in an eye-tracking study. The study looked at some other processing questions but included 10 short RC and 10 long RC sentences in order to observe attachment preference. Each RC sentence was followed by a question asking for the preferred noun to which the RC attaches. There were also random comprehension probes inserted to ensure that subjects read for meaning. Sample sentences included those in (115).

(115) (i) Tom will give you the cat that my dog chased after he buys a cage for it.
       (ii) The plumber adjusted the pipe of the sink that was cracked.

L2 Sentence Processing 175

We used an SMI EyeLink head-mounted eye-tracker. Total fixation time on N1 (e.g. *the pipe*) and N2 (e.g. *the sink*) were measured. Of the 9 DH subjects, 5 preferred HA in short RCs, 1 preferred LA, and 3 showed no preference; 5 preferred HA in long RCs, and 4 showed no preference. Remember that, given the Implicit Prosody Hypothesis, the HA would be triggered when the RC was long enough to form a Major Phrase or perhaps when there was a prosodic break inserted before the RC. However, the fixation times on the noun immediately preceding the RC were *not* different for the two types of sentences, and hence there is no indication that the DH subjects were inserting a prosodic break here. Sagae (2007) speculates that the HA preference may be transferred from the L1, but given that RC attachment in ASL is unambiguous (indicated by spatial marking), this would have to be pursued further in laboratory experiments.

The RC attachment data, then, suggest that the DH subjects were not performing like hearing subjects in either offline or online tasks. This suggests that they have not yet incorporated the relevant prosodic alignment strategies into their L2 parsing procedure. Remember though that the subjects did seem to be consulting the PCR in their processing of other sentences.

5.2.7.8 ASL PHONOLOGY
Signed languages have ways of marking the Major Phonological Phrase (Sandler and Lillo-Martin 2006) even though there is a modality difference. The phrase can be delimited by such things as lengthening the preceding sign, pausing between signs, or repeating the sign. Relative clauses, however, are structured quite differently in ASL. Recall that in English, relative clause attachment can lead to ambiguity; the sentence in (116) is structurally ambiguous:

(116)   Someone photographed the servant of the actress who was on the balcony.

There is nothing in the surface string which tells the reader who was on the balcony. However, in ASL, the relationship between the relative clause and the head of that clause is indicated overtly. Imagine that we found the structure of (117).

(117)   Someone photographed [the servant]$_a$ of [the actress]$_b$ [$_{RC}$ who$_{ab}$ was on the balcony].

We could indicate whether the RC was coindexed with either *a* or *b*, and this is what ASL does. The coindexation is achieved spatially, and thus RC attachment in ASL is unambiguous.

5.2.7.9 SUMMARY

We have, then, mixed results on the question of whether Hard-of-Hearing subjects can acquire English phonological encoding. One battery of tests suggests *yes* while the other suggests *not yet*. I would suggest that the results are consistent with the notion that they can redeploy their L1 gestural phonology to acquire spoken phonological representations but that this redeployment takes time. ASL has ways of marking the Major Phrase, and the subjects can acquire L2 ways to do this even though it is in a different mode. However, when it comes to RC attachment, the machinery in their L1 is *not* there to redeploy, and they have to learn a completely new parsing strategy for indicating coreference, and this appears to be more difficult.

The reanalysis results suggest that the subjects have acquired the appropriate representations. However, the RC attachment results suggest that the subjects still are not using them in a nativelike fashion. This is entirely as we would expect in looking at parsing procedures, that performance measures would be implicated.

I believe that the data are not consistent with a representational deficit position, which would argue that the DH subjects had not acquired spoken phonological representations. As we seek to formalize the construct of *redeployment*, this type of cross-modal redeployment presents fascinating opportunities for further research.

5.3 L2 WH-QUESTIONS

This section looks at another aspect of the phonology/syntax interface related to the formation of WH-questions. Richards (2010, 2016) articulates a theory which accounts for the variation between (a) languages which move WH-elements to the left periphery, and (b) languages which allow WH-elements to stay in place. English generates WH-questions via WH-movement as shown in (118).

(118)   *Whom* should Bob call?

Japanese, on the other hand, allows the WH-word to remain *in situ*, as shown in (119):

(119)   Mito-ga   *nani*-o   katta   no?
         Mito-NOM what-ACC bought +Q
         'What did Mito buy?'

L2 WH-Questions

In this section, I investigate the second language acquisition of Japanese WH-questions in order to explore whether the interlanguage grammars of the learners are subject to the grammatical principles laid out in the syntactic and phonological literature.

5.3.1 Contiguity Theory

Richards (2010, 2016) argues that there are two strategies to achieve the *contiguity* of the WH-word and the interrogative feature [+Q]. In English, surface linear adjacency realizes contiguity by moving the WH-word to the specifier of the CP position at the left edge. The WH-word is thus adjacent to where the phonologically null [+Q] feature resides, as shown in (120).

(120)
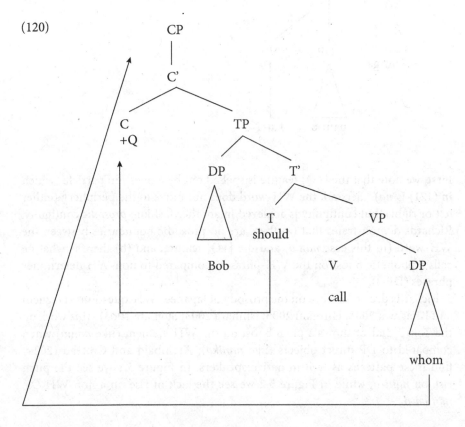

In Japanese, there are two noteworthy differences from the English structure, as we see in (121), 'What did Mito buy?'

(121)

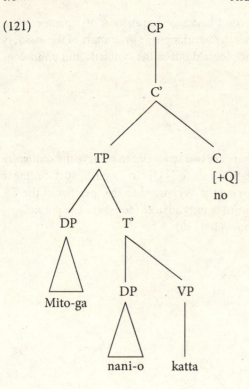

First, we note that the [+Q] feature is spelled out by a question particle (which in (121) is *no*).[2] Second, the WH-word does not move to the periphery (either left or right), but contiguity is achieved in another fashion: *prosodic* contiguity. Richards demonstrates that (a) there are no prosodic boundaries between the WH-word (in this case *nanio*) and the [+Q] feature, and (b) there is what he calls a phonetic boost on the WH-phrases (compared to non-WH determiner phrases (DPs)).

Richards draws on work on the prosody of Japanese WH-questions (Deguchi and Kitagawa 2002; Hirotani 2005; Ishihara 2003; Sughara 2003). This work on the Tokyo dialect shows a pitch boost on the WH-element (like *nanio*) when compared to DP direct objects (like *nanika*). Archibald and Croteau (2021) find these patterns as well in native speakers. In Figure 5.1 we see the pitch rise on *nani-o*, while in Figure 5.2 we see the lack of rise on a non-WH DP, *nanika-o*.

---

2. The particle *-ka* is used when there is a politeness marker in the sentence (see Miyagawa 2012).

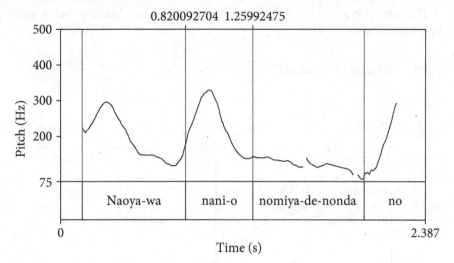

Figure 5.1. Pitch boost on a WH-question

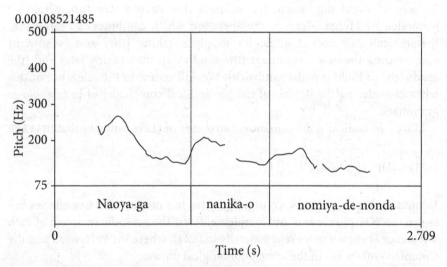

Figure 5.2. Lack of pitch boost on a declarative sentence

The structure for a Japanese interrogative would be (Japanese being right headed) as shown in (122):

(122) "What did Naoya buy?"

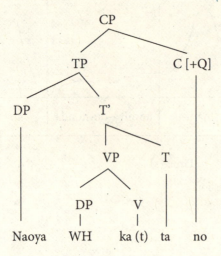

By way of slight digression, let me note that such a structure would be generated by Merge. Merge is the operation which combines categories into hierarchically structured units: for example, taking [the] and [sandwich] and building the new constituent [the sandwich], then taking [ate] and [the sandwich] to build [ate the sandwich]. We will return to the relevance of this when considering the denials of the hierarchical complexity of interlanguage grammars.

More schematically, the constituent structure of (122) would be that in (123):

(123)   [DP] [[$_{DP}$ WH] [V] $_{VP}$] C

Japanese achieves prosodic contiguity by having no prosodic boundaries between the WH-phrase and the Complementizer. The prosodic structure of such a sentence is shown more schematically in (124), where the WH-word and the Complementizer are in the same phonological phrase:

(124)   ($_\phi$ DP) ($_\phi$ WH   C)

Of course, in (119) there is only one word between the WH-word and the Complementizer. What of longer utterances? Longer utterances will have more phonological phrases. Richards (2010) follows Kubozono (2006) in the analysis that Japanese phonological phrases can be recursive, as shown in (125).

(125) "drank what at the bar?"

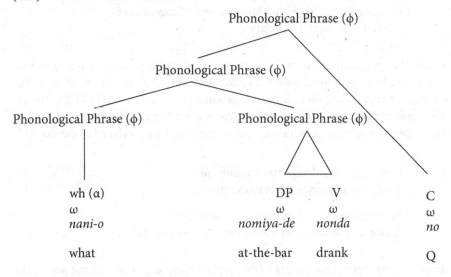

He refers to the highest phonological phrase as the WH-domain. Given a WH-phrase α and a Complementizer C, α and C must be separated by as few phonological phrase boundaries as possible.

This phonological phrasing would be generated in a fashion consistent with Match Theory (Elfner 2015; Selkirk 2011), which seeks to articulate the syntax-phonology interface. It was early on noted (Chomsky and Halle 1968: 372) that there could be a mismatch between phonological phrasing and syntactic phrasing as indicated non-technically in (126).

(126) a. Syntactic constituency: This is [$_{DP}$ the cat [$_{CP}$ that caught [$_{DP}$ the rat [$_{CP}$ that stole [$_{DP}$ the cheese]]]]]
b. Prosodic constituency: (This is the cat) (that caught the rat) (that stole the cheese)

In attempting to describe the domains of certain phonological phenomena, sometimes syntactic structures appear to be relevant. For example, English phrasal stress falls on the rightmost element in a syntactic phrase (Chomsky and Halle 1968), as shown in (127):

(127) [A syntactícian] and [a phonólogist] [walk into a bár]

Yet other phonological phenomena are predictable not by syntactic structures but rather by prosodic domains (examples from Nespor and Vogel 1986). Some patterns apply at the highest level of phonological utterance, such as Received Pronunciation English r-insertion which applies when there are adjacent vowels which can be adjacent even across sentences, as shown in (128).

(128) neve[r] again
       the giant Panda[r], as you know, is an endangered species
       That's a nice ca[r]. Is it yours?

Other changes, such as Tuscan spirantization (where stops become fricatives) are somewhat more restricted insofar as parenthetic material blocks the change. The domain of application, then, is the intonational phrase, as shown in (129). The orthographic 'c' words which are underscored are produced as the fricative [h] while the orthographic 'c' words which are not underscored are produced as the stop [k].

(129) i canarini congolesi costano molto cari
       'Congolese canaries are very expensive.'

       i canarini congolesi, come sai, costano molto cari
       'Congolese canaries, as you know, are very expensive.'

English stress retraction occurs within a phonological phrase but not across the boundary of two phonological phrases. The sentence in (130a) shows stress retraction while (130b) does not.

(130) (a) [pérseveres gladly]   (cf. persevéres)
       (b) [persevéres] [gládly and diligently]

So, how are syntactic and phonological structures related? A consensus view that has emerged recently (Yu 2019) is that there is, by default, a correspondence between the two. This correspondence can be violated under certain circumstances. Such correspondences are articulated in Match Theory (e.g. Selkirk 2011; Tyler 2019).

5.3.2 Match Theory

Match Theory, broadly speaking, begins with the assumption of syntax-prosody isomorphism. Phonological structure is modelled via the Prosodic Hierarchy (Nespor and Vogel 1986) with modifications to earlier proposals which recognize that (a) not all languages may encode all levels (see Özçelik 2017b), and (b) recursive structures are permissible. The preferential mapping is between (a) syntactic phrases (XPs) and phonological phrases (ϕ), and (b) syntactic heads (X⁰s) and prosodic words (ω)[3]. Furthermore, it is assumed that CPs are

---

3. These preferences are, in fact, modelled as violable constraints, the details of which are not crucial to my argument.

mapped on to intonational phrases (ι). Within such a model (e.g. Tyler (2019) using a Bare Phrase Structure tree to emphasize the isomorphy), an NP such as *shallow structure* would have the structural mapping shown in (131) at spell out:

(131)

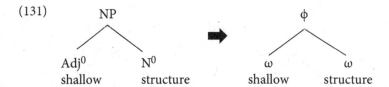

Remember we saw these correspondences in Chapter 4 when explaining the phonological and morphological properties of intraword code-switching.

Let us return to the Japanese structures in question. This transparent mapping between the syntax and the phonology would generate the structures (where the arrows indicate the mapping between the syntactic structure and the phonological structure) given in (132):

(132)

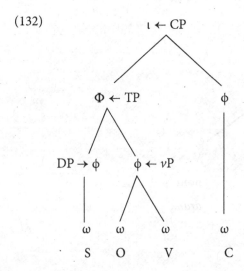

For the structure to be well formed the *in situ* WH-phrase must be followed by a minimal number of intervening φ-phrases.

Let us look at a specific example from Richards (2016). We begin with the declarative sentence 'Naoya drank something in the bar,' shown in (133):

(133)
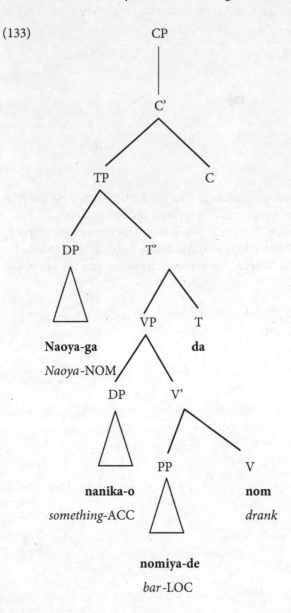

This syntactic structure would be mapped on the prosodic tree shown in (134):

(134)

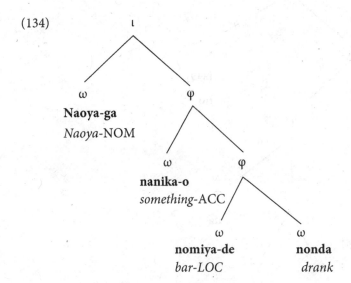

Richards argues that such prosodic trees (which, following van der Hulst (2010) and Féry (2010), are recursive) are generated by the narrow syntax as the derivation proceeds, not, as is standardly assumed, after the narrow-syntactic derivation is finished. Thus, abstract phonology is not merely a late spell-out routine. This, of course, has been recognized in the literature on derivation by phase (Dobler et al. n.d.). They also show that once phonological chunks get sent off to spell out, they tend not to be phonologically altered (the principle of phonological persistence).

Now let us consider the corresponding interrogative sentence 'What did Naoya drink at the bar?' shown in (135).

(135)

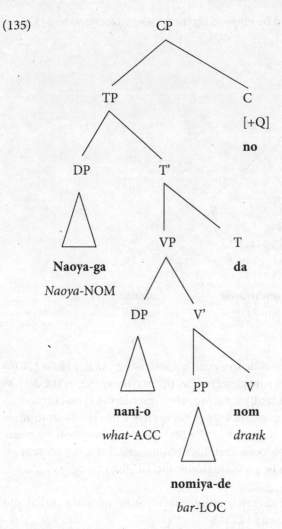

The generation of the prosodic tree proceeds through several intermediate steps which need not concern us here to arrive at the structure given in (136):

(136)

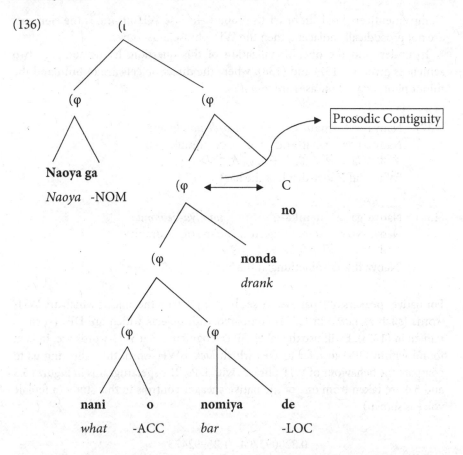

Each phonological phrase will have one prominent element. Note that *nanio nomiyade nonda* is a single phonological phrase. By having the pitch boost on *nanio*, it will be the most prominent element in the phrase, and there are no other prosodic peaks between *nanio* and *no*. In this way, prosodic contiguity is achieved and WH *in situ* is licensed.

5.3.3 What Is to Be Acquired?

The research question that arises out of probing the construct of prosodic contiguity is, *does Contiguity Theory hold for interlanguage grammars?* More specifically, we ask whether advanced L2 speakers are able to set up a phonological grammar with no prosodic boundaries between the WH-word and the Question

Complementizer ([+Q]) in order to properly license WH *in situ*. If the elements are not prosodically adjacent, then the WH-phrase must move.

To understand the operationalization of this question, let us compare two sentences given in (137) and (138), where the direct objects are in **bold** and the minor phonological phrases are in *italics*.

(137) Naoya-wa **nani**-o *nomiya-de nonda* no?
Naoya-TOP what-ACC bar-LOC drank +Q
ナオヤは、何を飲み屋で飲んだの？
'What did Naoya drink at the bar?'

(138) Naoya-ga **nanika**-o *nomiya-de nonda*.
Naoya-NOM something-ACC bar-LOC drank
ナオヤが、何かを飲み屋で飲んだ。
'Naoya drank something at the bar.'

For native speakers of Japanese, we see higher pitch on the objects which are WH-words (such as *nanio* in (137)) compared with objects which are DPs (such as *nanika* in (138)). I will use the label DP (recognizing that WH-words are, in fact, found within DPs) to refer to DPs which *lack* a WH-word, thus allowing us to compare the behaviour of WH-phrases with DPs. The spectrograms in Figures 5.3 and 5.4 are taken from one of the native speaker controls in this study (a female voice is shown).

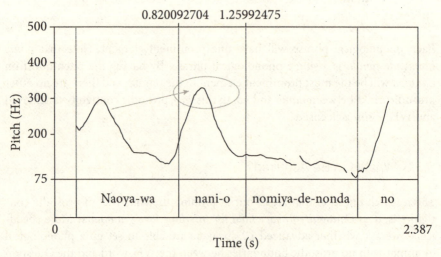

Figure 5.3. Pitch track of the WH-question shown in (137)

Note the pitch spike on the WH-phrase (*nanio*). Compare this with the declarative sentence of (138) produced by the same speaker shown in Figure 5.4.

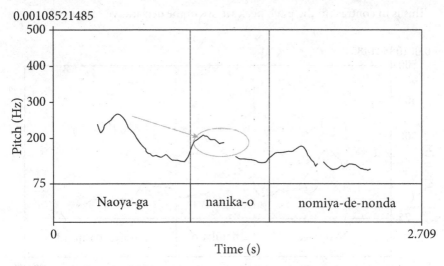

Figure 5.4. Pitch track of declarative sentence of (138) with DP object

Note the lower pitch (209 Hz) on the DP object (*nanika*). These pitch tracks are virtually identical to those given in Richards (2010: 144). Given this convergence, I assume that the production task is revealing the same properties of Japanese pitch as Ishihara (2003), and, thus, that native speakers of Japanese implement this pitch boost on WH-phrases.

Furthermore, there are no pitch peaks on the prosodic words (e.g. *nomiya de nonda*) which come between the WH-word and the [+Q] particle (as in Figure 5.5). The pitch tracks in Figures 5.5 and 5.6 are taken from one of our native speaker controls.

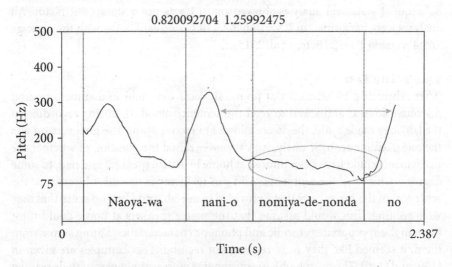

Figure 5.5. A native speaker recorded in our study demonstrating pitch compression

This is in contrast to the pitch peak we see in the declarative sentence:

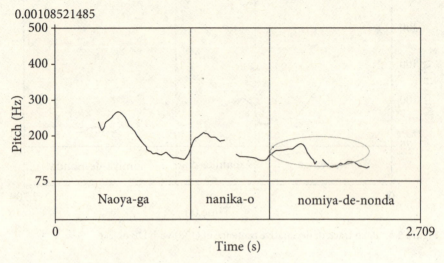

Figure 5.6. Native speaker pitch rise in declarative sentence

5.3.4 Methodology

Archibald and Croteau (2021) looked at 16 non-native speakers (NNS) of Japanese (and 6 native speaker controls) in a reading task to determine whether NNS of Japanese are able to acquire L2 grammars which observe this property of phonological contiguity. All non-native speakers were proficient in English, though four were native speakers of other languages (Cantonese, Mandarin, or Korean). Subsequent statistical analysis showed that L1 was not a significant factor. All analyses were performed in R version 3.2.3 (R Core Team 2015) with the package 'lme4' version 1.1-12 (Bates et al. 2015).

5.3.4.1 THE TASK

After rehearsing 19 sentences at home, subjects were told to assume a neutral discourse context and asked to read the sentence aloud. If, during recording in the lab, they made a slip, they were allowed to record again. The final version was the one used for acoustic analysis. A reviewer raised the question of whether the participants could have been tutored at home by native speakers and had, to some degree, memorized the sentences. All I can really say is that all subjects read the sentences of the paper copy that I provided in the lab, and I had no sense that they were reciting. This would assume that the native speakers at home could tutor them in the appropriate prosodic and phonetic characteristics. Sitting across from them, it seemed like they were reading not reciting. Two examples are given in (139) and (140). The morpheme-by-morpheme gloss was not part of their reading text. Both Roman and Japanese characters were included, however.

(139) Miki-wa   kinō   nani-o   kai-mashi-ta   ka?
      Miki-TOP   yesterday what-ACC   buy-POL-PAST   +Q
      ミキは、昨日何を買いましたか？
      'What did Miki buy yesterday?'

(140) Miki-wa   kinō   hon-o   kai-mashi-ta.
      Miki-TOP   yesterday book-ACC   buy-POL-PAST
      ミキは、昨日本を買いました。
      'Miki bought a book yesterday.'

Sentences were recorded on Audacity at 44.1 kHz, and pitch tracking was done via Praat 6.0.09 (Boersma and Weenink 2019) after exporting the .wav files from Audacity. An example of the pitch tracking from one of the non-native subjects is shown in Figure 5.7. Note the pitch rise on *nanio* and *no*.

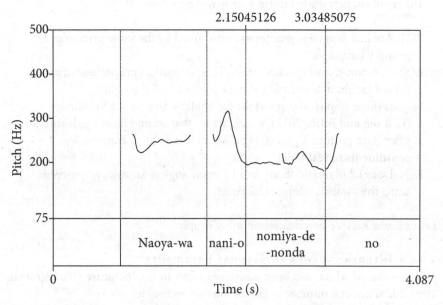

Figure 5.7. Visualization of the pitch patterns in a non-native speaker

The pitch peak was measured and entered into a spreadsheet for calculation. Pitch accent was controlled for in stimuli selection. All of the target words (both WH and DP) contained both high and low pitch accents, so any difference which could potentially emerge in the average across subjects and across lexical items cannot be attributed to some words having either all high or all low pitch accents.

5.3.4.2 The Structure of the Argument
Native speakers of Japanese boost the pitch on WH-words (compared to non-WH DPs) and compress the pitch between the WH-word and the Complementizer.

Richards (2016) builds a theory in which (a) the WH *in situ* is licensed by prosodic contiguity, and (b) the phonology/syntax interface is mediated by an architecture following Match Theory (Elfner 2015; Selkirk 2011), which predicts that the phonological and syntactic constituents should be largely isomorphic. Our study is designed to investigate these properties in second language learners. If the L2 subjects are producing prosodic contours which are nativelike in that they reflect L2 Japanese syntax, this is something that they could not have learned easily from classroom input or classroom instruction. We gave our subjects a reading task (not a grammaticality or acceptability judgement task) and assumed (following Levelt 1989) that the L2ers were generating a syntactic representation in production. So, given the syntactic structure of WH *in situ*, we are looking to see whether the produced utterances reflect nativelike prosody. There is much literature which demonstrates that syntactic constituent structure is invoked in silent reading tasks (e.g. Juffs and Harrington 1995; Kim, Montrul, and Yoon 2015; Pliatsikas and Marinis 2013), and I maintain this is true in production tasks as well.

The results of this study inform four major questions.

RQ1. Are interlanguage grammars constrained by the same principles as primary languages?

RQ2. Can non-native speakers attain L2 grammatical properties which are (a) not taught in class, and (b) not easily read off the input?

RQ3. Is there empirical support for the Shallow Structure Hypothesis (Clahsen and Felser 2017), which argues that second language learners often have problems processing abstract hierarchical grammatical constituents in real time?

RQ4. Does L2 phonetic ability and L2 phonological knowledge proceed along the same developmental path?

Let us probe each research question more deeply.

5.3.4.3 INTERLANGUAGES AS NATURAL LANGUAGES

This is a thread which has been addressed often in the literature (Bley-Vroman 1990, 2009) under a number of guises whether framed as

access to UG (Schwartz and Sprouse 1996),
whether interlanguages are natural languages (Adjémian 1976), or
structural conformity (Eckman 1991).

This is really a question of *domain specificity*. Many researchers have probed the question of whether interlanguage grammars are constrained by universal linguistic principles (White 2003). Of particular interest is the question of whether these universal properties are evident when there is no overt evidence for them in the L1. Will, for example, an L1 speaker who has no overt WH-movement show knowledge of constraints on WH-movement in the interlanguage? Berwick and colleagues (2011: 1207) outline the major arguments that invariant properties 'reflect an innate human endowment, as opposed to common experience'. These poverty of the stimulus cases are summarized nicely in the context of SLA by Özçelik and Sprouse (2016) and Özçelik (2017c). Some researchers maintain that knowledge of the L2 is the product of domain-general learning procedures (Wulff and Ellis 2018). A domain-general hypothesis-testing model would, I suggest, have difficulty arriving at the hypothesis *the WH-word is licensed to remain* in situ *because the pitch is compressed in the syntactic WH-domain*. Of course, such an argument could be presented in the future. To me, the most compelling position is that works from Archibald (1993) to Özçelik (2021) provide evidence that adult second language learners set up grammars which are constrained by Universal Grammar.

5.3.5 The Role of Input

Even though I take a modular, rationalist epistemological stance, I do not deny that the environmental input plays a critical role in L2 learning. See Yang and colleagues (2017), Yang (2017), and Lidz and Gagliardi (2015), for discussion of these issues. Universal Grammar is the locus of the deductive learning component, while learners also clearly evidence what Lidz and Gagliardi (2015) call the inferential component. L2 learners (like L1 learners) are sensitive to the statistical properties of the input, for example (see McDonough and Trofimovich 2016).

A novel aspect of this Contiguity study is that the subjects are classroom learners of Japanese as a foreign language. These learners have not received very much Japanese input (compared to naturalistic learners), and the structures in question (i.e. prosodic contiguity) have not been taught explicitly in class *at all*. Thus, if they acquire targetlike phonology and syntax while studying a foreign language at university, it seems highly unlikely that this learning is the result of a simple mapping of the classroom input. Once again, such a result would argue for domain-specific constraints on the nature of the interlanguage grammar.

5.3.6 Shallow Structure

Clahsen and Felser (2006) present the *Shallow Structure Hypothesis* (SSH), which attempts to account for some of the non-nativelike properties of interlanguage processing and interlanguage grammars by positing shallower, less-embedded syntactic representations in the non-native speakers. Clahsen and Felser (2017) revisit the model and note that the 'core claim of the SSH was that unlike native speakers, even highly proficient L2 speakers tend to have problems building or manipulating abstract syntactic representations in real time and are guided more strongly than native speakers by semantic, pragmatic, probabilistic, or surface-level information'. Furthermore, they make explicit that the claims of the SSH are expected to hold in production tasks as well as comprehension tasks.

They also argue that since the original research in 2006 (which focussed primarily on syntactic processing), there has been empirical evidence provided (Clahsen et al. 2010) which suggests that morphological processing is also affected. Thus, it would not be a stretch to infer that they would suspect that non-native speakers would also have difficulty 'building or manipulating' abstract *phonological* representations. Yes, I am putting words in their mouths, but while it is logically possible that a researcher could assume shallow morphological and syntactic structure but complex phonological structure, I know of no one who actually takes this stance. Given the nature of the syntax-phonology interface, our data (as we shall see) provide an argument that the complex phonology is a diagnostic of complex syntax, and this is also a counterargument to the Shallow Structure Hypothesis.

And while Clahsen and Felser acknowledge that non-native speakers can *have* hierarchical grammatical representations, they emphasize that the L2ers *underuse* abstract hierarchical representations in real-time processing. I argue that our research subjects were constructing and manipulating abstract syntactic and phonological categories in their production of L2 Japanese WH-questions.

5.3.7 Phonetics and Phonology

We are investigating (1) the phonetic property of the implementation of a pitch-level boost on WH-words, and (2) the grammatical property of phonological contiguity. In some respects, I am returning to the interface first discussed in Chapter 3 (phonetics/phonology), which just goes to show how the interfaces are connected. The logical possibilities are that our subjects will demonstrate targetlike performance in both phonology and phonetics, neither, or one. Given that they were university-age classroom learners of Japanese, it certainly seemed likely that their production would be accented phonetically but that they would have more of a chance to acquire the target phonology.

5.3.8 Results

The initial measurements were made and coded in Hertz. Then, to normalize the differences between male and female voices, we converted the Hertz scale to semitones. The difference between L1 English subjects and L1 other subjects was not significant ($p = .315$). When it comes to the pitch differences on WH-objects versus DP objects, I will report on all subjects together.

5.3.8.1 PITCH BOOST

Let us now turn to a discussion of the first component of Richards's notion of contiguity by looking at the instantiation of pitch boost by comparing sentences (in particular the bolded items) of the type shown in (141).

L2 WH-Questions

(141) a. Miki-wa   kino   **nani**-o   kai-mash-ita   ka?
Miki-TOP   yesterday what-ACC buy-POL-PAST [+Q]
'What did Miki buy yesterday?'

    b. Ponyo-wa   kino   **hon**-o   kai-mash-ita   ka?
Ponyo-TOP   yesterday book-ACC buy-POL-PAST [+Q]
'Did Ponyo buy a book yesterday?'

We compared (by paired t-test, since we have paired observations for the data in sentence pairs 1–3) the average pitch on DP direct objects versus WH direct objects in these sentences across all 16 subjects, shown in Table 5.2. None of the pairs of sentences had a significant difference in pitch.

Table 5.2. WH vs. DP PITCH LEVELS (IN SEMITONES) BY SENTENCE PAIR

Sentence pair	Object	Average pitch (sd)	Average difference in pitch (95% CI)	Significance from paired t-test
1	DP	12.98 (6.79)	−0.80 (−2.57, 0.97)	p = .349
	WH	12.18 (7.65)		
2	DP	13.59 (6.55)	−0.04 (−1.17, 1.08)	p = .935
	WH	13.54 (7.10)		
3	DP	11.16 (6.65)	−0.90 (−2.36, 0.56)	p = .207
	WH	10.26 (6.44)		

NOTE: sd = standard deviation; CI = confidence interval

Across all non-native Japanese speaking subjects, there is no difference in the mean pitch of WH- and DP-words (p = .801 on a paired t-test). This was revealed by a linear mixed model to account for the repeated measures on the same subjects, and this also revealed no significant difference between WH- and DP-words (p = .745).

The lack of significant difference between the two sentence types has two interesting implications. First, the non-native speakers were not phonetically implementing the WH-word pitch boost demonstrated by native speakers. Second, we are not seeing English echo questions produced here ('Ponyo bought WHAT?'), but rather L2 Japanese WH-questions. The L2 learners are not transferring English echo-question intonation here. For in addition to WH-moved questions ('What should Ponyo eat?'), English allows WH *in situ* questions with a particular pragmatic force. A sentence such as *Ponyo ate WHAT?* could be used to indicate shock or surprise at what Ponyo ate. It could also be used to indicate uncertainty on the part of the listener as to what was actually said. In either case, the *what* receives a boost in pitch to indicate the marked interpretation. If the L1 English speakers were transferring the intonation from these structures, then we might have expected a pitch boost on the Japanese *in situ* utterances. However, we see no significant boost. There is no reason to doubt that our subjects are producing Japanese WH-questions in our production task, as the task intended.

5.3.8.2 PROSODIC STRUCTURE

Let us turn to the second component of Contiguity Theory: prosodic contiguity.

Table 5.3 shows the data from two of the advanced speakers for the sentence given in (137). The boxed cells clearly indicate the basically level pitch between the WH-phrase (*nanio*) and the question particle (*no*). While the entire utterance shows a range of about five semitones, the area of interests shows a range of less than one semitone.

Table 5.3. PITCH LEVELS (IN SEMITONES) BETWEEN WH AND [+Q]

Subject #	nani-o WH	nomiya-de	nonda	no [+Q]
S1	5.94	0.511	1.33	5.82
S15	20.5	15.3	15.3	17.83

This almost completely level pitch contour between the WH-word and [+Q] is clearly consistent with Richards's hypothesis in that there is no prosodic boundary (as would be indicated by a pitch rise) in what he calls the *WH-domain*. The advanced subjects shown in Table 5.3 clearly show a nativelike prosodic pattern insofar as they maintain a level pitch contour between the WH-word and the question particle, with higher pitch on the WH-word and on the question particle. This particular sentence pair is used for illustration; the same pattern was found in other sentences. The pitch patterns in key sentences were tracked in four words of interest, as shown in Table 5.4.

Table 5.4. SENTENTIAL PITCH PATTERNS

Sentence	Word1	Word2	Word3	Word4
1	nani-o	nomiya-de	nonda	no
2	nani-o	mottekita	ndesu	ka
3	dare-ga	nani-o	kaimasita	ka
4	kino	nani-o	kaimasita	ka

The prediction was that in terms of pitch, Word3<Word2, Word3<Word1, and Word2<Word1. For each word pair comparison, two linear mixed models were fitted to the data: a full model where speakers were random effects and the fixed effects were word, proficiency, and the word-proficiency interaction, followed by a reduced model with the proficiency terms removed.

These analyses reveal that (a) the intermediate and advanced groups are behaving the same when it comes to pitch patterns, and (b) that there is a significant decline in fundamental frequency from Word1 to Word2 and from Word2 to Word3. In other words, there are no prosodic boundaries between Word1 and Word4.

5.3.8.3 ARCHITECTURAL IMPLICATIONS

The performance of these instructed learners suggests that they have acquired a grammar in which the phonological contiguity of the WH-phrase and the question particle is maintained. Note that (a) this is not a property which could have been transferred from L1 English, and (b) that this is not a property which was taught in class. Indeed, instructors and subjects alike confirmed in debriefing sessions that this was not covered in the textbooks or in the classroom instruction.

As Table 5.5 shows, the non-native speakers were not, however, behaving in a nativelike fashion when it comes to the pitch declination.

Table 5.5. Native vs. non-native pitch patterns

Sequence	Significance	Comparison
Word2 vs. Word1	p = .171	NS = NNS
Word3 vs. Word1	*p < .001	NS ≠ NNS
Word3 vs. Word2	*p = .001	NS ≠ NNS

For the pitch drop from Word1 to Word2, the non-native speakers were behaving like the native speakers, but for the other sequences (while there was, on average, a decline from Word2 to Word3 and from Word1 to Word3), these differences between groups were significant, meaning that the non-native speakers were not implementing the F0 decrease in a nativelike way.

It is worth noting that these two points are not incompatible: (1) the non-native speakers had significant categorical changes between all three target words, and (2) the changes were not the same as the changes native speakers make. The L2ers have acquired Japanese prosodic phrasing which matches the Japanese syntax. But they are not nativelike in the gradient pitch patterns implementing these phrases. They have accents.

Let us consider this in the broader context of assessing second language speech. There is a long tradition (often couched in the Critical Period Hypothesis) to see whether non-native speakers can perform a particular task (e.g. voice onset time, vowel contrast) with the range of native speakers. It is clear that Age of Acquisition correlates highly with accentedness of L2 speech. However, as Munro (2008: 194) notes, 'native pronunciation in the L2 is not only uncommon but unnecessary.' The nativelikeness measurement bar is a high bar and not the only bar. As Munro and Derwing (1995) have shown, heavily accented speech can be perfectly intelligible. So, our L2ers have acquired a targetlike phonology but have not acquired nativelike phonetics.

What we are seeing in the performance of our subjects is targetlike phonology which achieves prosodic contiguity but accented phonetic implementation.

5.3.8.4 Effects of Instruction / UG-Constrained Interlanguage
These results suggest that the L2 learners *are* able to acquire the target grammar insofar as they have no pitch peaks within the WH-domain. The interlanguage grammar licenses WH *in situ* by virtue of prosodic contiguity. I argue that the knowledge cannot be attributed to an effect of instruction but is rather the consequence of the interlanguage grammar being constrained by prosodic contiguity. The learners do not even consider hypotheses that are not found in other natural languages; phonological contiguity is an option provided in the

grammar-making toolbox that is UG. Such behaviour cannot be the result of an implicit analysis of the sentence intonation. The learners are not just 'imitating what they hear'. Crucially, there are some properties of Japanese speech that the L2 learners are *not* imitating correctly (e.g. the pitch boost on WH-words). Any theory would need to account for why some properties are acquired while others are not.

5.3.9 Interfaces

Sorace (2011) argues that interfaces between syntax and pragmatics show optionality or indeterminate acquisition. Furthermore, she suggests that the syntax/lexicon interface shows optionality when involving encyclopaedic knowledge or extralinguistic factors (external) but not with semantic roles (internal). Sorace summarizes, 'There is sufficient evidence for important developmental differences between linguistic structures that require conditions of a formal nature within the grammar, and structures that require the integration of contextual factors' (9). The structures under investigation here seem well suited to contributing to the literature on the Interface Hypothesis in two ways. First of all, this is an area where the structures in question are narrowly grammatical (and do not involve pragmatic or other external factors). The interface in question is the underexplored phonology-syntax interface which (with regard to these phenomena) seems to be acquirable by L2 learners.

Second, in probing what actually *causes* the residual optionality observed in the L2 learners for structures involving external interfaces, Sorace and colleagues (2009) and Serratrice and colleagues (2009) argue that it is restricted *input* which drives the incomplete acquisition. Slabakova (2013) expands this discussion in her *Bottleneck Hypothesis*, where she demonstrates the learnability of narrow syntax and narrow semantics but notes the environmental factors which can influence performance on certain tasks even by native speakers due to limited input. The examples she draws on are such structures as implausible passives (e.g. *The dog was bitten by the man*). Drawing on Dabrowska and Street (2006), the suggestion is that less-educated native speakers may perform differently owing to the lack of classroom input. I am not in a position to weigh in on the range of issues surrounding less-educated adults in SLA (see Young-Scholten 2013), but the role of formal education in acquisition is addressed in Kupisch and Rothman (2016).

The Contiguity study subjects were classroom learners of Japanese who had spent no extended periods in Japan. Their exposure to Japanese was not extensive. And yet the subjects *did* acquire the target structure of the phonological phrasing which licenses WH *in situ*.

These results then, appear to be consistent with the claims of the interface hypothesis (though the experiment was not designed to test this hypothesis) such that these formal properties are, indeed, acquirable and yet raise questions as to whether the acquisition is, in fact, input driven. Rather, it seems to suggest more that the L2 learner grammars are governed by universal properties (such as contiguity) which are not directly read off the input.

5.3.9.1 PHONETICS AND PHONOLOGY

These empirical results demonstrate a difference in ultimate attainment in the domains of phonetics and phonology. With respect to phonetics, the L2 learners were not implementing a phonetic boost on WH-elements compared to DP-elements (as has been reported in the literature (Hirotani 2005; Ishihara 2003; cited in Richards 2010)). However, they were encoding a representational system in which the grammars were constrained by universal principles, principles which cannot be directly inferred from the primary linguistic data and which are not addressed explicitly via instruction.

Given such poverty of the stimulus effects (see Özçelik and Sprouse 2016) in SLA, this has certain architectural implications which, in my mind, justify a well-defined phonetics/phonology demarcation. It is uncontroversial to note that phonology interfaces with other motoric and grammatical systems. The interface with morphology is crucial (Distributed Morphology (Embick 2010), Prosodic Morphology (McCarthy and Prince 1996; Zimmermann 2017)). The interface with syntax is critical (Selkirk 2011). However, there is much work which blurs the line between phonetics and phonology (Boersma and Pater 2016; Flemming 2017). This view is in opposition to the stance of phonology as cognition (Burton Roberts, Carr, and Docherty 2000; Reiss and Hale 2008). Such a computational model of phonology may well stem from the tenets of minimalist architecture, which has put less emphasis on the place of phonology in spell out. Even the work on the evolution of the language faculty (Berwick and Chomsky 2016) views the central development to be Merge but still considers phonology largely a production device. But Richards (2010, 2016) reminds us that there is an earlier interaction between phonology and syntax in which phonological properties may license syntactic structures. Drawing on work such as Selkirk (2011) and Elfner (2015), we see evidence for syntactic constituents being mapped one to one onto prosodic domains (contra Nespor and Vogel 1986). Thus, phonological domains are also fundamentally recursive (see also Wagner 2010).

Therefore, we can view L2 phonology as cognition and recognize that a phonetics/phonology split actually helps to account for the knowledge and behaviour of L2 learners. They are more successful at the categorial phonological phenomena (i.e. groupings of prosodic phrases) than they are at gradient phonetic phenomena (i.e. pitch level of a particular syntactic category). This is consistent with aspects of the literature on L2 phonology and nativelikeness. It is well documented that adult second language learners rarely fall within the range of native speaker performance when it comes to gradient phonetic phenomena such as voice onset time or vowel quality (Abrahamsson and Hyltenstam 2009; Munro, Flege, and Mackay 1996). I am not proposing a causal connection here (i.e. that these new contrasts are difficult *because* they are gradient). Indeed, it is well established that some gradient contrasts are easier to acquire than others (Bohn 1995; Polka and Bohn 2011). What I am suggesting is that one way of interpreting the differential learner performance is that they have acquired the targetlike phonology but not targetlike phonetic implementation of Japanese WH-questions.

5.3.9.2 Return to Learnability

As Yang (2017) reminds us, language acquisition is a fundamentally psychological activity, and our acquisition models must take into account both universal constraints on the system (both linguistic and computational) and the type of input available to the learner.

I therefore note that the learnability of the two phonetic and phonological phenomena is quite different. Phonological representations are constrained by UG (Match Theory, Contiguity Theory). We can conceptualize the architecture along the following lines:

IF WH remains in situ *THEN no prosodic boundaries between WH and [Q] particle.*

The learners are unable to set up grammars which violate UG properties. This is consistent with other L2 UG properties (Archibald, Yousefi, and Alhemaid 2022; Özçelik and Sprouse 2016).

Language-specific phonetic implementation (given that motoric skills are not governed by universal properties of the language faculty), however, must be picked up only from the environment, and, in this case at least, the patterns are much subtler and potentially masked, as we saw in Chapter 3 when I discussed intake frequency. Garcia (2020) also tackles the issue of masking in input distributions. In the case of L2 Japanese learners, they must note the fundamental frequency from a range of speakers (men, women, children) on different syntactic categories (WH- and non-WH DPs), keep track of the effects of intonation and pragmatic factors such as presupposition and focus, and from this determine that WH-words should have higher pitch than DP objects. At the very least, we would expect it to take *longer* for the L2 learner to acquire this property of Japanese.

5.3.10 Summary

These non-native speakers of Japanese who are learning the L2 in university classes (thus with relatively limited input compared to naturalistic learners) are able to acquire grammars which are constrained by such universal properties proposed in Match Theory (Elfner 2015; Selkirk 2011) and Contiguity Theory (Richards 2010, 2016).

The fact that it was a reading task meant that they were provided with the correct word order. The classroom learners were given explicit instruction as to the word order of Japanese WH-questions in their university courses. This environmental mix appears to have been sufficient for them to acquire targetlike syntactic structure for the sentences they read aloud. This syntactic knowledge, in turn, generated a targetlike prosodic structure.

Conclusions

The data support the position that interlanguage grammars are constrained by universal grammatical principles of Contiguity and Match Theories which govern the prosodic contiguity of WH-phrase licensing. These results are also counter to the Shallow Structure Hypothesis, as both hierarchical phonology and syntax are evidenced by these learners.

5.4 CONCLUSIONS

In this chapter, we have looked at two examples which illuminate the phonology/syntax interface. The first provided evidence of the role of phonology in syntactic interpretation, where we saw how phonological properties can influence such operations as syntactic reanalysis and relative clause attachment. The second provided evidence of the role of phonology in the production of L2 Japanese WH-questions, where the prosodic structure licensed WH *in situ*. In each case, the behaviour of the subjects is explained with reference to hierarchical phonological structures such as the phonological phrase.

6

Underture

6.1 INTRODUCTION

What I have attempted to argue for in this extended treatise is a unified architecture of SLA which relies centrally on an abstract, complex, hierarchical phonological knowledge. Such a model captures the empirical facts observed at the interfaces of phonology with phonetics, morphology, and syntax. This is an indirect realist model where representation and computation based on those representations is paramount.

There are, of course, models of SLA which are built on very different assumptions. This is not the place for me to enumerate specific criticisms of what might be an SLA of Harmonic Serialism, or a Bayesian SLA; however, I think such models would face challenges concerning:

- the nature of input representations and illusory vowels,
- the architecture of the phonology/morphology and phonology/syntax interface, and
- the feasibility of prior likelihood assessment demands of Batch Learning.

As I said at the beginning of Chapter 1, we want more than a department store of SLA components. One of the advantages of such a GenSLA model is that modular unification can be achieved.

Let us take the example of a proposed Bayesian account of language acquisition (Wilson and Davidson 2013). Like its predecessors (Genetic Algorithms (Clark 1992), Triggering Learning (Gibson and Wexler 1994), and Robust Interpretive Parsing (Tesar and Smolensky 1998)) these appear to be reasonable ways of modelling courses of *action* or performance, but they are problematic when it comes to modelling the acquisition of *knowledge*. Bayesian models are 'inductive' (see Perfors et al. 2010). They are argued to be good at handling induction problems when there is 'insufficient data' and a decision must be made. The learners tend to converge on an appropriate end state. However, as with the questions raised by

Phonology in Multilingual Grammars. John Archibald, Oxford University Press. © John Archibald 2024.
DOI: 10.1093/oso/9780190923334.003.0006

Dresher (1999) about the other learning theories just mentioned, there are some thorny issues about Bayesian approaches when it comes to *which* decisions are made. This is a system which matches input to output without specific reference to a theory of intermediary representations. On the input side of the equation, there is the question of not all input being available to the second language learner at one time. As Dresher and Kaye (1990) would have said, learning does not take place in *batch mode*. And as I discussed in Chapter 3, some input gets processed before other input. On the output side of things, we must face the question of how to determine what is the best fit (i.e. a goodness-of-fit algorithm), which brings us to the question of an evaluation metric (see Yang 2017) or the Blame Assignment issue. Bayesian models (such as Maximum Entropy (MaxEnt)) assume a description of the *prior*, and this is matched with the correct output on training. It is not straightforward to determine which grammar is the best solution for a particular environmental set. The import of this question has re-emerged in the discipline relatively recently as we seek to tackle issues of what Archibald (2022b) calls *I-proximity* in third language acquisition (L3A). One key question in the field of L3A is to try to predict when the L1 will transfer and when the L2 will transfer. Westergaard (2021) has a model known as the *Linguistic Proximity Model*, in which it is argued that the structure which is most similar ('closest') to the L3 will transfer. Note that this requires a theory of proximity (see Archibald 2022a for further discussion).

6.1.1 Bayesian Epistemology

Wilson and Davidson (2013) argue that acoustic properties such as release duration, relativized release burst amplitude, or prevoicing determine goodness of fit. These acoustic properties of the stimuli influence the production of non-native speakers via the perceptual likelihood function. 'If recording {z} has characteristics that make it more auditorily similar to typical realizations of phonetic/phonological representation [x] according to the native system of phonetic implementation, then the perceptual likelihood of [x] given {z} is increased.' So, perceptual likelihood seems to be a high correlation between an input feature and an output form. Such an input-output model assumes a substantive direct realist model similar to that of Brannen (2011), which I discussed in Chapter 3.

As Dresher and van der Hulst (1995) point out in their discussion of global determinacy, in phonology the cues to a particular analysis may not be strictly local. Arriving at the targetlike end-state grammar is not merely a matter of *noticing* but of *learning*. Take the example of a listener/learner having to reverse engineer setting up the representations for words like *electric[k]* and *electric[s]ity*. Or the underlying forms when vowel harmony might apply, where there might be certain segments which block the vowel harmony. Or the non-local consequences of adding a particular suffix (e.g. *eléctric/electrícity*). Mental representations are the intermediaries between input and output. Notions such *likelihood* do not take this into account explicitly.

There is probably no one who has thought more about the learnability of phonological systems within the Rationalist tradition than Elan Dresher (1999, 2009, 2018). Dresher (1999) proposes a cue-based algorithm for the acquisition of metrical structure. He introduced two fundamental problems which *any* learning theory has to address:

(1) *The Credit Problem* (sometimes called the *Blame Assignment Problem*). 'Where there is a mismatch between a target form and a learner's grammar, there is no way of reliably knowing which parameter/ constraints must be reset to yield the correct output.'
(2) *The Epistemological Problem*. 'There is a gap between the vocabulary in terms of which parameters/constraints are couched and the learner's analysis of the input.'

We can think of the Epistemological Problem as being connected to the Bootstrapping Problem (Pinker 1989) in that the objects of the world do not come labelled or even reliably cued by sensory input. There aren't nouns or verbs or little *v*s out there, but there are nouns and verbs in our grammars. There aren't phonemes or onsets or moras or phonological phrases out there, but they are in our phonological grammars.

The Bayesian approach faces the epistemological problem where the formula is designed to connect perceptual likelihood and phonotactic probability (where the output form is not taken to be a mental representation at all). The vocabulary (i.e. representational primitives) of the environmental input is markedly different from the vocabulary of the grammar which is consulted in order to generate the output. Some sort of transducer is necessary to map them together. Phonology cannot be simply noticed in the environment. Therein lies the problem with direct realist models of perception. This is also a problem that is decidedly not solved by theories of 'embodied' cognition (e.g. Wilson and Golonka 2013); see Goldinger and colleagues (2016) for a compelling critique.

Bayesian models are often informed by a kind of simplicity metric which, in computational phonology (Hayes and Wilson 2008), has been labelled MaxEnt. We can place this kind of MaxEnt worldview within a broader context of Bayesian epistemology (BE). One of the basic constructs is *Bayesian conditionalization*, where new knowledge impacts a person's subjective probabilities. The probability of a given course of action is influenced by past experience and by new evidence. One of the criticisms levelled against BE is the extension of traditional epistemological *beliefs* to *degrees of belief*. According to Pollock (1991), people do not have *degrees* of belief. Again, we may find it explanatory to model action and behaviour and the states of physical systems via constructs of entropy, but to extend such a notion to knowledge is fraught.

Rich, complex, hierarchical models of phonological knowledge can explain L2 linguistic behaviour at the morphological and syntactic interfaces in a way that other models would struggle with. So let us turn to that elephant-in-the-room question of why there is so much more work going on in L2 (and L3) morphosyntax and semantics than in L2 (and L3) phonology. It was ever so in the GenSLA world.

6.2 WHY IS GenSLA PHONOLOGY THE PARIAH?

Imagine if you will a book called *Second Language Acquisition* that did not mention syntax, or grammar, or morphology. That would be a feat of imagination. Yet there are books about second language acquisition that don't say anything about phonology. Maybe a bit about phonetics, and probably the Speech Learning Model (Flege 1995), but that might be it. A notable exception is Snape and Kupisch's (2016) *Second Language Acquisition*. Why should this be the case? At the very first Generative Approaches to Second Language Acquisition (GASLA) conference at MIT, there were three phonology talks (one of them mine). One of the conference organizers confessed to me, with a twinkle in his eye, 'we scheduled phonology right before the party so that people would stay.' He wasn't kidding. At GASLA 15 (26 years later), there were two phonology talks (one of them mine). My point here is not my own unrelenting stubbornness (nor my proportionate increase (33% to 50%) in GASLA influence over 26 years). When I was a regular attender of the Boston University Conference on Language Development, acquisition of syntax talks were always in the auditorium, while the acquisition of phonology talks were, to paraphrase Douglas Adams, in a 'closet stuck in a disused lavatory with a sign on the door saying, "Beware of the Leopard"'. I am kidding.

There is, of course, a proud lineage of second language phonology with, as they say, a small but enthusiastic following. However, the environmental conditions may be about to change. The recent work showing the influence of phonology on morphology and syntax in SLA may intrigue the morphosyntacticians and get them working with phonologists (a kind of 'gateway' phonology). So much research is interdisciplinary now, the broader teams may tackle broader questions. Syntacticians such as Richards (2019) are proposing models where phonology licenses certain syntactic phenomena (such as we saw in terms of Contiguity) related to linearization. These models present new opportunities for acquisitionists to pursue.

Phonology: it's generative, it's learned (not noticed), it's representational. I would certainly argue that it's recursive (Davis 2009; Féry 2010; Itô and Mester 2012; van der Hulst 2010), though not all would agree (see Kabak and Revithiadou 2009; Vogel 2009). It's much more than just externalization; it's at the grammatical core, a full member in the generative enterprise. Let me give the last word in this section to Dresher (2014: 177):

> It has been suggested that only syntactic recursion is part of the narrow faculty of language (FLN; Hauser, Chomsky and Fitch 2002), and that phonology is outside FLN. However, the contrastive hierarchy has a recursive digital character, like other aspects of FLN. Like syntax, phonology takes substance from outside FLN and converts it to objects that can be manipulated by the linguistic computational system.

I haven't delved into the Contrastive Hierarchy here, but see Archibald (2022a, 2022b) for discussion of this model in relation to third language acquisition of phonology.

6.3 GenSLA AND PEDAGOGY

And as if that were not enough, there are pedagogic implications. Slabakova and colleagues (2020) tackle the pedagogic aspects nicely. GenSLA reveals the nature of competence. Pedagogy strives to help learners acquire an L2. Yet there are even more utilitarian connections. As VanPatten (2015) points out, linguists can be valuable resources in the so-called language departments (which he asserts are really 'literature' departments). When it comes to discussing things like proficiency, teaching approaches for pronunciation, and matters of testing, we can provide solid guidance. We can be myth busters about language, language learning, and language teaching. When it comes to pronunciation, we can be resources on the difference between intelligibility and nativelikeness (Levis 2020). We can draw on collections such as Archibald, O'Brien, and Sewell (2021), which brings together L2 phonology and L2 pronunciation. We can make clear the difference between *errors* (which reflect competence) and mistakes (which are performance artefacts). The points made by Rothman and Slabakova (2018) are relevant to L2 phonology too. GenSLA emphasizes the commonality and complexity of all human languages. One of my great pleasures at the end of the term in Intro Linguistics is the ask-me-anything session with students. I remember getting asked, 'How does linguistics make the world a better place?' My answer was that linguistic analysis revealed the global uniformity of the Human Language. GenSLA brings in the fact that interlanguages are natural languages. In a world where inclusivity and diversity are valued, discrimination based on language is surprisingly widespread. We can see instances where particular regional or social dialects are stigmatized (often the dialects of marginalized populations) and where speakers of those dialects may be judged negatively. This is also true when it comes to speakers of second languages. Non-native speakers sometimes face difficulty getting hired based on the characteristics of their speech. Listeners may even attribute negative personality factors or cognitive abilities to people with a foreign accent (Lippi-Green 2012; Munro 2003). We can tackle this important issue of equity and social justice. L2 phonologies are not 'deficient' or 'shallow'. Rather, they are rich, complex mental representations.

We can also reinforce that non-native production may not necessarily reveal non-native competence. Just because a students' vowel production or stress implementation may not be nativelike does not mean that they are not marking a contrast. This is important for teachers to understand.

We can demonstrate that codeswitching in a bilingual individual or social group is not evidence of lack of proficiency but rather a complex, rule-governed linguistic phenomenon that can actually be a marker of very high bilingual proficiency.

Teachers are translators. They don't teach with technical linguistic jargon, but they can understand what their students are doing via linguistic questioning. They don't have to memorize all the grammatical properties of all their students' native languages. Our goal in advising teachers is to foster a culture of curiosity. Why are my students doing what they are doing? *Why* is the beginning of science but also the beginning of compassion. In my view, pedagogy is not, will not ever be, and should not be a science. It is an art, a calling, and deeply personal professional endeavour.

6.4 WRAPPING UP

As someone who has been working in the field of language learnability for 30 years, I have come across the opinion occasionally from applied linguists or teachers that GenSLA phonology is engaged in a judgemental exercise where grammars are compared and some are found wanting. In the field of pronunciation this would be akin to holding non-native speakers to the bar of nativelikeness as a measure of success. I don't think that's what we're doing in GenSLA at all. In some ways, I think that what we are doing is much more like chemistry than judging figure skating. Chemists have proposed the periodic table (Figure 6.1) as a descriptive and classificatory device to understand the behaviour of elements.

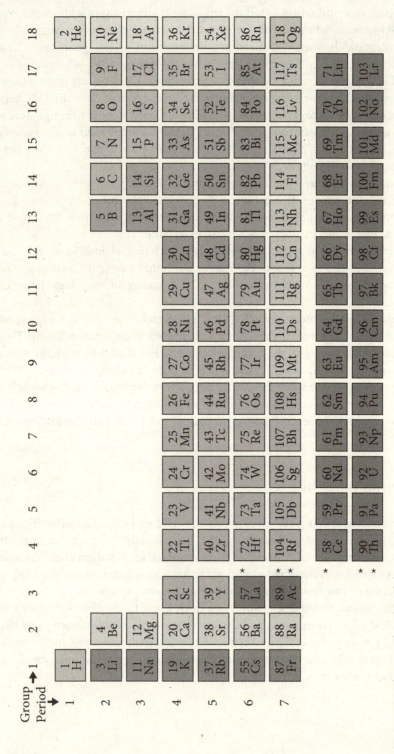

Figure 6.1. The periodic table of elements

Wrapping Up

Interlanguage grammars are like elements. Yes, hydrogen (H) is different from Helium (He), but it's not *better*. Hydrogen may share some properties with Lithium (Li) while Helium may share some properties with Argon (Ar). As acquisitionists, we look for patterns, we look for predictive factors, we look for individual variation. So, when we can construct a model that is internally consistent and accounts for a range of phenomena throughout our grammatical architecture, it is pleasing. I hope that I have taken a small step in this direction in this book, graphically represented in Figure 6.2.

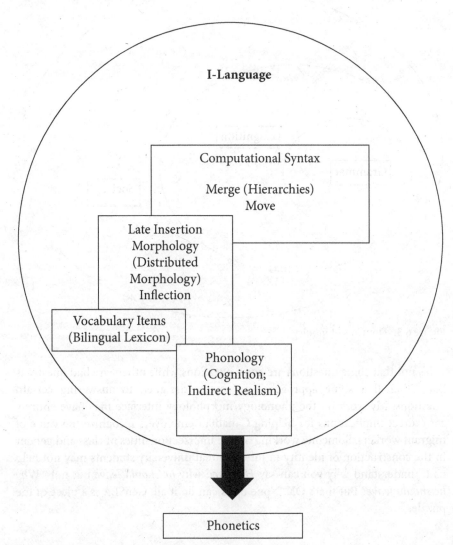

Figure 6.2. A unified architecture for L2 I-language

Of course, the language learners we study are more than grammars. Many researchers in applied linguistics are tackling very different questions from the ones I have been tackling here: questions of motivation, empathy, or anxiety; questions of power, colonialism, or identity; questions of feedback, medium of instruction, or task. Different approaches to research, whether they be the grammatical, the cognitive, or the social (as shown in Figure 6.3), ask different questions.

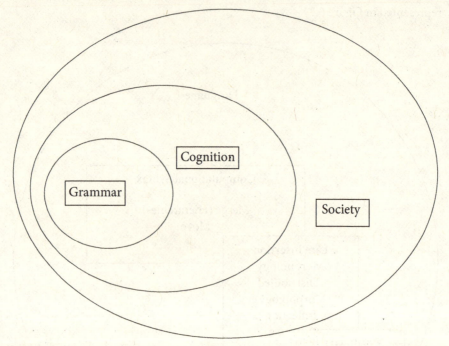

Figure 6.3. Domains of inquiry

It's not that some questions are good questions while others are bad questions but rather that some approaches are better designed to answering certain questions. My work on the phonology/morphology interface may have entirely zero direct implications for helping Canadian employers recognize the value of migrant workers. Someone working on the intersectionalities of class and gender in the construction of identity in international university students may not help us to understand why you can say *He asked why he should leave* but not **Why he should leave*? But that's OK. None of us can do it all. GenSLA is a piece of the puzzle.

6.5 EPILOGUE

We now imagine Prospero walking onto the stage and saying something like, *our revels now are ended*. So, where are we now? Which, yes, is a quote from a David

Epilogue

Bowie song which also has the line 'walking the dead' used to reminisce about his youthful days in Berlin. I'm not walking the dead yet in L2 phonology (as the field is not that old), but I am reminded of a Jackson Browne story: lamenting his senior statesmen years in the music world, he said that in every city he tours, there is a 'ghost on every corner'. For me, it's more like the Mexican Day of the Dead, though. I'm surrounded by my academic ancestors (not *ghosts*)—to reference Bruce Springsteen's fine autobiography—and it's a comfort.

It's also a comfort to see the new scholars in the field probing new questions and making new discoveries that build on what has gone before in this tradition with intellectual rigour and extraordinary vitality. My father, a professor of veterinary medicine (1949–1986 at the Ontario Veterinary College at the University of Guelph), always said that if we didn't train the next generation to go beyond what we knew, we had failed. And—while there have been dark days when I might have despaired that L2 phonology is still forgotten in textbooks; or that conference programs have few phonology talks compared to syntax, semantics, and processing; or that senior scholars might think that measuring voice onset time is the be-all and end-all of L2 phonology—there are young scholars out there whose research makes me think that it was not all for nought. As we learned in *Finding Dory*, just keep swimming.

I often exhort my students when preparing for defences to try to answer the question, *what do we know now that we didn't know before?* I suppose I should try to follow my own advice. If you have been stubborn enough to read to this point, what might you know that you didn't know before? Of course, you probably knew something about the subject when you picked the book up. A title like this isn't going to be competing for shelf space with Ian Rankin in airport news kiosks, so its readers are not a random population. Nevertheless, I hope that it has been sporadically instructive. Key points I have addressed include that phonology is

- cognition, abstract mental representation;
- more than the physics of muscle movement and audition;
- hierarchical and likely recursive, not 'shallow'; and
- learned, not 'noticed'.

Furthermore, we can take such a model of phonology and use it to characterize the interfaces with phonetics, morphology, and syntax. All the pieces can fit together.

L2 phonology is about much more than foreign accent. By understanding its role in the architecture of multilingual competence, we gain insight into the cognitive machinery of most of the brains on this planet. I have argued that the grammars of bilinguals are governed by such universal properties as the following:

- Representational universals respecting
  - syllable structure
  - metrical parameters
  - prosodic hierarchy

- association lines
- feature geometry
- Contiguity Theory
- Match Theory
- Phase Theory
- Aspects of lexical access (homophony and polysemy)
- Aspects of sentence processing (implicit prosody)

By looking at L2 phonology, we come to a deeper understanding of all of the components of an interlanguage grammar. The study of grammatical interfaces has, at times, been highlighted to probe the undeniably fascinating properties such as syntactic optionality or inflectional bottlenecks or segmental omission (which are, in fact, relatively local). But, to return to the department store metaphor from the opening of the book, the study of the interfaces has revealed that the architecture of bilingual grammar is not best described by a series of independent theories of phonology, morphology, and syntax. What has emerged is a complex, hierarchical, abstract L2 phonology which interacts with each of the other modules. Focussing in on this single component, in fact, allows us to bring the bigger picture into focus. L2 phonology helps us to understand the fundamental nature of the generative capacity of the multilingual language faculty.

APPENDIX A

Reading Sentences

1. Satsuki -ga   depāto -de   ojōsan -no   tame -ni ranpu -o eranda.
   Satsuiki-NOM dept.store-LOC daughter-GEN sake-DAT lamp-ACC chose
   サツキが、デパートでお嬢さんのためにランプを選んだ。
   'Satsuki chose a lamp for her daughter at the department store.'

2. Naoya -ga   nanika -o   nomiya -de nonda.
   Naoya-NOM something-ACC   bar-LOC   drank
   ナオヤが、何かを飲み屋で飲んだ。
   'Naoya drank something at the bar.'

3. Naoya -wa   nani -o   nomiya -de nonda no?
   Naoya-TOP what-ACC   bar-LOC   drank   Q
   ナオヤは、何を飲み屋で飲んだの？
   'What did Naoya drink at the bar?'

4. Umi -ga   depāto -de   dare -no   tame -ni   ranpu -o   eranda no?
   Umi-NOM dept. store-LOC who-GEN sake-DAT lamp-ACC chose   Q
   ウミが、デパートで誰のためにランプを選んだの？
   'Who did Umi choose a lamp for at the department store?'

5. Dare -ga   depāto -de dare- no   tame -ni ranpu -o eranda no?
   Who-NOM dept.store who-DAT
   誰が、デパートで誰のためにランプを選んだの？
   'Who chose a lamp for whom at the department store?'

6. Anata -wa Haru -ga   nani -o   suki -ka shitteimasu ka?
   you-TOP Haru-NOM   what-ACC   like Q   know   Q
   あなたは、ハルが何を好きか知っていますか？
   'What do you know Haru likes?'

7. Anata -wa dare -ga   Tatsuo -o   suki -ka shitteimasu ka?
   you-TOP who-NOM tatsuo-ACC like   Q know   Q
   あなたは、誰がタツオを好きか知っていますか？
   'Who do you think likes Tatsuo?'

8. Dare -ga   nani -o   kai-masita   ka?
   who-NOM what-ACC bought-POL Q
   誰が何を買いましたか？
   'Who bought what?'

9. Seiko -wa   dare -ga   tsukutta sushi -o   tabeta   no?
   Seiko-TOP who-NOM made   sushi-ACC ate   Q
   セイコは、誰が作った寿司を食べたの？
   'Seiko ate sushi that who made?'

10. Shiro -wa   hon'ya -de   nani -o   katta   no?
    Shiro-TOP bookstore-LOC whay-ACC bought Q
    シロは、本屋で何を買ったの？
    'What did Shiro buy at the bookstore?'

11. Kumiko -wa   doko -de   zasshi -o   katta   no?
    Kumiko-TOP where-LOC magazine-ACC bought Q
    クミコは、どこで雑誌を買ったの？
    'Where did Kumiko buy a magazine?'

12. Hayao -ga   senshū   katta   hon -ga   nakunatta
    Hayao-NOM last week bought book-NOM disappeared
    ハヤオが先週買った本が、無くなった。
    'The book Hayao bought last week disappeared.'

13. Masahiro -ga   katta   hon -ga   itsu   nakunatta   no?
    Masahiro-NOM bought book-NOM when disappeared Q
    マサヒロが買った本は、いつ無くなったの？
    'When did the book Masahiro bought disappear?'

14. Ponyo -wa   kinō   hon -o   kai-mashita   ka?
    Ponyo-TOP yesterday book-ACC bought-POL   Q
    ポニョは、昨日本を買いましたか？
    'Did Ponyo buy a book yesterday?'

15. Miki -wa   kinō   nani -o   kai-mashita   ka?
    Miki-TOP yesterday what-ACC bought-POL   Q
    ミキは、昨日何を買いましたか？
    'What did Miki buy yesterday?'

Appendix A

16. Miki -wa   kinō   hon -o   kai-mashita.
    Miki-TOP yesterday book-ACC   bought-POL
    ミキは、昨日本を買いました。
    'Miki bought a book yesterday.'

17. Noboru -wa   piza -o   mottekitandesu ka?
    Noburu-TOP   pizza-ACC   brought-POL   Q
    ノボルは、ピザを持って来たんですか？
    'Did Noburu bring pizza?'

18. Noboru -wa   kinō   piza -o   kai-mashita.
    Noburu-TOP yesterday pizza-ACC   bought-POL
    ノボルは、昨日ピザを買いました。
    'Nobouru brought pizza yesterday.'

19. Tarō -wa   nani -o   mottekitandesu ka?
    Taro-TOP   what-ACC   bought-POL   Q
    タローは、何を持って来たんですか？
    'What did Taro bring?'

APPENDIX B

Subject Profiles

Speaker	Sex	Proficiency	Either Parent Speaks Japanese	Mainly Instructed or Natural Input?	Length of Residency in Japan
TI	M	INT	N	Instructed	>1 Year
JM	F	INT	N	Instructed	<1 year
KR	F	INT	N	Instructed	<1 year
CS	F	ADV	N	Instructed	<1 month
A	M	ADV	N	Natural	<1 month
RKV	M	INT	N	Instructed	<1 year
KSD	F	ADV	N	Instructed	<1 month
ZM	M	ADV	N	Natural	<1 month
TF	F	ADV	N	I=N	>1 year
CJ	M	INT	N	Both	>1 year
OW	M	ADV	N	I=N	<1 year
AK	F	INT	Y	Natural	<1 year
JJ	F	INT	N	Natural	<1 year
RC	M	INT	N	Natural	<1 year
SK1	F	INT	Y	I=N	<1 year
NA	F	ADV	Y	Natural	<1 month
SK2	F	ADV	N	Natural	>1 year

REFERENCES

Abrahamsson, N. (2003). Development and recovery of L2 codas. *Studies in Second Language Acquisition* 25(3): 313–349.

Abrahamsson, N., and K. Hyltenstam (2008). The robustness of aptitude effects in near-native second language acquisition. *Studies in Second Language Acquisition* 30(4): 481–509.

Abrahamsson, N., and K. Hyltenstam (2009). Age of onset and nativelikeness in a second language: Listener perception versus linguistic scrutiny. *Language Learning* 59(2): 249–306.

Adjémian, C. (1976). On the nature, of interlanguage systems. *Language Learning* 26(2): 297–320.

Adriaans, F., and R. Kager (2010). Adding generalization to statistical learning: The induction of phonotactics from continuous speech. *Journal of Memory and Language* 62(3): 311–331.

Albright, A. (2009). Feature-based generalisation as a source of gradient acceptability. *Phonology* 26: 9–41.

Alexiadou, A., T. Lohndal, T. Åfarli, and M. Grimstad (2015). Language mixing: A distributed morphology approach. In T. Bui and D. Özyildiz, eds., *Proceedings of NELS*, vol. 45, Cambridge, MA: MIT Press. Pp. 25–38.

Alghmaiz, B. A. (2013). Word-initial consonant cluster patterns in the Arabic Najdi dialect. MA dissertation. Southern Illinois University, Carbondale.

Almalki, H. (2014). Acoustic investigation of production of clusters by Saudi second language learners of English. Thesis, Florida International University.

al-Mohanna, F. (1998). Syllabification and metrification in urban Hijazi Arabic: Between rules and constraints. PhD dissertation, Essex University.

Amaral, L., and Roeper, T. (2014). Multiple grammars and second language representation. *Second Language Research* 30(1): 3–36.

Anderson, S. (1992). *A-morphous Morphology*. New York: Cambridge University Press.

Archibald, J. (1993a). *Language Learnability and L2 Phonology: The Acquisition of Metrical Parameters*. Dordrecht: Kluwer.

Archibald, J. (1993b). The learnability of English metrical parameters by adult Spanish speakers. *International Review of Applied Linguistics* 31(2): 129–141.

Archibald, J. (1994). A formal model of learning L2 prosodic phonology. *Second Language Research* 10(3): 215–240.

Archibald, J. (1997a). The acquisition of English stress by speakers of nonaccented languages: Lexical storage versus computation of stress. *Linguistics* 35: 167–181.

Archibald, J. (1997b). Metrical parameters and lexical dependency. In S. Flynn, G. Martohardjono, and W. O'Neil, eds., *The Generative Study of Second Language Acquisition*. Mahwah, NJ: Erlbaum. Pp. 279–302.

Archibald, J. (1998). *Second language phonology*. Amsterdam: John Benjamins.

Archibald, J. (2000). Parsing procedures and the question of Full Access in L2 phonology. Plenary talk at New Sounds 2000. University of Amsterdam. September.

Archibald, J. (2003). Learning to parse second language consonant clusters. *Canadian Journal of Linguistics* 48(3/4): 149–178.

Archibald, J. (2004). Interfaces in the prosodic hierarchy: New structures and the phonological parser. *International Journal of Bilingualism* 8(1): 29–50.

Archibald, J. (2005). Second language phonology as redeployment of L1 phonological knowledge. *Canadian Journal of Linguistics* 50(1–4): 285–314.

Archibald, J. (2013). Reverse engineering the L1 filter: Bagging the elusive construct of intake frequency. Plenary speaker at New Sounds conference. Concordia. Montreal.

Archibald, J. (2017a). Second language processing and linguistic theory. In M. Aronoff, ed., *Oxford Research Encyclopedia in Linguistics*. Oxford University Press. https://doi.org/10.1093/acrefore/9780199384655.013.372

Archibald, J. (2017b). Transfer, contrastive analysis and interlanguage phonology. In R. Thompson, O. Kang, and J. Murphy, eds., *The Routledge Handbook of English Pronunciation*. London: Routledge. Pp. 9–24.

Archibald, J. (2018). Advanced level phonology and instructed SLA. In P. Malovrh and A. Benati, eds., *The Handbook of Advanced Proficiency in Second Language Acquisition*. Oxford: John Wiley. Pp. 241–263.

Archibald, J. (2019). A unified model of mono- and bilingual intelligibility: Psycholinguistics meets pedagogy. *Journal of Monolingual and Bilingual Speech* 1(1): 8–31.

Archibald, J. (2020). Turtles all the way down: Micro-cues and piecemeal transfer in L3 phonology. Commentary on Westergaard (2020) 'Microvariation in multilingual situations: The importance of property-by-property acquisition.' *Second Language Research* 37(3): 415–421.

Archibald, J. (2021). Speaking and hearing with an accent. *Frontiers for Young Minds: Understanding Neuroscience*. https://doi.org/10.3389/frym.2021.581824

Archibald, J. (2022a). Segmental and prosodic evidence for property-by-property phonological transfer in L3 English in northern Africa. *Languages* 7(1): 28. https://doi.org/10.3390/languages7010028

Archibald, J. (2022b). Phonological parsing via an integrated I-language: The emergence of property-by-property transfer effects in L3 phonology. *Linguistic Approaches to Bilingualism*. http://doi.org/10.1075/lab.21017.arc

Archibald, J. (2022c). Feature dependency and the poverty of the stimulus in the acquisition of L2 German plural allomorphy. In T. Leal, E. Shimanskya, and C. Isabelli, eds. *Generative SLA in the Age of Minimalism: Features, Interfaces, and Beyond (Selected Proceedings of the 15th Generative Approaches to Second Language Acquisition Conference)*. Philadelphia: John Benjamins. Pp. 117–136.

References

Archibald, J. (2023). Phonological redeployment and the mapping problem: Cross-linguistic E-similarity is the beginning of the story, not the end. *Second Language Research* 39(1): 287–297.

Archibald, J., and N. Croteau (2021). Acquisition of L2 Japanese WH questions: Evidence of phonological contiguity and non-shallow structures. *Second Language Research* 37(4): 649–679.

Archibald, J., and S. Jackson (2010). Phonological representations and perception of L2 contrasts. In M. Wrembel, M. Kul, and K. Dziubalska-Kolaczyk, eds., *Achievements and Perspectives in SLA of Speech: New Sounds 2010*. Frankfurt: Peter Lang. Pp. 161–170.

Archibald, J., and G. Libben (2019). Second language morphology: Representations, interfaces, and processing. In F. Masini and J. Audring, eds., *The Oxford Handbook of Morphological Theory*. Oxford: Oxford University Press. Pp. 522–540.

Archibald, J., M. O'Brien, and A. Sewell (2021). L2 phonology meets L2 pronunciation. *Frontiers in Communication: Language Sciences* 6.

Archibald, J., and M. Yousefi (2018). The redeployment of marked L1 Persian codas in the acquisition of marked L2 English onsets: Redeployment as a transition theory. Paper presented at Conference on Central Asian Language and Linguistics. Bloomington: Indiana University. March.

Archibald, J., M. Yousefi, and A. Alhemaid (2022). Redeploying appendices in L2 phonology: Illusory vowels in L1 Persian and Arabic acquisition of English sC initial clusters. *Journal of Monolingual and Bilingual Speech* 4(1): 76–108.

Armstrong, L. (1940). *The Phonetic and Tonal Structure of Kikuyu*. London: International African Institute.

Aronoff, M. (1994). *Morphology by Itself*. Cambridge, MA: MIT Press.

Atkey, S. (2001). The acquisition of L2 segmental contrasts: English speakers' perception and production of Czech palatal stops. MA thesis, University of Calgary.

Bader, M. 1998. Prosodic influences on reading syntactically ambiguous sentences. In J. D. Fodor and F. Ferreira, eds., *Reanalysis in Sentence Processing*. Dordrecht: Kluwer Academic. Pp. 1–46.

Badiola, L., R. Delgado, S. Sande, and S. Stefanich (2017). Code-switching attitudes and their effects on acceptability judgement tasks. *Linguistic Approaches to Bilingualism* 8: 5–24. https://doi.org/10.1075/lab.16006.bad

Baldi, P., ed. (1991). *Patterns of Change, Change of Patterns: Linguistic Changes and Reconstruction Methodology*. Berlin: De Gruyter.

Bale, A., and C. Reiss (2018). *Phonology: A Formal Introduction*. Cambridge, MA: MIT Press.

Bandi-Rao, S., and M. den Dikken (2014). Light switches: On V as a pivot in codeswitching, and the nature of ban on word-internal switches. In J. MacSwan, ed., *Grammatical Theory and Bilingual Codeswitching*. Cambridge, MA: MIT Press. Pp. 161–183.

Bates, D., M. Maechler, B. Bolker, and S. Walker (2015). Fitting linear mixed-effects models using lme4. *Journal of Statistical Software* 67(1): 1–48. https://doi.org/10.18637/jss.v067.i01

Berent, I. (2018). Algebraic phonology. In S. J. Hannah and A. Bosch, eds., *The Routledge Handbook of Phonological Theory*. Routledge Handbooks in Linguistics. Abingdon: Routledge. Pp. 569–588.

Beretta, A., R. Fiorentino, and D. Poeppel (2005). The effect of homonymy and polysemy on lexical access: An MEG study. *Cognitive Brain Research* 24(1): 57–65.

Bermúdez-Otero, R. (2017). Stratal phonology. In S. J. Hannahs and A. R. K. Bosch, eds., *The Routledge Handbook of Phonological Theory*. Abingdon: Routledge. Pp. 100–134.

Berwick, R., and N. Chomsky (2016). *Why Only Us?* Cambridge, MA: MIT Press.

Berwick, R., P. Pietroski, B. Yankama, and N. Chomsky (2011). Poverty of the stimulus revisited. *Cognitive Science* 35: 1207–1242.

Berwick, R., and E. Stabler, eds. (2019). *Minimalist Parsing*. Oxford: Oxford University Press.

Best, C. (1995). A direct realist view of cross-language speech perception. In W. Strange, ed., *Speech Perception and Linguistic Experience: Issues in Cross-language Research*. Timonium, MD: York Press. Pp. 171–206.

Best, C., and M. Tyler (2007). Nonnative and second-language speech perception. In O.-S. Bohn and M. Munro, eds., *Language Experience in Second Language Speech Learning*. Amsterdam: John Benjamins. Pp. 13–34.

Best, C. T., et al. (1988). Examination of perceptual reorganization for nonnative speech contrasts: Zulu click discrimination by English-speaking adults and infants. *Journal of Experimental Psychology: Human Perception and Performance* 14: 345–360.

Birdsong, D. (1992). Ultimate attainment in second language acquisition. *Language* 68(4): 706–755.

Blanco-Elorrieta, E., K. Emmorey, and L. Pylkkänen (2018). Language switching decomposed through MEG and evidence from bimodal bilinguals. *PNAS* 115(39): 9708–9713.

Blanco-Elorrieta, E., L. Gwilliams, A. Marantz, and L. Pylkkänen (2021). Adaptation to mis-pronounced speech: Evidence for a prefrontal-cortex repair mechanism. *Scientific Reports* 11(97). https://doi.org/10.1038/s41598-020-79640-0

Blanco-Elorrieta, E., and L. Pylkkänen (2015). Brain bases of language selection: MEG evidence from Arabic-English bilingual language production. *Frontiers of Human Neuroscience* 9: 1–19.

Blanco-Elorrieta, E., and L. Pylkkänen (2016). Bilingual language control in perception versus action: MEG reveals comprehension control mechanisms in anterior cingulate cortex and domain-general control of production in dorsolateral prefrontal cortex. *Journal of Neuroscience* 36(2): 290–301.

Bley-Vroman, R. (1990). The logical problem of foreign language learning. *Linguistic Analysis* 20: 3–49.

Bley-Vroman, R. (2009). The evolving context of the fundamental difference hypothesis. *Studies in Second Language Acquisition* 31(2): 175–198. https://doi.org/10.1017/S0272263109090275

Blumstein, S. E., and K. N. Stevens (1981). Phonetic features and acoustic invariance in speech. *Cognition* 10(1–3): 25–32.

Boersma, P., and J. Pater (2016). Convergence properties of a gradual learning algorithm for Harmonic Grammar. In John J. McCarthy and Joe Pater, eds., *Harmonic Grammar and Harmonic Serialism*. Sheffield: Equinox. Pp. 389–434.

Boersma, P., and D. Weenink (2019). Praat: Doing phonetics by computer. Version 6.0.55. http://www.praat.org/

References

Bohn, G., and R. Santos (2018). The acquisition of pre-tonic vowels in Brazilian Portuguese. *Alfa* 62(1): 191–221.

Bohn, O.-S. (1995). Cross language speech perception in adults: First language transfer doesn't tell it all. In W. Strange, ed., *Speech Perception and Linguistic Experience: Issues in Cross-Language Research*. Timonium, MD: York Press. Pp. 279–304.

Bohn, O.-S., and J. E. Flege (1992). The production of new and similar vowels by adult german learners of english. *Studies in Second Language Acquisition* 14: 131–158.

Bohn, O.-S., and M. Munro, eds. (2007). *Language Experience in Second Language Learning: In Honor of James Emil Flege*. Amsterdam: John Benjamins.

Bonet, E., and D. Harbour (2012). Contextual allomorphy. In J. Trommer, ed., *Morphology and Phonology of Exponence*. Oxford: Oxford University Press. Pp. 195–235.

Bongaerts, T., C. van Summeren, B. Planken, and E. Schils (1997). Age and ultimate attainment in the pronunciation of a foreign language. *Studies in Second Language Acquisition* 19: 447–465.

Booij, G. (2010). *Construction morphology*. Oxford: Oxford University Press.

Borgman, D. (1990). Sanuma. In D. Derbyshire and G. Pullum, eds., *Handbook of Amazonian Languages*. Berlin: De Gruyter. Pp. 15–248.

Boudaoud, M. (2008). The variable development of /s/ + consonant onset clusters in the interlanguage of Farsi ESL leaners. Master's thesis, Concordia University.

Brannen, K. (2011). The perception and production of interdental fricatives in second language acquisition. PhD dissertation, McGill University.

Broersma, M., and A. Cutler, (2007). Phantom word activation in L2. *System* 36: 22–34.

Bromberger, S., and M. Halle (2000). The ontology of phonology (revised). In N. Burton Roberts, P. Carr, and G. Docherty, eds., *Phonological Knowledge: Conceptual and Empirical Issues*. Oxford: Oxford University Press. Pp. 19–38.

Broś, K., M. Meyer, M. Kliesch, and V. Dellwo (2021). Word stress processing integrates phonological abstraction with lexical access—an ERP study. *Journal of Neurolinguistics* 57.

Broselow, E. (1992). Transfer and universals in second language epenthesis. In S. Gass and L. Selinker, eds., *Language Transfer in Language Learning*. Philadelphia: John Benjamins. Pp. 71–86.

Broselow, E., S.-I. Chen, and C. Wang (1998). The emergence of the unmarked in second language phonology. *Studies in Second Language Acquisition* 20(2): 261–280.

Broselow, E., and D. Finer (1991). Parameter setting in second language phonology and syntax. *Second Language Research* 7(1): 35–60.

Brown, C. (2000). The interrelation between speech perception and phonological acquisition from infant to adult. In J. Archibald, ed., *Second Language Acquisition and Linguistic Theory*. Oxford: Blackwell. Pp. 4–63.

Brown, C., and J. Matthews (2004). When intake exceeds input: Language specific perceptual illusions induced by L1 prosodic constraints. *International Journal of Bilingualism* 8(1): 5–27.

Burkholder, M. (2018). Language mixing in the nominal phrase: Implications of a Distributed Morphology perspective. *Languages* 3(2): 10. https://doi.org/10.3390/languages3020010

Burton Roberts, N., P. Carr, and G. Docherty, eds. (2000). *Phonological Knowledge: Conceptual and Empirical Issues*. Oxford: Oxford University Press.

Bybee, J. (2010). *Language, Usage, and Cognition*. Cambridge: Cambridge University Press.

Cabrelli Amaro, J. (2017). The role of prosodic structure in the acquisition of L2 Spanish stop lenition. *Second Language Research* 33(2): 233–269.

Cardoso. W. (2007). The development of sC onset clusters in interlanguage: Markedness vs. frequency effects. In *Generative Approaches to Second Language Acquisition Proceedings*. Somerville, MA: Cascadilla Press.

Cardoso, W., P. John, and L. French (2009). The variable perception of /s/ + coronal onset clusters in Brazilian Portuguese English. In M. Watkins, A. Rauber, and B. Baptista, eds., *Recent Research in Second Language Phonetics/Phonology*. Newcastle upon Tyne: Cambridge Scholars. Pp. 203–233.

Carlisle, R. (2001). Syllable structure universals and second language acquisition. *International Journal of English Studies* 1: 1–19.

Carroll, S. (2001). *Input and Evidence: The Raw Material of Second Language Acquisition*. Amsterdam: John Benjamins.

Chafe, W. (1977). Accent and related phenomena in the Five Nations Iroquois languages. In Larry Hyman, ed., *Studies in Stress and Accent*. Los Angeles: University of California Press. Pp. 169–181.

Chang, C. B. (2019). Language change and linguistic inquiry in a world of multicompetence: Sustained phonetic drift and its implications for behavioral linguistic research. *Journal of Phonetics* 74: 96–113.

Cheng, B., X. Zhang, S. Fan, and Y. Zhang (2019). The role of temporal acoustic exaggeration in high variability phonetic training: A behavioral and ERP study. *Frontiers in Psychology* 10. https://doi.org/10.3389/fpsyg.2019.01178

Chomsky, N. (1986). *Knowledge of Language*. New York: Praeger.

Chomsky, N. (1999). Derivation by phase. *MIT Occasional Papers in Linguistics* 18: 1–52.

Chomsky, N. (2015). Problems of projection: Extensions. In E. Di Domenico, C. Hamann, and S. Matteini, eds., *Structures, Strategies and Beyond: Studies in Honour of Adriana Belletti*, vol. 223. Amsterdam: John Benjamins. Book section 1, pp. 3–16.

Chomsky, N. (2017). Two notions of modularity. In R. de Almeida and L. Gleitman, eds., *On Concepts, Modules, and Language: Cognitive Science at Its Core*. Oxford: Oxford University Press. Pp. 25–41.

Chomsky, N., and M. Halle (1968). *The Sound Pattern of English*. New York: Harper & Row.

Clahsen, H., and C. Felser (2006). Grammatical processing in language learners. *Applied Psycholinguistics* 27(1): 3–42.

Clahsen, H., and C. Felser (2017). Some notes on the shallow structure hypothesis. *Studies in Second Language Acquisition* 40(3): 693–706. https://doi.org/10.1017/S02722631170000250

Clahsen, H., C. Felser, K. Neubauer, M. Sato, and R. Silva (2010). Morphological structure in native and nonnative language processing. *Language Learning* 60(1): 21–43.

Clark, R. (1992). The selection of syntactic knowledge. *Language Acquisition* 2: 83–149.

Clarke, C. M., and M. F. Garrett (2004). Rapid adaptation to foreign-accented English. *Journal of the Acoustical Society of America* 116: 3647–3658.

Clements, G. N. (2009). The role of features in phonological inventories. In E. Raimy and C. Cairns, eds., *Contemporary Views on Architecture and Representations in Phonology*. Cambridge, MA: MIT Press. Pp. 19–68.

References

Colantoni, L., J. Steele, and P. Escudero (2015). *Second Language Speech.* Cambridge: Cambridge University Press.

Cole, D. T. (1967). *Some Features of Ganda Linguistic Structure.* Johannesburg: Witwatersrand Press.

Coleman, John, and Janet B. Pierrehumbert (1998). Stochastic phonological grammars and acceptability. In *Proceedings of the Third Meeting of the ACL Special Interest Group in Computational Phonology.* Somerset, NJ: Association for Computational Linguistics. Pp. 49–56.

Collins, C., and E. Stabler (2016). A formalization of Minimalist syntax. *Syntax* 19(1): 43–78.

Collins, L., P. Trofimovich, J. White, M. Horst, and W. Cardoso (2006). Acquiring language efficiently: Research and teaching (ALERT Project). Funded by the Fonds québécois de la recherche sur la société et la culture (FQRSC). Concordia University.

Coppieters, R. (1987). Competence differences between native and near-native speakers. *Language* 63(3): 544–573.

Corcoran, D. W. J. (1966). An acoustic factor in letter cancellation. *Nature* 210: 658.

Corcoran, D. W. J. (1967). Acoustic factor in proof reading. *Nature* 214: 851–852.

Corder, S. P. (1967). The significance of learners' errors. *IRAL* 5: 161–169.

Correia, S., J. Butler, M. Vigário, and S. Frota (2015). A stress 'deafness' effect in European Portuguese. *Language and Speech* 58(1): 48–67.

Coté, M.-H. (2000). Consonant cluster phonotactics: A perceptual approach. Doctoral dissertation, Massachusetts Institute of Technology.

Cowper, E., and D. C. Hall (2019). Scope variation in contrastive hierarchies of morphosyntactic features. In D. Lightfoot and J. Havenhill, eds., *Variable Properties in Language: Their Nature and Acquisition.* Washington, DC: Georgetown University Press. Pp. 27–41.

Cuetos, F., and D. C. Mitchell (1988). Cross-linguistic differences in parsing: Restrictions on the use of the late closure strategy in Spanish. *Cognition* 30: 73–105.

Cummins, R. (1983). *The Nature of Psychological Explanation.* Cambridge, MA: MIT Press.

Curtin, S., H. Goad, and J. Pater (1998). Phonological transfer and levels of representation: The perceptual acquisition of Thai voice and aspiration by English and French speakers. *Second Language Research* 14(4): 389–405.

Cutler, A. (2012). *Native Listening: Language Experience and the Recognition of Spoken Words.* Cambridge, MA: MIT Press.

Dabrowska, E., and J. Street, (2006). Individual differences in language attainment: Comprehension of passive sentences by native and non-native English speakers. *Language Sciences* 28: 604–615.

Darcy, I., et al. (2012). Direct mapping of acoustics to phonology: On the lexical encoding of front rounded vowels in L1 English–L2 French acquisition. *Second Language Research* 28(1): 5–40.

Darcy, I., H. Park, and C.-L. Yang (2015). Individual differences in L2 acquisition of English phonology: The relation between cognitive abilities and phonological processing. *Learning and Individual Differences* 40: 63–72.

Davidson, L. (2006). Phonology, phonetics, or frequency: Influences on the production of non-native sequences. *Journal of Phonetics* 34: 104–137.

Davis, S. (2009). On the foot-based analysis of aspiration in American English. Paper presented at the CUNY Conference on the Foot, New York, NY, January 15–17.

de Almeida, R. (2017). A Fodor's guide to cognitive science. In R. de Almeida and L. Gleitman, eds., *On Concepts, Modules and Language: Cognitive Science at Its Core*. Oxford: Oxford University Press. Pp. 1–21.

de Almeida, R., and L. Gleitman, eds. (2017). *On Concepts, Modules, and Language: Cognitive Science at Its Core*. Oxford: Oxford University Press.

de Groot, A. M. (1992). Determinants of word translation. *Journal of Experimental Psychology: Learning, Memory, and Cognition* 18(5): 1001–1018.

Deguchi, M., and Y. Kitagawa (2002). Prosody and *WH*-questions. In Masako Hirotani, ed., *Proceedings of NELS 32*. Amherst: GLSA, University of Massachusetts. Pp. 73–92.

Dehaene-Lambertz, G., E. Dupoux, and A. Gout, (2000). Electrophysiological correlates of phonological processing: A cross-linguistic study. *Journal of Cognitive Neuroscience* 12(4): 635–647. https://doi.org/10.1162/089892900562390

Dekydtspotter, L., R. A. Sprouse, and K. Swanson (2001). Reflexes of the mental architecture in second language acquisition: The interpretation of discontinuous *combien* extractions in English-French interlanguage. *Language Acquisition* 9: 175–227.

Dijkstra, T., J. Grainger, and W. J. B. Van Heuven (1999). Recognition of cognates and interlingual homographs: The neglected role of phonology. *Journal of Memory and Language* 41(4): 496–519.

Ding, N., L. Melloni, H. Zhang, X. Tian, and D. Poeppel (2015). Cortical tracking of hierarchical linguistic structures in connected speech. *Nature Neuroscience* 19(1): 158–164.

Dobler, E., H. Newell, G. Piggott, T. Skinner, M. Sugimura, and L. Travis. Narrow syntactic movement after spell-out (unpublished ms, n.d.).

Dörnyei, Z., and M. Scott (2002). Communication strategies in a second language: Definitions and taxonomies. *Language Learning* 47(1): 173–210.

Dresher, E. (1999). Charting the learning path: Cues to parameter setting. *Linguistic Inquiry* 30(1): 27–67.

Dresher, E. (2009). *The Contrastive Hierarchy in Phonology*. Cambridge: Cambridge University Press.

Dresher, E. (2014). The arch not the stones: Universal feature theory without universal features. *Nordlyd* 41(2): 165–181.

Dresher, E. (2018). Contrastive hierarchy theory and the nature of features. In W. Bennett, L. Hracs, and D. Storoshenko, eds., *Proceedings of the 35th West Coast Conference on Formal Linguistics*. Somerville, MA: Cascadilla Proceedings Project. Pp. 18–29.

Dresher, E., and J. Kaye (1990). A computational learning model for metrical phonology. *Cognition* 34: 137–195.

Dresher, E., and H. van der Hulst (1995). Global determinacy and learnability in phonology. In. J. Archibald, ed., *Phonological Acquisition and Phonological Theory*. Hillsdale, NJ: Erlbaum. Pp. 1–22.

Dresher, E., and H. van der Hulst (1998). Head-dependent asymmetries in phonology: Complexity and visibility. *Phonology* 15: 317–352.

Dretske, F. (2003). Experience as representation. *Philosophical Issues (Philosophy of Mind)* 13: 67–82.

Duanmu, S. (2000). *The Phonology of Standard Chinese*. Oxford: Oxford University Press.

Duanmu, S. (2007). *The Phonology of Standard Chinese*. 2nd edition. Oxford: Oxford University Press.

References

Dulay, H., and M. Burt (1974). Natural sequences in child second language acquisition. *Language Learning* 24(1): 37–53.

Dupoux, E., K. Kakehi, Y. Hirose, C. Pallier, and J. Mehler (1999). Epenthetic vowels in Japanese: A perceptual illusion? *Journal of Experimental Psychology: Human Perception and Performance* 25(6): 1568–1578.

Dupoux, E., C. Pallier, N. Sebastián, and J. Mehler (1997). A distressing 'deafness' in French? *Journal of Memory and Language* 36(3): 406–421.

Dupoux, E., S. Peperkamp, and N. Sebastián-Galles (2001). A robust method to study stress 'deafness'. *Journal of the Acoustical Society of America* 11(3): 1606–1618.

Dupoux, E., N. Sebastián-Galles, E. Navarrete, and S. Pepperkamp (2008). Persistent stress 'deafness': The case of French learners of Spanish. *Cognition* 106: 682–706.

Dyck, C. (1995). Constraining the phonetics-phonology interface. PhD dissertation, University of Toronto.

Eckman, F. (1991). The structural conformity hypothesis and the acquisition of consonant clusters in the interlanguage of ESL learners. *Studies in Second Language Acquisition* 13(1): 23–41.

Eckman, F. (2008). Typological markedness and second language phonology. In J. Hansen and M. Zampini, eds., *Phonology and Second Language Acquisition*. Amsterdam: John Benjamins. Pp. 95–116.

Eckman, F. R., A. Elreyes, and G. K. Iverson (2003). Some principles of second language phonology. *Second Language Research* 19(3): 169–208.

Eckman, F., and G. Iverson (1994). Pronunciation difficulties in ESL: Coda consonants in English interlanguage. In M. Yavas, ed., *First and Second Language Phonology*. San Diego: Singleton Press. Pp. 251–265.

Eckman, F., and G. Iverson (1997). Structure preservation in interlanguage phonology. In S. J. Hannahs and M. Young-Scholten, eds., *Focus on Phonological Acquisition*. Amsterdam: John Benjamins. Pp. 183–207.

Elfner, E. (2015). Recursion in prosodic phrasing: Evidence from Connemara Irish. *Natural Language & Linguistic Theory* 33(4): 1169–1208.

Embick, D. (2010). *Localism Versus Globalism in Morphology and Phonology*. Cambridge, MA: MIT Press.

Escudero, P., R. Hayes-Harb, and H. Mitterer (2008). Novel second-language words and asymmetric lexical access. *Journal of Phonetics* 36: 345–360.

Escudero, P., and K. Wanrooij (2010). The effect of L1 orthography on non-native vowel perception. *Language and Speech* 53(3): 343–365.

Everett, D. (2005). Cultural constraints on grammar and cognition in Pirahã: Another look at the design features of human language. *Current Anthropology* 46:621–646.

Farris-Trimble, A., and A.-M. Tesser (2019). The effect of allophonic processes on word recognition: Eye-tracking evidence from Canadian raising. *Language* 95(1): e136–e160.

Fatemi, M. A., A. Sobhani, and H. Abolhassani (2012). Difficulties of Persian learners of English in pronouncing some English consonant clusters. *World Journal of English Language* 2(4): 69–75.

Fernández, E. M. (1998). Language dependency in parsing: Evidence from monolingual and bilingual processing. *Psychologica Belgica* 38: 197–230.

Fernández, E. M. (2003). *Bilingual Sentence Processing: Relative Clause Attachment in English and Spanish*. Amsterdam: John Benjamins.

Ferreira, F., and J. M. Henderson (1991). Recovery from misanalysis of garden-path sentences. *Journal of Memory and Language* 30:725–745.

Féry, C. (2010). Recursion in prosodic structure. *Phonological Studies (Kaitakusha, Tokyo)* 13:51–60.

Fikkert, P. (1994). *On the Acquisition of Prosodic Structure*. Holland Institute of Linguistics Dissertations.

Flege, J. (1995). Second language speech learning: Theory, findings and problems. In W. Strange, ed., *Speech Perception and Linguistic Experience: Issues in Cross-Language Research*. Baltimore: York Press. Pp. 233–272.

Flege, J. (2018). It's input that matters most, not age. *Bilingualism: Language and Cognition* 21(5): 919–920. https://doi.org/10.1017/S136672891800010X

Flege, J. E., and O.-S. Bohn (2021). The revised Speech Learning Model (SLM-r). In R. Wayland, ed., *Second Language Speech Learning: Theoretical and Empirical Progress*. Cambridge: Cambridge University Press. Pp. 3–83.

Fleischhacker, H. (2001). Cluster-dependent epenthesis asymmetries. *UCLA Working Papers in Linguistics* 7: 71–116.

Flemming, E. (2017). Dispersion theory and phonology. In M. Aronoff, ed., *The Oxford Research Encyclopedia of Linguistics*. Oxford: Oxford University Press. https://doi.org/10.1093/acrefore/9780199384655.013.110

Flemming, E. (2021). Comparing maxent and noisy harmonic grammar. *Glossa: A Journal of Generative Linguistics* 6(1): 1–42.

Fodor, J. (1983). *The Modularity of Mind*. Cambridge, MA: MIT Press.

Fodor, J. (2002). Prosodic disambiguation in silent reading. In M. Hirotani, ed., *Proceedings of the North East Linguistics Society* 32. Amherst: GSLA, University of Massachusetts. Pp. 112–132.

Fodor, J., and Z. Pylyshyn.(1988). Connectionism and cognitive architecture: A critical analysis. *Cognition* 28:3–71.

Fodor, J. D. (1998a). Parsing to learn. *Journal of Psycholinguistic Research* 27(3): 339–374.

Fodor, J. D. (1998b). Learning to parse? *Journal of Psycholinguistic Research* 27:285–319.

Frazier, L. (1978). On Comprehending Sentences: Syntactic Parsing Strategies. PhD dissertation, University of Connecticut, Storrs. Distributed by the Indiana University Linguistics Club, Bloomington, IN.

Frazier, L., and C. Clifton (1996). *Construal*. Cambridge, MA: MIT Press.

Frazier, L., and K. Rayner (1982). Making and correcting errors during sentence comprehension: Eye movements in the analysis of structurally ambiguous sentences. *Cognitive Psychology* (14):178–210.

Gallistel, R. (2017). The neurobiological bases for the computational theory of mind. In R. de Almeida and L. Gleitman, eds., *On Concepts, Modules, and Language: Cognitive Science at Its Core*. Oxford: Oxford University Press. Pp. 275–296.

Gallistel, R., and A. P. King (2010). *Memory and the computational Brain: Why Cognitive Science will Transform Neuroscience*. New York: Wiley-Blackwell.

Garcia, G. D. (2020). Language transfer and positional bias in English stress. *Second Language Research* 36(4): 445–474.

Gass, S., and L. Selinker (2001). *Second Language Acquisition: An Introductory Course*. Mahwah, NJ: Erlbaum.

Gibson, E. (1991). A computational theory of human linguistic processing. PhD dissertation, Carnegie Mellon University, Pittsburgh, PA. Available as Center for Machine Translation Technical Report CMU-CMT-91-125.

References

Gibson, E. (2000). Dependency locality theory: A distance-based theory of linguistic complexity. In A. Marantz, Y. Miyashita, and W. O'Neil, eds., *Image, Language, Brain: Papers from the First Mind Articulation Project Symposium*. Cambridge, MA: MIT Press Pp. 95–126.

Gibson, E., and K. Wexler (1994). Triggers. *Linguistic Inquiry* 25:407–454.

Gierut, J., and K. O'Connor (2002). Precursors to onset clusters in acquisition. *Journal of Child Language* 29: 495–517.

Goad, H. (2016). Phonotactic evidence from typology and acquisition for a coda+onset analysis of initial sC clusters. In K.-M. Kim et al., eds., *Proceedings of 33rd WCCFL*. Somerville, MA: Cascadilla Press. Pp. 17–28.

Goad, H., N. B. Guzzo, and L. White (2020). Parsing ambiguous relative clauses in L2 English: Learner sensitivity to prosodic cues. *Studies in Second Language Acquisition* 43(1): 83–108.

Goad, H., and L. White (2004). Ultimate attainment of L2 inflection: Effects of L1 prosodic structure. In S. Foster-Cohen, M. S. Smith, A. Sorace, and M. Ota, eds., *Eurosla Yearbook*, vol. 4. Amsterdam: John Benjamins. Pp. 119–145.

Goad, H., and L. White (2006). Ultimate attainment in interlanguage grammars: A prosodic approach. *Second Language Research* 22(3): 243–268.

Goad, H., and L. White (2019). Prosodic effects on L2 grammars. *Linguistic Approaches to Bilingualism* 9(6): 769–808.

Gold, E. M. (1967). Language identification in the limit. *Information and Control* 10(5): 447–474.

Goldinger, S., M. Papesh, A. Barnhart, W. Hansen, and M. Hout (2016). The poverty of embodied cognition. *Psychological Bulletin Review* 23(4): 959–978. doi 10.3758/ s13423-015-0860-1

Gollan, T., K. Forster, and R. Frost (1997). Translation priming with different scripts: Masked priming with cognates and noncognates in Hebrew-English bilinguals. *Journal of Experimental Psychology: Learning, Memory and Cognition* 23: 1122–1139.

González Poot, A. (2011). Conflict resolution in the Spanish SLA of Yucatec ejectives: L1, L2, and universal constraints. PhD dissertation, University of Calgary.

González Poot, A. (2014). Conflict resolution in the Spanish L2 acquisition of Yucatec ejectives: L1, L2 and universal constraints. In *The Proceedings of the Annual Conference of the Canadian Linguistic Association*. https://cla-acl.artsci.utoronto.ca/wp-content/ uploads/GonzálezPoot-2014.pdf

González-Vilbazo, K., L. Bartlett, S. Downey, S. Ebert, J. Heil, B. Hoot, et al. (2013). Methodological considerations in code-switching research. *Studies in Hispanic Lusophone Linguistics* 6: 119–138. https://doi.org/10.1515/shll-2013-1143

González-Vilbazo, K., and L. López (2011). Some properties of light verbs in code-switching. *Lingua* 121(5): 832–850.

Gorrell, P. (1995). *Syntax and Parsing*. Cambridge: Cambridge University Press.

Goto, H. (1971). Auditory perception by normal Japanese adults of the sounds 'l' and 'r'. *Neuropsychologia* 9(3): 317–323.

Greenberg, Joseph (1963). Some universals of grammar with particular reference to the order of meaningful elements. In Joseph Greenberg, ed., *Universals of Language*. London: MIT Press. Pp. 73–113.

Gregg, K. (1993). Taking explanation seriously; or, Let a couple of flowers bloom. *Applied Linguistics* 14(3): 276–294.

Gregg, K. (2006). Taking a social turn for the worse: The language socialization paradigm for second language acquisition. *Second Language Research* 22: 413–442.

Green, D. (2018). Language control and code-switching. *Languages* 3: 8. https://doi.org/10.3390/languages3020008

Green, D. W., and J. Abutalebi (2013). Language control in bilinguals: The adaptive control hypothesis. *Journal of Cognitive Psychology* 25: 1–16. https://doi.org/10.1080/20445911.2013.796377

Grenon, I., M. Kubota, and C. Sheppard (2019). The creation of a new vowel category by adult learners after adaptive phonetic training. *Journal of Phonetics* 72: 17–34.

Grosjean, F. (2012). An attempt to isolate, and then differentiate, transfer and interference. *International Journal of Bilingualism* 16: 11–21.

Guion, S., J. Flege, S. Liu, and G. Yeni-Komshian (2000). Age of learning effects on the duration of sentences produced in a second language. *Applied Psycholinguistics* 21:205–228.

Guion, S., and E. Pederson (2007). Investigating the role of attention in phonetic learning. In O.-S. Bohn and M. Munro, eds., *Second Language Speech Learning: The Role of Language Experience in Speech Perception and Production*. Amsterdam: John Benjamins. Pp. 99–116.

Gwilliams, L., T. Linzen, D. Poeppel, and A. Marantz (2018). In spoken word recognition, the future predicts the past. *Journal of Neuroscience* 38(35): 7585–7599.

Haber, L. R. and R. N. Haber (1982). Does silent reading involve articulation? Evidence from tongue twisters. *American Journal of Psychology* 95: 410–419.

Hakulinen, L. (1961). *The Structure And Development of the Finnish Language*. Trans. John Atkinson. Bloomington: Indiana University Press.

Hale, M., and C. Reiss (2000). Phonology as cognition. In N. Burton Roberts, P. Carr, and G. Docherty, eds., *Phonological Knowledge: Conceptual and Empirical Issues*. Oxford: Oxford University Press. Pp. 161–184.

Hall, D. C. (2017). Contrastive specification in phonology. In M. Aronoff, ed., *Oxford Research Encyclopedia of Linguistics*. https://doi.org/10.1093/acrefore/9780199384655.013.26

Halle, M., and A. Marantz (1993). Distributed morphology and the pieces of inflection. In K. Hale and J. Keyser, eds., *The View from Building 20*. Cambridge, MA: MIT Press. Pp. 111–176.

Hancin-Bhatt, B. (1994). Segment transfer: A consequence of a dynamic system. *Second Language Research* 10(3): 241–269.

Hansen Edwards, J., and M. Zampini, eds. (2008). *Phonology and Second Language Acquisition*. Amsterdam: John Benjamins.

Hanson, V. L., E. W. Goodell, and C. A. Perfetti (1991). Tongue-twister effects in the silent reading of hearing and deaf college students. *Journal of Memory and Language* 30: 319–330.

Harley, B. (1986). *Age in Second Language Acquisition*. Clevedon: Multilingual Matters.

Harris, A. (2017). *Multiple Exponence*. Oxford: Oxford University Press.

Haugen, J. (2008). *Morphology at the Interfaces: Reduplication and Noun Incorporation in Uto-Aztecan*. Amsterdam: John Benjamins.

Haugen, J., and D. Sidiqi (2013). Roots and the derivation. *Linguistic Inquiry* 44(3): 493–517.

Hauser, M., N. Chomsky, and T. Fitch (2002). The faculty of language: What is it, who has it, and how did it evolve? *Science* 298: 1569–1579.

References

Hawkins, R., and C. Y.-H. Chan (1997). The partial availability of Universal Grammar in second language acquisition: The 'Failed Functional Features Hypothesis'. *Second Language Research* 13: 187–226.

Hawkins, R., and H. Hattori (2006). Interpretation of multiple *WH*-questions by Japanese speakers: A missing uninterpretable account. *Second Language Research* 22: 269–301.

Hawkins, R., and S. Liszka (2003). Locating the source of defective past tense marking in advanced L2 English speakers. In R. van Hout, A. Hulk, F. Kuiken and R. Towell, eds., *The Lexicon-Syntax Interface in Second Language Acquisition*. Amsterdam: John Benjamins. Pp. 21–44.

Hayes, B. (1995). *Metrical Stress Theory: Principles and Case Studies*. Chicago: University of Chicago Press.

Hayes, Bruce., and C. Wilson (2008). A maximum entropy model of phonotactics and phonotactic learning. *Linguistic Inquiry* 39: 379–440.

Hayes-Harb, R., and K. Masuda (2008). Development of the ability to lexically encode novel L2 phonemic contrasts. *Second Language Research* 24(1): 5–33.

Hellmuth, S. (2016). Non-persistent 'stress-deafness' in L1 English-speaking advanced learners of L2 Spanish. New Sounds 2016. Aarhus, Denmark.

Herschensohn, J. (2000). *The Second Time Around—Minimalism and L2 Acquisition*. Philadelphia: John Benjamins.

Hestvik, A., and K. Durvasula (2016). Neuobiological evidence for voicing under-specification in English. *Brain & Language* 152:28–43.

Hirotani, M. (2005). Prosody and LF interpretation: Processing Japanese WH-questions. Doctoral dissertation, University of Massachusetts, Amherst.

Holland, J., K. Holyoak, R. Nisbett, and P. Thagard (1986). *Induction: Processes of Inference, Learning and Discovery*. Cambridge, MA: MIT Press.

Howe, D., and D. Pulleyblank (2004). Harmonic scales as faithfulness. *Canadian Journal of Linguistics* 49(1): 1–50.

Hsieh, M.-L. (2008). *The Internal Structure of Noun Phrases in Chinese*. Monograph series. Taiwan: Taiwan Journal of Linguistics.

Hudson, R. (2010). *An Introduction to Word Grammar*. Cambridge: Cambridge University Press.

Hunyadi, L. (2010). Cognitive grouping and recursion in prosody. In Harry van der Hulst, ed., *Recursion and Human Language*. Berlin: De Gruyter. Pp. 343–370.

Hurford, J. (2014). *The Origins of Language: A Slim Guide*. Oxford: Oxford University Press.

Hyltenstam, K., and N. Abrahamsson (2000). Who can become native-like in a second language? All, some, or none? On the maturational constraints controversy in second language acquisition. *Studia Linguistica* 54(2): 150–166.

Ishihara, S. (2003). Intonation and interface conditions. Doctoral dissertation, MIT.

Itô, J., and A. Mester (2012). Recursive prosodic phrasing in Japanese. In Toni Borowsky, Shigeto Kawahara, Takahito Shinya, and Mariko Sugahara, eds., *Prosody Matters: Essays in Honor of Elisabeth Selkirk*. Sheffield: Equinox. Pp. 280–303.

Itô, J., and A. Mester (2017). The structure of the phonological lexicon. In N. Tsujimura, ed., *The Handbook of Japanese Linguistics*. Malden, MA: Wiley. Pp. 62–100. https://doi.org/10.1002/9781405166225.ch3

Iverson, G., and J. Salmons (1995). Aspiration and laryngeal features in Germanic. *Phonology* 12: 369–396.

Iverson, P., and B. G. Evans (2009). Learning English vowels with different first language vowel systems II: Auditory training for native Spanish and German speakers. *Journal of the Acoustical Society of America* 126(2): 866–877.

Jackson, S. (2009). Non-native perception of laryngeal features. MA thesis, University of Calgary.

Jakobson, R. (1941/1968). *Child Language, Aphasia and Phonological Universals.* The Hague: Mouton. (Revised version of *Kindersprache, Aphasie und allgemeine Lautgesetze*, Uppsala, 1941).

Jakobson, R., and M. Halle (1956). *Fundamentals of Language.* The Hague: Mouton.

James, A. (1988). *The Acquisition of a Second Language Phonology.* Tübingen: Gunter Narr.

Jensen, I., R. Slabakova, and M. Westergaard (2019). The Bottleneck Hypothesis in L2 acquisition: L1 Norwegian learners' knowledge of syntax and morphology in L2 English. *Second Language Research* 36(1): 3–29. https://doi.org/10.1177/026765831 8825067

Jesney, K. (2005). Chain shift in phonological acquisition. MA thesis, University of Calgary.

Jesney, K. (2007). Child chain shifts as faithfulness to input prominence. In A. Belikova et al., eds., *Proceedings of the 2nd Conference on Generative Approaches to Language Acquisition North America (GALANA).* Somerville, MA: Cascadilla Proceedings Project. Pp. 188–199.

Johnson, K. (2005). *Decisions and Mechanisms in Exemplar-based Phonology.* UC Berkeley Phonology Lab Annual Report. Pp. 289–311.

Juffs, A., and M. W. Harrington (1995). Parsing effects in L2 sentence processing: Subject and object asymmetries in wh-extraction. *Studies in Second Language Acquisition* 17(4): 483–516.

Jusczyk, P. (1997). *The discovery of spoken language.* Cambridge, MA: MIT Press.

Kabak, B., and W. Idsardi (2007). Perceptual distortions in the adaptation of English consonant clusters: Syllable structure or consonantal contact constraints? *Language and Speech* 50(1): 23–52.

Kabak, B., and A. Revithiadou (2009). An interface approach to prosodic word recursion. In J. Grijzenhout and B. Kabak, eds., *Phonological Domains: Universals and Deviations.* Berlin: De Gruyter. Pp. 105–134.

Kamide, Y., and D. C. Mitchell (1997). Relative clause attachment: Non-determinism in Japanese parsing. *Journal of Psycholinguistic Research* 26: 247–254.

Karimi, S. (1987). Farsi speakers and the initial consonant clusters in English. In G. Ioup and S. H. Weinberger, eds., *Interlanguage Phonology: The Acquisition of a Second Language Sound System.* Cambridge, MA: Newbury House. Pp. 305–318.

Kawagoe, I. (2003). Acquisition of English word stress by Japanese learners. In J. Liceras et al., eds., *Proceedings of the 6th Generative Approaches to Second Language Acquisition Conference.* Somerville, MA: Cascadilla Press. Pp. 161–167.

Kawahara, S. (2015). The phonology of Japanese accent. In H. Kubozono, ed., *Handbook of Japanese Phonetics and Phonology.* Berlin: De Gruyter. Pp. 313–362.

Kaye, J. (1990). *Phonology: A Cognitive View.* Mahwah, NJ: Erlbaum.

Kaye, J. (1992). Do you believe in magic? The story of s+C sequences. *SOAS Working Papers in Linguistics* 2: 293–313.

References

Kaye, J., J. Lowenstamm, and J.-R. Vergnaud (1990). Constituent structure and government in phonology. *Phonology* 7(2): 193–231.

Keating, P. A. (1990). Phonetic representations in a generative grammar. *Journal of Phonetics* 18: 321–334.

Kehrein, W., and C. Golston (2004). A prosodic theory of laryngeal contrasts. *Phonology* 21: 325–357.

Keyser, S. J., and K. Stevens (2006). Enhancement and overlap in the speech chain. *Language* 82(1): 33–63.

Kijak, A. (2009). *How stressful is L2 stress?* Utrecht: LOT.

Kim, E., S. Montrul, and J. Yoon (2015). The on-line processing of binding principles in second language acquisition: Evidence from eye tracking. *Applied Psycholinguistics* 36(6): 1317–1374.

Kim, E.-S., and D. Pulleyblank (2009). Glottalization and lenition in Nuuchah-nulth. *Linguistic Inquiry* 40(4): 567–617.

Kim, Y., N. Tracy-Ventura, and Y. Jung (2016). A measure of proficiency or short-term memory? Validation of an elicited imitation test for SLA research. *Modern Language Journal* 100: 655–673.

Kimball, J. (1973). Seven principles of structure parsing in natural languages. *Cognition* 2: 15–47.

Kingston, J., and R. Diehl (1994). Phonetic knowledge. *Language* 70(3): 419–454.

Kiparsky, P. (1982). From cyclic phonology to lexical phonology. In H. van der Hulst and N. Smith, eds., *The Structure of Phonological Representation*. Part 1. Dordrecht: Foris. Pp. 131–176.

Kiparsky, P. (2003). Syllables and moras in Arabic. In C. Féry and R. van de Vijver, eds., *The Syllable in Optimality Theory*. Cambridge: Cambridge University Press. Pp. 147–182.

Kubozono, H. (2006). Where does loanword prosody come from? A case study of Japanese loanword accent. *Lingua* 116(7): 1140–1170.

Kucera, H., and N. Francis (1967). *Computational Analysis of Present-Day American English [The Brown Corpus]*. Providence, RI: Brown University Press.

Kulikov, V. (2010). Features, cues, and syllable structure in the acquisition of Russian palatalization by L2 American learners. In M. Wrembel, M. Kul, and K. Dziubalska-Kolaczyk, eds., *Achievements and Perspectives in SLA of Speech: New Sounds 2010*. Frankfurt: Peter Lang. Pp. 193–204.

Kupisch, T., and J. Rothman, (2016). Terminology matters! Why difference is not incompleteness and how early child bilinguals are heritage speakers. *International Journal of Bilingualism* 22(5): 564–582. https://doi.org/10.1177/1367006916654355

LaCharité, D., and P. Prévost (1999). Le rôle de la langue maternelle et de l'enseignement dans l'acquisition des segments anglais langue seconde par les apprenants francophones. *Revue de langues et linguistique* 25: 81–109.

Ladd, R. (2014). *Simultaneous Structure in Phonology*. Oxford: Oxford University Press.

Lado, R. (1957). *Linguistics Across Cultures: Applied Linguistics for Language Teachers*. Ann Arbor: University of Michigan Press.

Lago, S., M. Scharinger, Y. Kronrod, and W. J. Idsardi (2015). Categorical effects in fricative perception are reflected in cortical source information. *Brain & Language* 143: 52–58.

Lahiri, A., and H. Reetz (2002). Underspecified recognition. In C. Gussenhoven and N. Warner, eds., *Laboratory Phonology 7*. Berlin: Mouton. Pp. 637–675.

Lahiri, A., and H. Reetz (2010). Distinctive features: Phonological underspecification in representation and processing. *Journal of Phonetics* 38(1): 44–59.

Lardiere, D. (2007). *Ultimate Attainment in Second Language Acquisition*. Mahwah, NJ: Erlbaum.

Larson-Hall, J. (2004). Predicting perceptual success with segments: A test of Japanese speakers of Russian. *SLR* 20(1): 33–76.

Lassetre, P., and P. Donegan (1998). Perception in Optimality Theory: The frugality of the base. In B. Bergen, M. Plauch, and A. Bailey, eds., *Proceedings of the 24th Annual Meeting of the Berkely Linguistics Society*. Linguistic Society of America. Pp. 346–355.

Lee, D.-Y. (1998). *Korean Phonology: A Principle-Based Approach*. Munich: LINCOM Europa.

Lee, S. S. (2000). Chain shift in second language phonological acquisition. *Journal of the Pan-Pacific Association of Applied Linguistics* 4(1): 175–199.

Legate, J., and C. Yang (2007). Morphosyntactic learning and the development of tense. *Language Acquisition* 14(3): 315–344.

Lemhöfer, K., T. Dijkstra, and M. Michel, (2004). Three languages, one ECHO: Cognate effects in trilingual word recognition. *Language and Cognitive Processes* 19(5): 585–611.

Levelt, W. J. M. (1989). *Speaking: From Intention to Articulation*. Cambridge, MA: MIT Press.

Levis, J. (2020). Revisiting the intelligibility and nativeness principles. *Journal of Second Language Pronunciation* 6(3): 310–328.

Levy, E. (2004). Effects of language experience and consonantal context on perception of French front rounded vowels by adult American L2 learners of French. PhD dissertation, City University of New York.

Libben, G. (2000). Representation and processing in the second language lexicon: The homogeneity hypothesis. In J. Archibald, ed., *Second Language Acquisition and Linguistic Theory*. Malden, MA: Blackwell. Pp. 228–248.

Libben, G. (2021). Psycholinguistics. In W. O'Grady and J. Archibald, eds., *Contemporary Linguistic Analysis*. 9th edition. North York: Pearson.

Libben, G., and M. Goral (2015). How bilingualism shapes the mental lexicon. In J. Schwieter, ed., *The Cambridge Handbook of Bilingual Processing*. Cambridge: Cambridge University Press. Pp. 631–644.

Libben, M., and D. Titone (2009). Bilingual lexical access in context: Evidence from eye movements during reading. *Journal of Experimental Psychology: Learning, Memory, and Cognition* 35(2): 381–390.

Liberman, A. M., and I. G. Mattingly (1985). The motor theory of speech perception revised. *Cognition* 21(1): 1–36.

Lidz, J., and A. Gagliardi (2015). How nature meets nurture: Universal grammar and statistical learning. *Annual Review of Linguistics* 1: 12.1–12.21.

Lieberman, M. (2013). The importance of comprehension to a rounded view of second language acquisition. Paper presented at the Department of Linguistics, University of Utah, Salt Lake City, UT, January.

Lightfoot, D. (1991). *How to set parameters: Arguments from language change*. Cambridge, MA: MIT Press.

Lightfoot, D. (2020). *Born to parse: How children select their languages*. Cambridge, MA: MIT Press. https://doi.org/10.7551/mitpress/12799.001.0001

Lin, Y-H. (2001). Syllable simplification strategies: a stylistic perspective. *Language Learning* 51(4): 681–718.

References

Lippi-Green, R. (2012). *English with an Accent: Language, Ideology, And Discrimination in the United States*. 2nd edition. New York: Routledge.

Lombardi, L. (2003). Second language data and constraints on manner: Explaining substitutions for the English interdentals. *Second Language Research* 19(3): 225–250. https://doi.org/10.1177/026765830301900304

Long, M. H. (1990). Maturational constraints on language development. *Studies in Second Language Acquisition* 12(3): 251–285.

López, L. (2020). *Bilingual Grammar: Toward an Integrated Model*. Cambridge: Cambridge University Press.

López, L., A. Alexiadou, and T. Veenstra (2017). Code-switching by phase. *Languages* 2(3): 9. https://doi.org/10.3390/languages2030009

MacSwan, J., and S. Colina (2014). Some consequences of language design: Codeswitching and the PF Interface. In J. MacSwan, ed., *Grammatical Theory and Bilingual Codeswitching*. Cambridge, MA: MIT Press. Pp. 185–210.

MacWhinney, B. (1987). The competition model. In B. MacWhinney, ed., *Mechanisms of Language Acquisition*. Hillsdale, NJ: Erlbaum. Pp. 249–308.

MacWhinney, B., and W. O'Grady, eds. (2015). *The Handbook of Language Emergence*. Malden, MA: Wiley Blackwell.

Maddieson, I. (1984). *Patterns of Sounds*. Cambridge: Cambridge University Press.

Mah, J. (2003). *The Acquisition of Phonological Features in a Second Language*. MA thesis, University of Calgary.

Mah, J., and J. Archibald (2003). The acquisition of L2 length contrasts. In J. Liceras et al., eds., *Proceedings of GASLA*. Somerville MA: Cascadilla Press. Pp. 208–212.

Mah, J., H. Goad, and K. Steinhauer (2016). Using event-related brain potentials to assess perceptibility: The case of French speakers and English [h]. *Frontiers in Psychology* 7: 1469. https://doi.org/10.3389/fpsyg.2016.01469

Major, R. (2001). *Foreign Accent: The Ontogeny and Phylogeny of Second Language Phonology*. Mahwah, NJ: Erlbaum.

Major, R. C. (2008). Transfer in second language phonology: A review. In J. Hansen Edwards and M. Zampini, eds., *Phonology and Second Language Acquisition*. Philadelphia: John Benjamins. Pp. 63–94.

Marantz, A. (2001). Words. Paper presented at the West Coast Conference on Formal Linguistics 20. Los Angeles, CA.

Marcel, A. J. (1983). Conscious and unconscious perception: Experiments on visual masking and word recognition. *Cognitive Psychology* 15: 197–237.

Marr, D. (1982). *Vision*. San Francisco: Freeman.

Matthews, J., and C. Brown (2004). When language intake exceeds input: Language specific perceptual illusions induced by L1 prosodic constraints. *International Journal of Bilingualism* 8(1): 5–27.

Matthews, P. (1974). *Morphology*. Cambridge: Cambridge University Press.

McAllister, R. (2007). Strategies for realization of L2-categories: English /s/- /z/. In O.-S. Bohn and M. Munro, eds., *Language Experience in Second Language Speech Learning*. Amsterdam: John Benjamins. Pp. 153–166.

McCarthy, J., and A. Prince (1996). Prosodic morphology. In J. Goldsmith, ed. *The Handbook of Phonological Theory*. Cambridge, MA: Blackwell. Pp. 318–366.

McCutchen, D., and C. Perfetti (1982). The visual tongue-twister effect: Phonological activation in silent reading. *Journal of Verbal Learning and Verbal Behavior* 21: 672–687.

McDonough, K., and P. Trofimovich (2008). *Using Priming Methods in Second Language Research*. New York: Routledge.

McDonough, K., and P. Trofimovich (2016). The role of statistical learning and working memory in L2 speakers' pattern learning. *Modern Language Journal* 100(2): 428–445.

McGinnis, M. (2016). Distributed morphology. In A. Hippisley and G. Stump, eds., *The Cambridge Handbook of Morphology*. Cambridge: Cambridge University Press. Pp. 390–423.

McGuian, F. J., and A. B. Dollins (1989). Patterns of covert speech behavior and phonetic coding. *Pavlovian Journal of Biological Science* 24: 19–26.

Meisel, J. (2011). *First and Second Language Acquisition*. Cambridge: Cambridge University Press.

Miyagawa, S. (2012). Agreements that occur mainly in the main clause. In L. Aelbrecht, L. Haegeman, and R. Nye, eds., *Main Clause Phenomena: New Horizons*. Philadelphia: John Benjamins. Pp. 79–112.

Miyagawa, S., S. Ojima, R. Berwick, and K. Okanoya (2014). The integration hypothesis of human language evolution and the nature of contemporary languages. *Frontiers in Psychology*. doi: 10.3389/fpsyg.2014.00564

Monahan P. J., E. F. Lau, and W. J. Idsardi (2013). Computational primitives in phonology and their neural correlates. In C. Boeckx and K. K. Grohmann, eds., *The Cambridge Handbook of Biolinguistics*. Cambridge: Cambridge University Press. Pp. 233–256.

Monreal, S. T., and R. S. Hernández (2005). Reading levels of Spanish deaf students. *American Annals of the Deaf* 150(4): 379–387.

Montrul, S. (2011). Multiple interfaces and incomplete acquisition. *Lingua* 121: 591–604.

Munro, M. (2008). Foreign accent and speech intelligibility. In J. Hansen Edwards and M. Zampini, eds., *Phonology and Second Language Acquisition*. Amsterdam: John Benjamins. Pp. 193–218.

Munro, M. (2021). On the difficulty of defining 'difficult' in second-language vowel acquisition. *Frontiers in Communication: Language Sciences* 6. https://doi.org/10.3389/fcomm.2021.639398

Munro, M., and T. Derwing (2015). A prospectus for pronunciation research in the 21st century: A point of view. *Journal of Second Language Pronunciation* 1(1): 11–42.

Munro, M., J. Flege, and I. Mackay (1996). The effects of age of second language learning on the production of English vowels. *Applied Psycholinguistics* 17: 313–335. https://doi.org/10.1017/S0142716400007967

Munro, M. J. (2003). A primer on accent discrimination in the Canadian context. *TESL Canada Journal* 20(2): 38–51.

Munro, M. J., and T. M. Derwing (1995). Foreign accent, comprehensibility, and intelligibility in the speech of second language learners. *Language Learning* 45(1): 73–97.

Munro, M. J. (2003). A primer on accent discrimination in the Canadian context. *TESL Canada Journal* 20(2): 38–51.

Muroi, K. (1995). Problems of perception and production of Japanese morae: The case of native English speakers. *Sophia Linguistica* 38:41–60.

Nakayama, M., and J. Archibald (2005). Eyetracking and interlingual homographs. *Proceedings of the Canadian Linguistic Association*. Pp. 1–14. https://cla-acl.ca/actes/actes-2005-proceedings.html

References

Nakayama, M., C. Sears, Y. Hino, and S. Lupker (2013). Masked translation priming with Japanese-English bilinguals: Interactions between cognate status, target frequency and L2 proficiency. *Journal of Cognitive Psychology* 25(8): 949–981.

Nakayama, M., R. Verdonschot, C. Sears, and S. Lupker (2014). The masked cognate translation priming effect for different-script bilinguals is modulated by the phonological similarity of cognate words: Further support for the phonological account. *Journal of Cognitive Psychology* 26(7): 714–724.

Nearey, T. (1990). The segment as a unit of speech perception. *Journal of Phonetics* 18: 347–373.

Nearey, T. (1992). Context effects in a double-weak theory of speech perception. *Language and Speech* 35(1/2): 153–171. https://doi.org/10.1177/002383099203500213

Nemser, W. (1971). *An Experimental Study of Phonological Interference in the English of Hungarians*. Bloomington: Indiana University Press.

Nespor, M., and I. Vogel (1986). *Prosodic Phonology*. Dordrecht: Foris.

Nevins, A., D. Pesetsky, and C. Rodrigues (2009). Pirahã exceptionality: A reassessment. *Language* 5(2): 355–404.

Newell, H., and G. Piggott (2014). Interactions at the syntax—phonology interface: Evidence from Ojibwe. *Lingua* 150: 332–362.

O'Grady, W. (2005). *Syntactic Carpentry*. Mahwah, NJ: Erlbaum.

Ohala, J. (1986). Against the direct realist view of speech perception. *Journal of Phonetics* 14:75–82.

Ohala, J. J. (1983). The origin of sound patterns in vocal tract constraints. In P. F. MacNeilage, ed., *The Production of Speech*. New York: Springer-Verlag. Pp. 189–216.

Ortega-Llebaria, M. (2006). Phonetic cues to stress and accent in Spanish. In M. Diaz-Campos, ed., *Selected Proceedings of the 2nd Conference on Laboratory Approaches to Spanish Phonology*. Somerville, MA: Cascadilla Press. Pp. 104–118.

Ou, S-C., and Ota, M. (2004). Metrical computation in L2 stress acquisition: Evidence from Chinese-English interlanguage. Paper presented at Laboratory Phonology 9. Indiana.

Özçelik, Ö. (2017a). The prosodic acquisition path hypothesis: Towards explaining variability in L2 acquisition of phonology. *Glossa* 1(1): 1–48.

Özçelik, Ö. (2017b). The foot is not an obligatory constituent of the Prosodic Hierarchy: 'Stress' in Turkish, French and child English. *Linguistic Review* 34(1): 157–213.

Özçelik, Ö. (2017c). Universal grammar and second language phonology: Full transfer/ prevalent access in the L2 acquisition of Turkish 'stress' by English and French speakers. *Language Acquisition* 25(3): 1–36. https://doi.org/10.1080/10489223.2017.1293672

Özçelik, Ö. (2021). L2 acquisition of a complex stress pattern: UG-constrained learning paths in Khalkha Mongolian. *Frontiers in Psychology: Language Sciences* 12. https://doi.org/10.3389/fpsyg.2021.627797

Özçelik, Ö., and R. Sprouse (2016). Emergent knowledge of a universal phonological principle in the L2 acquisition of vowel harmony in Turkish: A 'four'-fold poverty of the stimulus in L2 acquisition. *Second Language Research* 33(2): 179–206.

Pater, J. (1997a). Metrical parameter missetting in second language acquisition. In S. J. Hannahs and M. Young-Scholten, eds., *Focus on Phonological Acquisition*. Amsterdam: John Benjamins. Pp. 235–261.

Pater, J. (1997b). Minimal violation and phonological development. *Language Acquisition* 6(3): 201–253.

Peperkamp, S., and E. Dupoux (2002). A typological study of stress 'deafness'. In C. Gussenhoven and N. Warner, eds., *Laboratory Phonology 7*. Berlin: Mouton de Gruyter. Pp. 202–240.

Peperkamp, S., I. Vendelin, and E. Dupoux (2010). Perception of predictable stress: A cross linguistic investigation. *Journal of Phonetics* 38(3): 422–430.

Perfors, A., J. Tenenbaum, E. Gibson, and T. Regier, (2010). How recursive is language? A Bayesian exploration. In H. van der Hulst, ed., *Recursion and Human Language*. 1st edition. Berlin: Mouton de Gruyter. Pp. 159–175.

Phillips, C. (1996). Order and structure. Doctoral dissertation, Massachusetts Institute of Technology.

Phillips, C., and L. Ehrenhofer (2015). The role of language processing in language acquisition. *Linguistic Approaches to Bilingualism* 5(4): 409–453.

Phillips, C., T. Pellathy, A. Marantz, E. Yellin, K. Wexler, D. Poeppel, M. McGinnis, and T. Roberts (2000). Auditory cortex accesses phonological categories: An MEG mismatch study. *Journal of Cognitive Neuroscience* 12(6): 1038–1055.

Pienemann, M. (1998). *Language Processing and Second Language Development: Processability Theory*. Amsterdam: John Benjamins.

Pierrehumbert, J. (2001). Exemplar dynamics: Word frequency, lenition and contrast. In Joan L. Bybee and P. Hopper, eds., *Frequency and the Emergence of Linguistic Structure*. Amsterdam: John Benjamins. Pp. 137–157.

Pierrehumbert, J., M. Beckman, and R. Ladd (2000). Conceptual foundations of phonology as a laboratory science. In N. Burton Roberts, P. Carr, and G. Docherty, eds., *Phonological Knowledge: Conceptual and Empirical Issues*. Oxford: Oxford University Press. Pp. 273–304.

Pinget, A.-F., R. Kager, and H. Van de Velde (2020). Linking variation in perception and production in sound change: Evidence from Dutch obstruent devoicing. *Language and Speech* 63(3): 660–685.

Pinker, S. (1984). *Language Learnability and Language Development*. Cambridge, MA: Harvard University Press.

Pinker, S. (1989). *Learnability and Cognition: The Acquisition of Argument Structure*. Cambridge, MA: MIT Press.

Pinker, S., and R. Jackendoff (2005). The faculty of language: What's special about it? *Cognition* 95(2): 201–236.

Pliatsikas, C., and T. Marinis (2013). Processing empty categories in a second language: When naturalistic exposure fills the (intermediate) gap. *Bilingualism: Language and Cognition* 16(1): 167–182.

Poeppel, D., W. Idsardi, and V. van Wassenhove (2008). Speech perception at the interface of neurobiology and linguistics. *Philosophical Transactions of the Royal Society* 363: 1071–1086.

Polka, L., and O.-S. Bohn (2011). Natural Referent Vowel (NRV) framework: An emerging view of early phonetic development. *Journal of Phonetics* 39(4): 467–478. https://doi.org/10.1016/j.wocn.2010.08.007

Pollock, J. (1991). How to use probabilities in reasoning. *Philosophical Studies* 64: 65–85.

Pollock, J. (2006). *Thinking About Acting*. New York: Oxford University Press.

Prévost, P., and L. White (2000). Missing surface inflection or impairment in second language acquisition? Evidence from tense and agreement. *Second Language Research* 16(2): 103–133. https://doi.org/10.1191/026765800677556046

References

Pulleyblank, D. (2006). Minimizing UG: Constraints upon constraints. In D. Baumer et al., eds. *Proceedings of WCCFL: 25*. Somerville, MA: Cascadilla Press. Pp. 15–39.

Pye, C., D. Ingram, and H. List (1987). A comparison of initial consonant acquisition in English and Quiché. In K. Nelson and A. van Kleeck, eds., *Children's Language*, vol. 6 Hillsdale, NJ: Erlbaum. Pp. 175–190.

Pylkkänen, L., R. Llinás, and G. Murphy (2006). The representation of polysemy: MEG evidence. *Journal of Cognitive Neuroscience* 18(1): 97–109, 175–190.

Pylyshyn, Z. (1984). *Computation and Cognition*. Cambridge, MA: MIT Press.

Pynte, J., and S. Colonna (2000). Decoupling syntactic parsing from visual inspection: the case of relative clause attachment in French. In A. Kennedy, R. Radach, D. Heller, and J. Pynte eds., *Reading as a Perceptual Process*. Oxford: Elsevier. Pp. 529–547.

R Core Team (2015). R: A language and environment for statistical computing. R Foundation for Statistical Computing, Vienna, Austria. https://www.R-project.org/

Raimy, E., and C. Cairns, eds. (2009). *Contemporary Views on Architecture and Representation in Phonology*. Cambridge, MA: MIT Press.

Rast, R. (2008). *Foreign Language Input: Initial Processing*. Clevedon: Multilingual Matters.

Rayner, K., and A. Pollatsek (1989). *The Psychology of Reading*. New York: Prentice-Hall.

Reinisch, E., and A. Weber (2012). Adapting to suprasegmental lexical stress errors in foreign accented speech. *Journal of the Acoustical Society of America* 132(2): 1165–1176.

Reiss, C. (2017). Substance free phonology. In. S. J. Hannahs and A. Bosch, eds. *The Routledge Handbook of Phonological Theory*. Abingdon: Routledge. Pp. 425–452.

Reiss, C., and M. Hale (2008). *The Phonological Enterprise*. Oxford: Oxford University Press.

Rice, K. (1992). On deriving sonority: A structural account of sonority relationships. *Phonology* 9:61–99.

Rice, K., and P. Avery (1995). Variability in a deterministic model of language acquisition: a theory of segmental elaboration. In J. Archibald, ed., *Phonological Acquisition and Phonological Theory*. Mahwah, NJ: Erlbaum. Pp. 23–42.

Richards, N. (2010). *Uttering Trees*. Cambridge, MA: MIT Press.

Richards, N. (2016). *Contiguity Theory*. Cambridge, MA: MIT Press.

Richards, N. (2019). Detecting contiguity-prominence. Unpublished manuscript.

Ringen, C., and O. Heinämäki (1999). Variation in Finnish vowel harmony: An OT account. *Natural Language and Linguistic Theory* 17: 303–337.

Rochet, B. (1995). Perception and production of second-language speech sounds by adults. In W. Strange, ed., *Speech Perception and Linguistic Experience*. Baltimore: York Press. Pp. 379–410.

Roeper, T., and E. Williams (1987). *Parameter Setting*. Dordrecht: Reidel.

Rothman, J., J. González Alonso, and E. Puig-Mayenco (2019). *Third Language Acquisition and Linguistic Transfer*. New York: Cambridge University Press.

Rothman, J., and R. Slabakova (2018). The generative approach to SLA and its place in modern second language studies. *Studies in Second Language Acquisition* 40(2): 417–442.

Sagae, S. (2007). Sentence processing and prosody: A comparison between hearing-loss and hearing readers. MA thesis, University of Calgary.

Saleemi, A. (1992). *Universal Grammar and Language Learnability*. Cambridge: Cambridge University Press.

Salem, S. T. (2014). *The Modification of English /s/ + Consonant Onset Clusters by Levant Arabic Speakers*. Lethbridge, Canada: University of Lethbridge, Faculty of Education.

Samarajiwa, C., and R. M. Abeysekera (1964). Some pronunciation difficulties of Sinhalese learners of English as a foreign language. *Language Learning* 14:45–50.

Sandler, W. (2012). The phonological organization of sign languages. *Language and Linguistic Compass* 6(3): 162–182. https://doi.org/10.1002/lnc3.326

Sandler, W., and D. Lillo-Martin (2006). *Sign Language and Linguistic Universals*. Cambridge: Cambridge University Press.

Sapir, E. (2008/1933). The psychological reality of phonemes. In P. Swiggers, ed., *The Collected Works of Edward Sapir*, vol. 1. Berlin: De Gruyter. Pp. 539–554.

Schmidt, R. (1990). The role of consciousness in second language learning. *Applied Linguistics* 11:129–158.

Scholz, B., F. J. Pelletier, G. Pullum, and R. Nefdt (2022). Philosophy of linguistics. In Edward N. Zalta, ed., *The Stanford Encyclopedia of Philosophy*. https://plato.stanford.edu/archives/spr2022/entries/linguistics/

Schütze, C. T., and J. Sprouse (2014). Judgment data. In R. Podesva and D. Sharma, eds., *Research Methods in Linguistics*. Cambridge: Cambridge University Press. Pp. 27–50. https://doi.org/10.1017/CBO9781139013734.004

Schwab, S., N. Giroud, M. Meyer, and V. Dellwo (2020). Working memory and not acoustic sensitivity is related to stress processing ability in a foreign language: An ERP study. *Journal of Neurolinguistics* 55. https://doi.org/10.1016/j.jneuroling.2020.100897

Schwartz, B. D., and R. A. Sprouse (1996). L2 cognitive states and the Full Transfer / Full Access model. *Second Language Research* 12: 40–72.

Schwartz, B. D., and R. Sprouse (2021). The Full Transfer / Full Access model and L3 cognitive states. *Linguistic Approaches to Bilingualism* 11(1): 1–29.

Schwartz, B. D., and R. Sprouse (2020). In defense of 'copying and restructuring'. *Second Language Research* 37(3): 489–493. https://doi.org/10.1177/0267658320975831

Schwartz, M., and H. Goad (2017). Indirect positive evidence in the acquisition of a subset grammar. *Language Acquisition* 24(3): 234–264.

Scovel, T. (1988). *A Time to Speak*. Cambridge: Newbury House.

Selinker, L. (1972). Interlanguage. *International Review of Applied Linguistics* 10:209–231.

Selkirk, E. (2000). The interactions of constraints on prosodic phrasing. In M. Horne, ed., *Prosody: Theory and Experiment*. Dordrecht: Kluwer Academic. Pp. 231–261.

Selkirk, E. (2011). The syntax-phonology interface. In J. Goldsmith et al., eds., *The Blackwell Handbook of Phonological Theory*. 2nd edition. Oxford: Wiley-Blackwell. Pp. 435–484.

Serratrice, L., A. Sorace, F. Filiaci, and M. Baldo (2009). Bilingual children's sensitivity to specificity and genericity: Evidence from metalinguistic awareness. *Bilingualism: Language and Cognition* 12: 1–19.

Sharwood Smith, M., and J. Truscott (2014). *The Multilingual Mind: A Modular Processing Perspective*. Cambridge: Cambridge University Press.

Shinohara, Y., and P. Iverson (2018). High variability identification and discrimination training for Japanese speakers learning English /r/-/l/. *Journal of Phonetics* 66: 242–251.

Singh, R. (1985). Prosodic adaptation in interphonology. *Lingua* 67: 269–282.

Singleton, D. (1989). *Language acquisition: The age factor*. Clevedon: Multilingual Matters.

Slabakova, R. (2013). What is easy and what is hard to acquire in a second language: A generative perspective. In M. García Mayo, M. J. Gutiérrez Mangado, and M. Martínez-Adrián, eds., *Contemporary Approaches to Second Language Acquisition*. Amsterdam: John Benjamins. Pp. 5–28.

Slabakova, R., T. Leal, A. Dudley, and M. Stack (2020). *Generative Second Language Acquisition*. Cambridge: Cambridge University Press.

Snape, N., and T. Kupisch (2016). *Second language acquisition*. London: Red Globe Press.

Sorace, A. (2011). Pinning down the concept of interface in bilingual development. *Linguistic Approaches to Bilingualism* 2(2): 209–216.

Sorace, A., L. Serratrice, F. Filiaci, and M. Baldo (2009). Discourse conditions on subject pronoun realization: Testing the linguistic intuitions of older bilingual children. *Lingua* 119: 460–477.

Stefanich, S. (2019). A morphological account of Spanish/English word-internal codeswitching. Ph.D. thesis. University of Illinois at Chicago.

Stefanich, S., and J. Cabrelli (2018). Phonological factors of Spanish/English word-internal code-switching. In L. López, ed., *Code-Switching Experimental Answers to Theoretical Questions: In Honor of Kay González-Vilbazo*. Amsterdam: John Benjamins. Pp. 195–222.

Stefanich, S., J. Cabrelli, D. Hilderman, and J. Archibald (2019). The morphophonology of intraword codeswitching: Representation and processing. *Frontiers in Communication: Language Sciences* 4: 54. https://doi.org/10.3389/fcomm.2019.00054

Steinberg, J., H. Truckenbrodt, and T. Jacobsen (2010). Preattentive phonotactic processing as indexed by the mismatch negativity. *Journal of Cognitive Neuroscience* 22(10): 2174–2185. https://doi.org/10.1162/jocn.2009.21408

Steriade, D. (1982). Greek prosodies and the nature of syllabification. Doctoral dissertation, Massachusetts Institute of Technology.

Steriade, D. (2009). The phonology of perceptibility effects: The p-map and its consequences for constraint organization. In K. Hanson and S. Inkelas, eds., *The Nature of the Word: Studies in Honor of Paul Kiparsky*. Cambridge, MA: MIT Press. Pp. 151–179.

Strange, W., ed. (1995). *Speech Perception and Linguistic Experience: Issues in Cross-Language Research*. Baltimore: York Press.

Strange, W., and V. Shafer (2008). Speech perception in second language learners: The re-education of selective perception. In J. Hansen Edwards and M. Zampini, eds., *Phonology and Second Language Acquisition*. Amsterdam: John Benjamins. Pp. 153–192.

Suárez, J. (1983). *The Mesoamerican Indian Languages*. Cambridge: Cambridge University Press.

Sughara, M. (2003). Downtrends and post-FOCUS intonation in Tokyo Japanese. Doctoral dissertation, University of Massachusetts, Amherst.

Summerell, F. (2007). The L2 acquisition of Japanese length contrasts. MA thesis, University of Calgary.

Taylor, B. (2011). Do English learners of Japanese produce isolated nouns with Standard Japanese lexical accent? *Second Language* 10: 15–31.

Taylor, B., and S. Hellmuth (2012). Exploring 'stress deafness' in English listeners: An experimental study. Paper presented at the University of York Workshop on Second Language Phonology.

Taylor, C. (1985). *Nkore-Kiga*. London: Croom Helm.

Tesar, B., and P. Smolensky (1998). Learnability in Optimality Theory. *Linguistic Inquiry* 29: 229–268.

Tessier, A.-M., and K. Jesney (2014). Learning in Harmonic Serialism and the necessity of a richer base. *Phonology* 31:155–178. https://doi.org/10.1017/S0952675714000062

Treiman, R., and K. Hirsh-Pasek (1983). Silent reading: Insights from second-generation deaf readers. *Cognitive Psychology* 15: 39–65.

Tremblay, A. (2008). Is L2 lexical access prosodically constrained? On the processing of word stress by French Canadian L2 learners of English. *Applied Psycholinguistics* 29: 553–584.

Trofimovich, P., and W. Baker (2006). Learning second language suprasegmentals: Effect of L2 experience on prosody and fluency characteristics of L2 speech. *Studies in Second Language Acquisition* 28(1): 1–30.

Trommer, J. (2015). Moraic affixes and morphological colors in Dinka. *Linguistic Inquiry* 46(1): 77–112.

Trommer, J. (2018). The subsegmental structure of German plural allomorphy. Talk given at the University of Victoria.

Tsimpli, I. M., and M. Dimitrakopoulou (2007). The interpretability hypothesis: Evidence from WH-interrogatives in second language acquisition. *Second Language Research* 23(2): 215–242.

Tyler, M. (2019). Simplifying MATCH WORD: Evidence from English functional categories. *Glossa* 4(1): 1–32.

Van de Weijer, J. (2019). Where now with Optimality Theory? *Acta Linguistica Academica* 66(1): 115–136.

van der Hulst, Harry (2010). A note on recursion in phonology. In Harry van der Hulst, ed., *Recursion and Human Language*. Berlin: De Gruyter. Pp. 301–342.

van der Pas, B., and W. Zonneveld (2004). L2 parameter resetting for metrical systems: An assessment and a reinterpretation of some core literature. *Linguistic Review* 21:125–170.

Vanderweide, T. (2005). Cue-based learning and the acquisition of pre-vocalic clusters. PhD dissertation, University of Calgary.

Van Heuven, W., and T. Dijkstra (2001). The Semantic, Orthographic and Phonological Interactive Activation Model. Poster presented at the 12th conference of the European Society for Cognitive Psychology. Edinburgh, Scotland.

van Leerdam, M., A. Bosman, and A. de Groot (2009). When MOOD rhymes with ROAD: Dynamics of phonological coding in bilingual visual word perception. *Mental Lexicon* 4: 303–335.

Van Leussen, J.-W., and P. Escudero (2015). Learning to perceive and recognize a second language: The L2LP model revised. *Frontiers in Psychology: Language Sciences* 6. https://doi.org/10.3389/fpsyg.2015.01000

VanPatten, B. (2015). Where are the experts? *Hispania* 98(1): 2–13.

Vaux, B., and A. Wolfe (2009). The appendix. In E. Raimy and C. Cairns, eds., *Contemporary Views on Architecture and Representations in Phonology*. Cambridge: MIT Press. Pp. 101–143.

Voga, M., and J. Grainger (2007). Cognate status and cross-script translation priming. *Memory and Cognition* 35: 938–952.

Vogel, Irene (2009). Universals of prosodic structure. In Sergio Scalise, Elisabetta Magni, and Antonietta Bisetto, eds., *Universals of Language Today*. Berlin: Springer. Pp. 59–82.

Wagner, M. (2010). Prosody and recursion in coordinate structures and beyond. *Natural Language and Linguistic Theory* 28: 183–237.

Wang, Y., A. Jongman, and J. Sereno (2003). Acoustic and perceptual evaluation of Mandarin tone productions before and after perceptual training. *Journal of the Acoustic Society of America* 113(2): 1033–1043.

Watanabe, S., and J.-T. Chien, eds. (2015). *Bayesian Speech and Language Processing*. Cambridge: Cambridge University Press.

Watumull, J., M. D. Hauser, I. G. Roberts, and N. Hornstein (2014). On recursion. *Frontiers in Psychology* 4: 1–7.

Weber, S. (2014). The role of foot structure on the intelligibility of L2 stress errors. PhD thesis, University of Calgary.

Weinberger, S. (1988). Theoretical Foundations of Second Language Phonology. PhD. dissertation, University of Washington.

Weinreich, U. (1953). *Languages in Contact: Findings and Problems*. The Hague: Mouton.

Werker, J. F., and J. S. Logan (1985). Cross-language evidence for three factors in speech perception. *Perception & Psychophysic* 37(1): 35–44.

Westergaard, M. (2021). Microvariation in multilingual situations: The importance of property-by-property acquisition. *Second Language Research* 37(3): 379–407.

Wexler, K., and P. Culicover (1980). *Formal Principles of Language Acquisition*. Cambridge, MA: MIT Press.

White, B., B. Muradás-Taylor S. Hellmuth. (2016). Non-persistent 'stress-deafness' in L1 English-speaking advanced learners of L2 Spanish. Paper presented at the *New Sounds* conference, Aarhus, Denmark.

White, L. (2003). *Second Language Acquisition and Universal Grammar*. Cambridge: Cambridge University Press.

White, L. (2011). Second language acquisition at the interfaces. *Lingua* 121: 577–590.

White, L., and F. Genesee (1996). How native is near-native? The issue of ultimate attainment in adult second language acquisition. *Second Language Research* 12(3): 233–265.

Wiese, R. (1996). *The Phonology of German*. Oxford: Oxford University Press.

Wilson, A. D., and S. Golonka (2013). Embodied cognition is not what you think it is. *Frontiers in Psychology* 4(58): 1–13. https://doi.org/10.3389/fpsyg.2013.00058

Wilson, C., and L. Davidson (2013). Bayesian analysis of non-native cluster production. In S. Kan, C. Moore-Cantwell, and R. Staub, eds., *Proceedings of NELS 40*. Amherst, MA: University of Massachusetts Graduate Linguistics Student Association. Pp. 265–278.

Wright, R. (2001). Perceptual cues in contrast maintenance. In E. Hume and K. Johnson, eds., *The Role of Speech Perception in Phonology*. San Diego: Academic Press. Pp. 252–277.

Wright, R. (2004). A review of perceptual cues and cue robustness. In B. Hayes, R. Kirchener, and D. Steriade, eds. *Phonetically Based Phonology*. Cambridge: Cambridge University Press. Pp. 34–57.

Wulff, S., and N. C. Ellis (2018). Usage-based approaches to second language acquisition. In D. T. Miller, F. Bayram, J. Rothman, and L. Serratrice, eds., *Bilingual Cognition and Language: The State of the Science Across Its Subfields*. Amsterdam: John Benjamins. Pp. 37–56.

Wunderlich, D. (1999). German noun plural reconsidered. *Behavioral and Brain Sciences* 22(0): 1044–1045.

Yan, X., Y. Maeda, J. Lv, and A. Ginther (2016). Elicited imitation as a measure of second language proficiency: A narrative review. *Language Testing* 33(4). https://doi.org/10.1177/0265532215594643

Yang, C. (2017). Rage against the machine: Evaluation metrics in the 21st century. *Language Acquisition* 24(2): 100–125. https://doi.org/10.1080/10489223.2016.1274318

Yang, C. (2018). A formalist perspective on language acquisition. *Linguistic Approaches to Bilingualism* 8(6): 665–706.

Yang, C., S. Crain, R. Berwick, N. Chomsky, and J. Bolhuis (2017). The growth of language: Universal Grammar, experience, and principles of computation. *Neuroscience and Biobehavioral Reviews* 81(Part B): 103–119.

Yang, H. (2005). Plurality and modification in Mandarin noun phrases. PhD Dissertation, University of Texas at Austin.

Ylinen, S., M. Uther, A. Latvala, S. Vepsäläinen, P. Iverson, R. Akahane-Yamada, and R. Näätänen (2009). Training the brain to weight speech cues differently: A study of Finnish second-language users of English. *Journal of Cognitive Neuroscience* 22(6): 1319–1332.

Young-Scholten, M. (1993). *The Acquisition of Prosodic Structure in a Second Language*. Tubingen: Max Niemeyer.

Young-Scholten, M. (2013). Low-educated immigrants and the social relevance of second language acquisition research. *Second Language Research* 29(4): 441–454.

Young-Scholten, M., and J. Archibald (2000). Second language syllable structure. In J. Archibald, ed., *Second Language Acquisition and Linguistic Theory*. Oxford: Blackwell. Pp. 64–101.

Yu, K. M. (2019). Parsing with minimalist grammars and prosodic trees. In R. Berwick and E. Stabler, eds., *Minimalist Parsing*. Oxford: Oxford University Press. Pp. 69–109.

Yuan, Q., and J. Archibald (2022). Modified input training and cue reweighting in second language vowel perception. *Frontiers in Educational Research* 5(6): 65–75. https://doi.org/10.25236/FER.2022.050613

Zec, D. (1995). Sonority constraints on syllable structure. *Phonology* 12: 85–129.

Zhang, N. (2014). Expressing number productively in Mandarin Chinese. *Linguistics* 52(1): 1–34.

Zimmermann, E. (2017). *Morphological Length and Prosodically Defective Morphemes*. Oxford: Oxford University Press.

INDEX

For the benefit of digital users, indexed terms that span two pages (e.g., 52–53) may, on occasion, appear on only one of those pages.

Abrahamsson, N, 73–74, 121–22, 131–33, 141–43

abstract representations, 4, 6–7, 14–16, 80, 83, 170

Abutalebi, J., 140–41

accented speech, 11–13, 37–38, 53–54, 160, 197

acquisition, 8–9, 18–20, 50, 92–93, 95

 See also L2 grammar; L2 learners; L2 phonology; L2 speech; learnability; nativelikeness

age effects, 35–36, 37–38

Alexiadou, A., 161

algebraic phonology, 14

Alhemaid, A., 118, 119

allomorphs, 139–40

allomorphy, 145–49, 150–51

Almalki, H., 116

ambiguity, 165, 169, 175

American Sign Language (ASL), 171–75

 See also gestural languages

appendices, 117, 118–20, 121, 127–28

approximants, 65, 68–69, 125–26

Arabic, 28, 71, 90–91, 113–21, 126

aspiration, 20–21, 62, 85

association lines, 151, 155–56

Atkey, S., 123–24

auditory discrimination, 18–19, 23–24, 99–100

auditory distance, 85–89

Avery, P., 57–58

Bader, M., 166

Bayesian epistemology, 202–5

Beckman, M., 98

Berretta, A., 138–39

Berwick, R., 91–92, 192–93

Best, C., 86–87, 91–92, 94

bilingual lexicon, 133, 134–39, 140–41, 152, 198

Birdsong, D., 37–38

Blame Assignment, 202–3

 See also Credit Problem, The

Blanco-Elorrieta, E., 75, 123, 160

Bley-Vroman, R., 34

block transfer hypothesis, 161

Bohn, G., 57–58

Bohn, O.-S., 46

bootstrapping problem, 91–92, 204

bottleneck hypothesis, 198

Boudaoud, M., 115

Brannen, K., 82–83, 85–87, 88–90, 91

Brazilian Portuguese (BP), 29–30, 85, 113–14, 118, 120–21

 See also Portuguese

Broersma, M., 125–26

Broś, K., 14–15

Broselow, E., 28, 63, 70, 71, 126–27

Brown, C., 18–21, 92–93, 112, 124

Burkholder, M., 140–41

Cardoso. W., 29, 30–31, 85, 113, 114–15

chain shifts, 58–60

Chen, S.-I., 126–27
Chinese, 17–20, 32–33, 48–49, 50–52,
    131–32
    See also Mandarin
Chomsky, N., 5, 7, 8, 91–92
Clahsen, H., 193–94
Clements, G., 97–98
Clifton, C., 172
coda condition hypothesis, 76
codas, 69, 75–79, 81, 99–103, 131–32,
    141–44
code switching. *See* intraword code
    switching (ICS)
cognition, 2–4, 13–15, 16, 57, 98, 164–65,
    199–200
Collins, C., 160
Colonna, S., 168
communication strategies, 132–33
competence, 53, 81–82, 206–7, 211
condition-action rule, 72
consonant clusters
    acquisition and, 8–9
    epenthetic vowels and, 73–75
    inflectional morphology and, 131–33
    perception of, 112–21
    release burst and, 85
    syllables and, 25–28, 61–70, 113–21,
        131–32
    See also codas; consonantal sequences;
        distributed morphology (DM);
        onsets; s-clusters
consonant place (CPlace) node, 155
consonantal contact hypothesis, 76
consonantal sequences, 70, 75–78, 83–84,
    112, 113–21
    See also codas; consonant clusters;
        distributed morphology (DM); onsets
contiguity theory, 177–82, 187–88, 196–97
    See also phonological contiguity
contrastive hierarchy, 14–15, 80–81,
    89–91, 206
contrastive stress, 38–40
Corcoran, D., 168
coronal, 20, 21–22, 59, 147–49, 151, 154–56
Correia, S., 44–45
Credit Problem, The, 204
    See also Blame Assignment

Croteau, N., 178, 190
Curtin, S., 20–21
Cutler, A., 15, 125–26
Czech, 123–24

Darcy, I., 54–55, 125–26
Davidson, L., 203
de Almeida, R., 13
deaf and hard of hearing (DH) subjects,
    171–75
deaf learners, 164
deficit hypothesis, 17–20
Dehaene-Lambertz, G., 73–74
Dekydtspotter, L., 75–76
deletion, 73–74, 122, 131–32
Dellwo, V., 52
derived environment constraint, 27–28
Derwing, T., 34–35, 160, 197
devoicing, 25–26
differential substitution, 82–83, 86, 92
Dijkstra, T., 134–35, 138
direct realist approach, 85–86,
    89–90
distributed morphology (DM), 133–34,
    138, 140–45, 160, 209
DMAP (direct mapping of acoustics to
    Phonology), 125–26
Dobler, E., 161
Dollins, A., 168
double-weak model, 89–90
Dresher, E., 14–15, 57–58, 74, 89–91,
    202–4, 206
Duanmu, S., 18, 51
Dupoux, E., 38–42, 46, 73–74, 75–76
Durvasula, K., 14–15
Dutch, 92, 134–36, 138–39
Dyck, C., 1–2, 14–15

Eckman, F., 26, 63, 126–27
ejectives, 23–24, 81, 83–84, 99–102
E-language, 13, 26, 27–28
elicited imitation, 116–17
Embick, D., 133, 134
emergentism, 13–14
Emmorey, K., 160
empiricist theories, 3–4
enhancement, 87–88, 97–98

Index

epenthesis
  illicit consonantal sequences and, 72–77
  illusory vowels and, 72–73, 110–11, 112–13
  repair strategy and, 32–34, 131–33
  sC onsets and, 118–23
Epistemological Problem, The, 204
errors
  epenthetic vowels and, 32–34, 112
  homophones and, 171
  morphology and, 142, 150–54
  onset clusters and, 63, 113–14
  with stress, 39–45
Escher's problem, 111
essentialism, 14–16
European French, 88–89, 92
  See also French; Quebec French
Evans, B., 97–98
event-related potential (ERP), 14–15, 22, 24–25
evolution, 91–92
exemplar theory, 2, 81, 127–28
externalism, 13
eye-tracking, 4, 135, 172, 173–75

Farris-Trimble, A., 4
feature dependency, 148, 151
feature geometry, 147–49
feature hierarchies, 89–90, 125
feature spreading, 155
feature weighting, 87
features. *See* morphosyntactic features; phonological features
Felser, C., 193–94
Finer, D., 63, 126–27
Finnish, 38, 41–42, 49, 62–70, 97–98
Fiorentino, R., 138–39
Flege, J., 81–82, 83, 94
Fodor, J., 4, 168–71
foot structure, 15–16, 47–48, 131
  See also metrical representations; stress
Frazier, L., 172
French, 21–22, 24–25, 38–46, 47–50, 52, 90–92, 138–40
  See also European French; Quebec French
French, L., 29, 30–31

frequency, intake, 85–86, 93–95, 97–98, 99–103
full access, 36
full transfer, 36–38
  See also prosodic transfer hypothesis; transfer

Gagliardi, A., 5
Garcia, G., 200
garden-path sentences, 165
geminates, 109–10
GenSLA (generative approaches to second language acquisition), 16, 205–7, 210
German, 11–12, 130–31, 145–54, 156–57
gestural languages, 164, 171–75
Giroud, N., 52
Goad, H., 20–21, 24, 129, 130–31
González Poot, A., 14, 23, 81, 84, 99–102
Goodell, E., 171
Gout, A., 73–74
government phonology (GP), 60–61
Grainger, J., 134–35, 138
grammatical interfaces, 212
Green, D., 140–41
Greenberg, J., 26, 102
Gregg, K., 27
Grosjean, F., 7

Haber, L., 168
Haber, R., 168
Hakulinen, L., 64
Hale, M., 14
Hanson, V., 171
hard of hearing and deaf (DH) subjects, 171–75
Haugen, J., 140
hearing loss, 171–75
Hellmuth, S., 43–44
Hestvik, A., 14–15
high attachment (HA), 167–70, 174–75
Hindi, 28, 85, 91, 126
Hirsh-Pasek, 171
Holland, J., 72
homogeneity hypothesis, 137–39, 140–41
homographs, 134–36, 138–39

homophones, 134–36, 138–40
Hungarian, 41–42, 46, 47–49
Hurford, J., 91–92

iambic feet, 47, 127
identity map lexical-learning strategy, 127–28
Idsardi, W., 75, 76, 77, 78, 112–13
IL grammar, 9, 36, 126, 163
  See also interlanguage grammars; universal grammar (UG)
I-language, 26, 27–28, 91–92, 159, 209
illusory vowels, 110–23, 126, 127–28
implicit prosody hypothesis (IPH), 168–71, 174–75
  See also prosody
indirect realist approach, 85–86, 91–92, 202
individual differences, 52–54, 62
inference engine, 5, 54
inner speech, 165, 171
input
  as cognition, 199–200
  cues, 25, 46
  frequency of, 29–31
  intake vs., 93
  linguistic, 3–5, 7
  parsing of, 72–74
  processing of, 46
  robustness of, 20–22, 23–25
  working memory and, 54–46
input effects, 9–11
input signal, 97
intake frequency, 85–86, 93–95, 97–98, 99–103
intelligibility, 34–36, 81, 121, 206–7
interface hypothesis, 198–99
interfaces
  grammatical, 212
  indirect realist model and, 202
  L2 WH-questions and, 176–77
  morphology/syntax, 205
  with phonetics, 211
  phonetics/phonology, 176–77, 194, 199–200
  phonology/lexicon, 136–41
  phonology/morphology, 129–30, 132–45, 160–62

phonology/syntax, 164, 198
syntax/lexicon, 198
syntax/pragmatic, 198
  See also bottleneck hypothesis; interface hypothesis; match theory
interlanguage grammars
  constraints on, 197–98
  contiguity theory and, 187–88
  L2 phonology and, 3–7
  model of, 209
  multilingualism and, 7
  shallow structure and, 193–94
  See also IL grammar; universal grammar (UG); universals
interlingual allomorphs, 139–40
interlingual homographs, 134–36, 138
interlingual homophones, 134–36, 138
interrogatives, 176–81, 185–89, 194–98
intra-constituent licensing, 60–61, 67–70
intraword code switching (ICS), 133, 157–59, 162
Iverson, G., 63
Iverson, P., 46, 97–98

Jackendoff, R., 91–92
Jackson, S., 85, 91
James, A., 92
Japanese
  accent placement in, 48–49
  acquisition of /l/ and /r/ by speakers of, 18–20
  contiguity theory and, 187–93
  English s-clusters and speakers of, 72–76
  match theory and, 182–87
  new features to speakers of, 95–96
  perception of illusory vowels by speakers of, 111–12, 120–21
  phonemic length in, 103–10
  speakers of, learning Russian, 20
  stress deafness and, 50–51
  WH-questions in, 176–82, 194–200
Jesney, K., 58–60, 127–28
John, P., 29, 30–31
Jung, Y., 116–17

Kabak, B., 75, 76, 77, 78, 112–13
Kawagoe, I., 48–49, 50, 51, 52

Index

Kaye, J., 6, 202–3
Keyser, S., 87
Kijak, A., 43
Korean, 59–60, 62–63, 64–70
Kruskal-Wallis test, 107–8

L2 grammar, 6–7
L2 learners, 3–7, 23–24
L2 phonology
  acquisition of, 3–7
  cognitive science and, 2–3
  linguistic input and, 5
  perception and, 94
  phonetics and, 199–200
  proficiency and, 53
  role of perception in, 82, 94
  of Swedish, 141–43
  theories of, 1
L2 speech, 2, 7, 57–58, 83, 197
L2 WH-questions, 176–77
LaCharité, D., 21–22
Ladd, R., 80, 98
Lago, S., 14–15
language change, 9–10
language faculty, 3–4, 8, 26, 199
language learnability. *See* learnability
Language of Thought, The
  (Fodor), 4
language tags, 7, 140–41, 162
Lardiere, P., 17, 145
Larson-Hall, J., 20
lateralization, 76–77
learnability, 3, 5, 6–7, 200, 204
Lee, D.-Y., 62
Lee, S., 59
Legate, J., 9–10
length contrasts, 103–4, 107, 110
lexical access, 105, 134–36
lexical decision task (LDT), 137
lexicon, bilingual, 133, 134–39, 140–41,
  152, 198
Libben, G., 137–38, 140–41
licensing, 60–61, 67–68
  See also universals
Lidz, J., 5
Lightfoot, D., 11
Lin, Y.-H., 32–34

linguistic environment, 2–4, 5, 9, 52–53,
  93, 127
linguistic input, 3–5, 7
linguistic proximity model, 202–3
Llinás, R., 136
López, L., 140–41, 161
low attachment (LA), 167–70, 174–75

Maddieson, I., 63–64
Mah, J., 22, 24
main stress rule (SPE), 6
major phonological phrases, 169–70, 175
Mandarin, 121, 131–32, 141–45
  See also Chinese
Mann-Whitney U test, 106, 108
Marantz, A., 161
markedness, 25–26, 27–28, 29–30, 126–27
match theory, 161–62, 181, 182–87,
  191–92
Matthews, J., 112, 146
McDonough, K., 116
McGuian, F., 168
Mehler, J., 38–39
memory, working, 54–57
mental representations, 4, 14–15, 55–56,
  80–81, 137
Merge operation, 91–92, 134, 160, 180, 199
metalinguistic knowledge, 39–40
metrical representations, 50
Meyer, M., 52
minimal sonority distance (MSD), 63, 64–65
minor phonological phrases, 169–70
Modularity of the Mind, The (Fodor), 4
morphology, 131–33, 158–59
morphology/syntax interface, 205
morphosyntactic features, 129–30, 134,
  144–45, 147–49, 177–78
  See also tense marking
multilingualism, 7, 140–41
multiple exponence, 146–47
Munro, M., 34–35, 160, 197
Muradás-Taylor, B., 43–44
Murphy, G., 136

Nakayama, M., 7, 135, 136
nasalization, 76–77
nativelikeness, 34–35, 37–38, 53–54, 197

Navarrete, E., 38–39
Nearey, T., 89–90
Nespor, M., 169
no crossing constraint, 155–57
nonce words, 116

O'Brien, M., 206–7
onsets, 18–19, 23–24, 62–63, 68–69, 81
ontogeny/phylogeny model, 126–27
Orwell's problem, 5, 7, 97–98
Ota, M., 48–49, 50, 51, 52
Ou, S.-C., 48–49, 50, 51, 52
Özçelik, Ö., 48, 52, 57–58, 127, 154,
    155–56, 192–93

Pallier, C., 38–39
Park, H., 54–55
parsers, 68–70, 72–73, 165–66
parsing, 66–75, 121, 176
Pater, J., 20–21, 50
pedagogy and GenSLA, 206–7
Pelletier, F., 13
Peperkamp, S., 38–40, 41–42, 45
perceptibility, 82–86, 96
    See also auditory distance; perception
perception
    errors of, 113–21
    features causing inaccurate, 95–96
    illusory vowels and, 110–13
    of non-L1 features, 96
    of palatal stops, 123–24
    of phonological features, 84–86, 95–96
    vs production, 22–23, 81–82
    production study and, 114–20
    role of in acquisition, 81–86
    of s-clusters, 30–32
    See also production
Perceptual Assimilation Model
    (PAM-L2), 94
Perfetti, C., 171
Persian, 73, 113–20, 121–23
phase head hypothesis, 161
Phillips, C., 80–81
phonetics/phonology interface, 176–77,
    194, 199–200
phonological contiguity, 194, 196–98
    See also contiguity theory

phonological features
    abstract, 14–15, 80–81
    acquisition of, 18–20, 92–93, 95
    auditory distance and, 86–89
    chain shifts and, 58–60
    contrastive hierarchies of, 89–90
    deficit hypothesis and, 17–20
    of ejectives, 23–24, 99–102
    intake and, 97–98
    L1 vs. L2, 12–13
    learning difficulty of, 22
    perceptibility of, 84–86, 95–96
    phonetic features vs., 89–91
    redeployment of, 123–24
    robustness of, 97–98
    secondary articulations of, 155–56
    vowel harmony and, 154
    See also coronal; enhancement; feature
        geometry; preferential feature
        preservation; voicing
phonological knowledge, 13
phonological parsing, 70–75
phonological persistence, 161
phonological phrases. *See* major
    phonological phrases; minor
    phonological phrases
phonological switching, 160
phonology, L2, 3–5
phonology/lexicon interface, 136–41
phonology/morphology interface, 129–30,
    132–45, 160–62
phonology/syntax interface, 164, 198
phylogeny/ontogeny model, 126–27
picture identification task, 105, 108
Pierrehumbert, J., 98
Pinker, S., 91–92
pitch boost, 194–95
place nodes, 154
Plato's problem, 7
plural marking, 143–54
Poeppel, D., 138–39
Polish, 38, 41–43, 46, 49
Pollatsek, A., 165
Pollock, J., 204–5
polysemy, 138–39, 140
Portuguese, 43–45, 82–83, 113–14
    See also Brazilian Portuguese (BP)

poverty of the stimulus, 156–57, 199
preferential feature preservation, 58–60
Prévost, P., 21–22
primary linguistic data (PLD), 93, 199
priming, 137–39, 140
processing speed, 54–57
production
  DMAP and, 125
  epenthetic vowels and, 73–75, 121–23
  of geminates, 109–10
  illusory vowels and, 110–11
  of inflectional morphology, 131–33
  L2 accent in, 11–13
  markedness and, 30–32
  morphology and, 131–33
  native vs non-native, 34–35
  vs perception, 22–23
  perception study and, 114–20
  verb morphology and, 158–59
  See also perception
proficiency, 37, 43–44, 53, 105–8, 122–23
pronunciation, 34–35, 37–38, 197, 206–7
prosodic constraints on reanalysis (PCR),
  166, 172–75
prosodic hierarchy, 130, 161–62, 182–83
prosodic transfer hypothesis, 129, 130–31,
  145
prosodic tree, 185–86
prosodic words (PWd), 130–31
prosody, 166–71
psycholinguistics, 137, 139, 152
Pullum, G., 13
Pylkkänen, I., 123, 136, 160
Pylyshyn, Z., 4, 98
Pynte, J., 168

Quebec French, 88–89, 92
  See also European French; French
Quechua, 9–10

rationalist theory, 3–4
Rayner, K., 165
reading, 135, 152, 168, 171–74
realism, 75–77, 91–92
reanalysis, 143–45, 166, 173–74
recoverability, 32, 100–1, 141–43
recursion, 91–92, 206

redeployment, 60–61, 68–70, 103–10,
  113–21
relative clause (RC) attachment, 166–71,
  174–76
repair strategies, 28–34, 120, 126–27,
  131–32
representational realism, 75–77
Richards, N., 176, 177–82, 184–92, 194,
  196, 205
robustness, 11, 20–22, 23–25, 83–84,
  97–98, 103
Rochet, B., 12, 82–83
Rothman, J., 206–7
rounding, 87, 97–98
Russian, 20–21, 92, 95–96

Sagae, S., 164, 172, 174–75
saliency. *See* robustness
Sanskrit, 29
Scholz, B., 13
Schwab, S., 52
s-clusters, 28–32, 121–22, 126
  See also consonant clusters; consonantal
    sequences
Scovel, T., 11–12
Sebastián, N., 38–39
Sebastián-Galles, N., 38–40, 42
second language speech. *See* L2
  phonology; L2 speech
Selkirk, E., 160, 169
Serratrice, L., 198
Sewell, A., 206–7
shallow structure, 193–94
Siddiqi, D., 140
signed languages, 175
  See also gestural languages
silent reading, 135, 152, 168, 171–74
Singh, R., 28, 126
Sinhalese, 29
Slabakova, R., 198, 206–7
SLM. *See* speech learning model (SLM)
social justice, 206–7
sonorant voice (SV) node, 148
sonority, 81
  See also minimal sonority distance
    (MSD); sonority sequencing principle
    (SSP)

sonority sequencing principle (SSP), 25, 28–29, 71–72, 117, 126
Sorace, A., 198
Sound Pattern of English, The (Chomsky and Halle), 6
Spanish, 9–10, 22, 23–24, 39–45, 158–59
speech, L2, 2
speech learning model (SLM), 81–82, 83, 94, 205
Sprouse, R., 154, 155–56, 192–93
Stabler, E., 160
Stefanich, S., 140–41, 158–60
Steinhauer, K., 24
Stevens, K., 87
stress, 6, 20–21, 38–40, 46–50
   See also metrical representations; stress deafness
stress deafness, 38–39, 42–46, 49, 50–52
stridents, 59–60, 81, 84, 87–88, 100–2
structural conformity hypothesis, 26, 126–27
substitution, 82–83, 86, 92
successive division algorithm, 15, 90–91
Summerell, F., 103–5
Swedish, 32, 121, 131–32, 141–45
switching. *See* intraword code switching (ICS); phonological switching
syllables
   clusters in, 25–26, 61–70, 113–21, 131–32
   constraints on structure of, 61–62, 76
   typological patterns of, 67–68
   weight of, 51–52, 109–10
   See also stress
syntax/lexicon interface, 198
syntax/pragmatics interface, 198

tags. *See* language tags
Taylor, B., 43–44
tense marking, 9–10, 17, 129–30, 131–32, 141–45, 165
   See also morphosyntactic features
tense vowels, 46, 108–9
Tessier, A.-M., 4, 127–28
Thai, 20–21, 112

tongue twisters, 168, 171
transfer
   features and, 60, 86
   full, 36–38
   of L1 to L2, 11–12
   licensing and, 68
   parameter settings and, 48, 50
   sentences and, 195
   syllables and, 118
   See also block transfer hypothesis; prosodic transfer hypothesis
translation equivalents, 139–40
Treiman, R., 171
Tremblay, A., 50
trochaic feet, 47, 50, 51, 127
Trofimovich, P., 116
Trommer, J., 147, 148, 156
Turkish, 52, 154
typological universals, 26–28, 63–64, 102
   See also universal grammar (UG); universals

ultimate attainment, 34–37, 199
umlaut, 146–47, 148, 149–54, 156
universal grammar (UG), 3–4, 8–9, 26, 197–98
   See also typological universals; universals
universals, 26–28, 126–27
   See also typological universals

van der Hulst, H., 74, 203–4
Van Heuven, W., 134–35, 138
Vanderweide, T., 83–84
VanPatten, B., 206–7
Veenstra, T., 161
Vendelin, I., 41, 45
vocabulary insertion, 134
Vogel, I., 169
voicing, 85, 89–90, 159
vowel harmony, 154
vowel place (VPlace) node, 154
vowel reduction, 43–45
vowels. *See* epenthesis; illusory vowels; tense vowels

Index 253

Wang, C., 32, 126–27
Weber, S., 81
Weighting. *See* feature weighting
Weinberger, S., 131–32
Westergaard, M., 165
White, I., 43–44, 129, 130–31
WH-questions, 176–81,
    196–97
  See also interrogatives
Wiese, R., 145

Wilson, C., 203
working memory, 54–57
Wright, R., 83–84, 97–98

Yan, X., 116–17
Yang, C., 200
Yang, C.-L., 9–10, 54–55
Young-Scholten, M., 64–65
Yousefi, M., 119
Yucatec Maya, 23–24, 81, 99–102